BUYING, OWNING *and* SELLING A HOME
in Canada

SECOND EDITION

Margaret Kerr
&
JoAnn Kurtz

JOHN WILEY & SONS CANADA, LTD
Toronto   New York   Chichester   Weinheim   Brisbane   Singapore

John Wiley & Sons Canada Ltd
22 Worcester Road
Etobicoke, Ontario
M9W 1L1

Canadian Cataloguing in Publication Data
Kerr, Margaret Helen, 1954 −
    Buying, owning and selling a home in Canada

2nd ed.
Includes index.
ISBN 0-471-64191-X

1. House buying — Canada.   2. Home ownership — Canada.
3. House selling — Canada.   4. Home ownership — Law and legislation —
Canada.   5. Vendors and purchasers — Canada.
I. Kurtz, JoAnn, 1951 −   . II. Title.

HD1379.K47 1997   643'.12'0971   C96-932059-0

Production Credits
Cover & text design: Christine Rae
Printer: Trigraphic Printing Ltd.

Printed in Canada
10 9 8 7 6 5 4 3 2 1

CONTENTS

CONTENTS

ACKNOWLEDGEMENTS

We thank the following for their help:

Michael Kerr, Elaine Chelin, Joe Agostino, Michael Engelberg, Joan Emmans, Sophie Ouellette, J. Brian Cornish, Denis Noel, W. Richey Clarke, Darryl Drover, Terence Morrison, Herbert Suderman, Bryan Salte, Jack Webster, Jane Eagleson, Insurance Bureau of Canada, Canada Mortgage and Housing Corporation, Canadian Real Estate Association, Canadian Gas Association, Canadian Standards Association, Canada Post Corporation, Consumer's Gas, Monnex Insurance Brokers Limited, Sedgwick Limited, Armor Moving & Storage Ltd., AbbeyWood Moving and Storage Inc., Abell Pest Control, Addiction Research Foundation, Nova Scotia Real Estate Association, Ontario Real Estate Association, Prince Edward Island Real Estate Association, Ontario New Home Warranty Plan, Ontario Association of Architects, Office of the Land Registrar of Ontario, Halifax and Dartmouth Real Estate Board, Greater Toronto Homebuilders' Association, Toronto Humane Society—and a special thanks to anyone in Canada who didn't interrupt us while we were working.

This book is dedicated to

Helen Kathleen Porter Wood

and to

George and Irene Kurtz

buying a home

1 A MANUAL FOR HOMEOWNERS

DECIDING TO BUY A HOME
(OR AT LEAST THIS BOOK)

If you've picked up this book and you don't already own a home, you're probably thinking about buying one. But buying a home can take a long time and you've got the itch to buy something *right away*. So now you're thinking about buying this book. We want to encourage you to do that. You may think that we are acting only out of self interest, but in fact we're doing you a tremendous service. After all, if you're going to buy something on impulse, it's better to buy a book about buying a home than it is to buy a home.

Actually, even a lot of people who put a great deal of time and effort into finding a home might as well be buying on impulse, for all they really know about buying, owning and eventually selling a home.

That's where this book comes in. You wouldn't buy a car without researching the available models, their features and price, and you wouldn't drive the car without first having a look at the owner's manual. A car only costs a fraction of what a home costs, yet the kind of information that you can easily get about cars is difficult, or even impossible, to get about homes. We think that you should have access to at least as much information about your home as about your car.

ONCE YOU OWN A HOME

If you already own a home, you still need this book. Your relationship with your home is a complex one and is just beginning when you buy a home. Buying is the first stage, but it's followed by owning and then selling. Each stage has its joys, problems, and concerns. You don't need our help to experience your own kind of joy, and you don't need our help to find the problems either—they'll find you. But this book should help you cope with the problems as they arise, and help you identify and deal with the important concerns.

Some of the problems and concerns of home ownership are legal, some are practical, and some are both. Practical books on home ownership tend to focus on hands-on matters like financing or plumbing. Legal books on home ownership are written for lawyers, and even lawyers don't always understand them. This book, on the other hand, is both legal and practical. It's designed to help you to avoid problems as much as to solve them. And it's designed to give you the information you need all in one place and in language that you can understand.

However, this book is not a substitute for legal or other professional advice. There are times when you need a real estate agent, home inspector, mover, insurance broker, contractor, exterminator—even a lawyer. We try to tell you when it's time to hire a professional. And we try to send you off with enough knowledge to make sure that the person you hire serves you well.

QUESTIONS THIS BOOK ANSWERS

Here's a sampling of some of the questions this book answers.

About Buying a Home

- When's a good time to buy a home?
- What does it cost to buy a home?
- How much can you afford to pay for your home?
- How large a down payment will you need, and where on earth will you find the money?
- How much will you have to pay for your home each month?
- What should you look for in a neighbourhood and a home?
- What can a real estate agent do for you, and can you do it yourself instead?

- How do you make an offer to purchase a home?
- Do you need a lawyer to buy a home?
- What is a mortgage and how do you get one?
- How can you survive moving day?
- What do you do if there are problems with your new home?

About Owning a Home

- What kind of home insurance do you need and how do you get it?
- How do you make an insurance claim?
- What renovations will increase the value of your home?
- How do you find a reliable contractor?
- How do you live through a renovation?
- What are construction or builders' liens and how do you avoid them?
- What steps can you take to make your home secure against break-ins?
- How can you prevent accidents in your home?
- What happens if someone gets hurt on your property?
- Who is a trespasser and what can you do about one?
- How do you get rid of stray and wild animals?
- What do you do about noisy neighbours?
- Can you get your neighbour to pay for part of your fence?
- Can your neighbour cut down your tree?
- Can you object to your neighbour's construction project?
- Can you do anything if your property taxes are too high?
- What happens if you can't pay your mortgage?

About Selling a Home

- When is the best time to sell?
- Should you buy first or sell first?
- Do you need a real estate agent, or can you sell your home yourself?
- How do you make your home attractive to potential purchasers?
- Do you need a lawyer to sell your home?
- What must you leave behind when you move?
- How much money will you get from your sale?

Having the answers to these and other questions dealt with in this book should help you prevent many potential problems and solve others, either on your own or with professional help.

IT'S GREAT TO LIVE IN CANADA ... BUT ...

Canada is a big country and the law may vary considerably from province to province. (And don't even get us started about the weather.) Because we've tried to write a book for all of Canada, we've often had to talk in very general terms. This means that we haven't been able to take provincial variations into account on every topic. If you need specific legal advice, don't just rely on this book. Speak to a lawyer.

2 WHAT CAN YOU AFFORD?

No matter how much money you have, the home of your dreams will always cost more than you can afford. That's one of the universal truths of looking for a new home. You can take comfort from knowing that while the place you end up buying may not be your dream home, it is probably the dream home of someone who has even less money than you do.

We know it's hard to put up with someone telling you to be realistic when you are all set to climb ev'ry mountain and follow ev'ry rainbow in search of your dream, and a lot of people don't listen. But a lot of people also buy their dream home only to have it turn into a nightmare—when they wake up and realize how much they have to keep paying for it.

You can avoid the nightmare of buying a home that's too expensive for you by knowing what you can afford before you start looking. This will help you concentrate your hunting efforts on homes in your price range. A good way to keep yourself from buying a home you can't afford is *not to look at* homes you can't afford. In this chapter we'll help you figure out what you *can* afford.

WHEN IS THE BEST TIME TO BUY?

People often wonder whether they can get a deal on a home—or, put another way, afford a home that they couldn't otherwise afford—if they buy at a certain time of year. The answer is maybe yes, maybe no. There are times (like Christmas vacation) when almost no one wants to go house-hunting. If you find something you like at that time of year, you may be able to buy it for a good price because there are very few purchasers competing with you for it. There are other times of the year when almost everyone is out looking. The home you find at that time of year may cost you more because other purchasers are interested in it too.

You may think, then, that it makes sense to shop when no one else is shopping. But sellers also know that they may get less for their home during slow periods, so there will probably be fewer properties on the market for you to choose from. Sellers are more likely to put their homes up for sale when they think there will be a lot of buyers. So you can choose between a smaller selection of homes at (maybe) a lower price, and a larger selection at (maybe) a higher price. If you want to try to buy during a slow sales period, ask a real estate agent for advice about when that might be in your area.

Whatever the time you're looking, you may be lucky enough to find a "motivated seller," someone who has to sell quickly for their own personal reasons. The reason is often divorce (and a split-up of family property) or a job-related move to another city. You can ask your real estate agent if he or she knows of any sellers who are anxious to make a deal.

Finding a suitable home can take a while, so even if you think you know when to buy to get the best price, you have to start looking before then. The best time to start looking for a home is when you've decided you want to buy a home. And if you find a home that you like at a price you can afford, that's the home to buy and that's the best time to buy it.

KNOWING WHAT YOU CAN AFFORD

To know what you can afford, you have to know

- what it costs to buy and maintain a home
- how much money you have for a down payment
- how large a mortgage you can afford

The most complicated of these three things is calculating how large a mortgage you can afford. This means preparing a budget...something you've probably put off longer than cleaning your oven—and you're probably moving to get away from that dirty oven. Well, you can run, but you can't hide. It's either cleaning your oven and staying put, or doing a budget.

WHAT DOES IT COST TO BUY AND OWN A HOME?

The cost of buying and running a home is probably higher than you think. The actual cost of buying a home includes more than the purchase price, and the ongoing monthly costs of owning it include more than your mortgage payments. If you make the mistake of failing to take these additional costs into account, you will end up buying a more expensive home than you can afford.

What Are the One-Time Costs of Buying a Home?

The one-time costs of buying a home are all the things you pay for at the time the home is purchased. They include

- the purchase price
- sales taxes
- lawyer's fees and related expenses
- professional home inspection
- mortgage costs
- adjustments
- new home warranty costs (optional in most provinces), if you're buying a newly-constructed home
- relocation costs
- renovation costs

Some of the money you thought you could use for a down payment has to be used to pay these one-time costs. So you'll either have less money for your down payment than you thought, or you will have to borrow more money than you planned.

The Purchase Price

The purchase price is what you agree to pay for the home itself. Many people think of this amount as the entire cost of their home. While it is the major part of the cost, it is not the only cost—as you'll see if you keep going.

Sales Taxes

In several provinces there is a special kind of sales tax charged on the sale of real estate, called a **land transfer tax**. This tax is calculated as a percentage of the purchase price and can be several hundred to several thousand dollars.

You pay this tax to the provincial government at the time you close the deal for your home. Ask your lawyer or your real estate agent if there's such a tax in your province, and for an estimate of what it would be for a home in your price range.

The purchase price of your home may include things like appliances and curtains which are being sold with the home. (These things are called **chattels**.) If so, you will also have to pay **provincial retail sales tax** (H.S.T. where applicable) on the value of the chattels.

If you are buying a newly constructed home, you will have to pay **G.S.T.** (G.S.T. is often included in the purchase price and not calculated separately—ask your builder whether it's included). But if your house costs less than $450,000, you can apply for a G.S.T. rebate of up to 2.5 per cent of the purchase price. Your builder will help you with the paperwork.

Lawyer's Fees and Related Expenses

Your lawyer will charge you for legal services provided in helping you buy your home. The amount of lawyer's fees varies greatly, but you can expect to pay at least several hundred dollars, and up to several thousand dollars if there are problems with completing the deal. We'll discuss the role of the purchaser's lawyer in more detail in Chapter 6.

Inspection Fees

Some people have their home inspected by a qualified home inspector before they complete the purchase, to make sure that it's in good structural condition and has no plumbing, wiring, or other problems. An inspection can cost several hundred dollars or more.

Mortgage Costs

If you are borrowing money by taking out a mortgage, the mortgage lender may insist on having the property **appraised** (inspected to decide its value). Sometimes mortgage lenders charge an appraisal fee in the range of $100 to $200. If you get your mortgage through a **mortgage broker** instead of an **institutional lender** like a bank or trust company, the broker may charge a brokerage fee. The fee charged could be 1 to 2 per cent of the amount borrowed.

Monthly mortgage payments are usually due on the first of the month. If your home purchase is **closing** (being legally completed) on another day of the month, the mortgage lender may deduct, from the mortgage money that is being given to you to close the deal, an amount to cover the interest for the time from the closing date to the first day of the next month. (That means you may have to come up with some extra money on closing day to cover any shortfall in the amount of money that the mortgage lender actually gives you.)

If your mortgage is for more than 75 per cent of the purchase price, you'll almost certainly have to get **mortgage insurance**, which is arranged through the Canada Mortgage and Housing Corporation (CMHC). If you need CMHC mortgage insurance, you will have to pay an insurance application fee of $75 if your mortgage lender provides an appraisal, or up to $235 if your lender does not. You will also have to pay a **premium** for the mortgage insurance. The amount of the premium varies with the value of the house and the size of the loan, but the highest rate charged is 4.25 per cent of the amount of the mortgage loan. You can make a one-time payment of the premium or have it added to your mortgage and pay it on a monthly basis.

There's much more about mortgages in Chapter 7. Flip there now if you can't stand the suspense.

Adjustments

If the person selling the home (the **vendor**) has paid such things as property taxes and utilities in advance, you may have to pay the vendor back for your share of these expenses. You have no way of knowing how much this will be at the time you make your offer to buy the home. Your lawyer will tell you the exact amount just before the deal closes.

New Home Warranty Costs

All provinces have warranty programs for newly constructed homes. Participation in these programs is optional in most provinces. If your new home comes with a warranty, there will be an **enrolment fee** that the builder will pass on to you, either by including it in the purchase price or as a separate charge. If you are buying a newly constructed home, be sure to find out whether there is an additional charge for a warranty. Depending on the province and the purchase price of the home, the charge can be between about $200 and $1200.

Extra Charges Associated with Newly-Constructed Homes

If you're buying a house in a new development, you may have to pay an extra charge for a lot that's wider or deeper than the standard lot, or that backs onto green space or that has a west-facing backyard or that's on a corner. If you're buying a condo in a high-rise, you'll pay an extra charge for a suite that's on a higher floor or that has a good view. These charges are typically a few thousand dollars.

You'll also have to pay more to **upgrade** from standard features. The model you look at may be full of upgrades (high quality carpeting, hardwood floors, expensive tiles and countertops, built-in kitchen appliances, luxury bathroom fixtures, central air), and you may not be thrilled with what the base purchase price will buy you. The upgrades you want could cost several hundred to several thousand dollars (although they could be less expensive if you arrange purchase or installation on your own later).

Relocation Expenses

You should budget for your moving costs, unless you'll be arriving at your new home with nothing but a suitcase and a can opener. The amount will depend on whether you hire a mover or boldly go yourself. If you hire a mover, the cost tends to go up the more things you have to move and the further you have to move them. Moving with a mover can cost several thousand dollars. We tell you all about moving with a mover in Chapter 9. If you're a do-it-yourself type, you can rent a small moving van or a trailer if you or your friends don't have a suitable vehicle. The rental cost varies with the length of time you need the van or trailer and the distance you drive it.

Once you are in your new home, you will have to get telephone and cable television service, not to mention hydro and water service and maybe natural gas or oil service. You'll have to pay a fee to open a new account or to transfer the services (you can probably figure on $25 to $50 per service). You may also have to pay installation fees for telephone and cable TV.

Renovation Expenses

Not many people move into a home that is in perfect condition, so don't forget to budget for renovations, repairs, redecoration, painting, and cleaning. Also, be sure that you have left yourself enough money to pay for any new appliances or furniture that you may need.

What Does All This Mean?

It means you need more money than you were planning to spend on your new home—maybe several thousand dollars more than you had planned on. It's a good thing you're reading this before you made an offer on a home that was calculated to take every penny you have! (At least we hope you're reading this *before*.)

What are the Monthly Expenses of Owning a Home?

Everybody knows there will be monthly mortgage payments after they buy a home, but many people forget about the other regular monthly expenses. These expenses include

- property taxes
- utilities
- home insurance
- maintenance and repairs

Mortgage Payments

A mortgage is a loan that is repaid in instalments, usually on a monthly basis. The monthly payments include an amount to repay the amount borrowed and an amount to pay interest. The amount of the payment will therefore depend on how much you borrow and the interest rate. If you had to get mortgage insurance and you elected not to make a one-time payment, the monthly payment will also include the insurance premium.

Property Taxes

Every municipality charges property taxes that are used to pay for municipal services and in most provinces for local schools. They are payable in instalments over the course of the year, sometimes monthly and sometimes at other intervals. Annual property taxes can be many thousands of dollars, depending on the value of your home and the tax rate set by the municipality. Some mortgage lenders pay property taxes for you and require you to repay them on a monthly basis with your mortgage.

Utilities

You should find out the approximate monthly cost of heating, water, and electricity for any home you are interested in buying to make sure you can afford these utility payments. Since they can vary greatly from home to home (especially heating costs), it's a good idea to find out what the current owner has paid in the last year. Your real estate agent will get the information for you.

Home Insurance

Every homeowner needs home insurance. The cost varies from home to home but will probably be $500 to $1000, or more, per year. Most insurance companies allow homeowners to make monthly premium payments instead of insisting on a single annual payment.

Maintenance and Repairs

If you don't want to spend time in the great Canadian outdoors shovelling your own driveway or mowing your own lawn, you should budget for snow removal and lawn care.

You should also keep in mind that things in your new home will break and have to be repaired or replaced—usually when you can least afford it. Make sure that your budget allows you to deal with these unexpected but necessary expenses.

What Does This Mean for You?

Whatever you think you can afford to pay on a monthly basis for a home, don't plan to spend it all on just your mortgage payments. If you spend too much on mortgage payments, you won't have enough money to cover your other expenses.

HOW MUCH MONEY DO YOU HAVE FOR YOUR NEW HOME?

When you buy your new home, you should pay only what you can afford. (It's amazing how often books like this one give you the same advice as your mother.) What you can afford depends on a combination of how much money you have for a down payment, plus how large a mortgage you can afford to carry.

TABLE 1: HOW MUCH MONEY DO YOU HAVE FOR A HOME?		
Your down + payment	A mortgage you can afford	= The amount you have to spend on your new home

DOWN PAYMENTS

A **down payment** is the part of the purchase price that you pay in cash when your offer to purchase a home is accepted by the vendor. The rest of the purchase price is financed by a mortgage.

It's usually easy to calculate how much you have for a down payment. It's the money you have saved in the bank, or the money you can beg or borrow from your family (we don't recommend stealing), or the money you can raise by selling property that you already own. Remember, though, that this money has to cover not only your down payment but all of the other one-time costs of buying a house, unless you're willing to take out a bigger mortgage (assuming that a mortgage lender is willing to give you a bigger mortgage).

Minimum Down Payments

For most people, a large part of a home's purchase price is financed by a mortgage. Institutional mortgage lenders (banks and trust companies) prefer you to have a down payment that covers at least 25 per cent of the purchase price of your home. A down payment of this size will qualify you for a **conventional mortgage**.

If you don't qualify for a conventional mortgage, you'll still be able to get a mortgage thanks to the Canada Housing and Mortgage Corporation. CMHC insures **high ratio mortgages** (mortgages for more than 75 per cent of the purchase price), thus calming the fears of the institutional lenders that you might be a deadbeat and unable to make your mortgage payments. If you can't keep up with your payments and default on your mortgage, and your home is sold for less than the outstanding amount of the mortgage, CMHC will pay your mortgage lender the shortfall. CMHC makes it possible to buy a home with a down payment as small as 5 per cent of the purchase price, leaving up to 95 per cent to be financed by a mortgage. You can check out CMHC's website at www.cmhc.ca.

Finding the Down Payment

If you already own a home, most of your down payment will probably come from the money you have left from the sale of that home, after paying off your mortgage and paying the other expenses of the sale.

If you don't own a home, or if you can't get as much as you need out of your home's sale price, you must look to other sources for your down payment, such as:

- savings in your bank account, bonds, or GICs
- any other investments
- gifts or loans from your family
- RRSPs
- provincial home ownership savings plans

RRSPs

The Canadian government will allow you to withdraw, without tax penalty, up to $20,000 per person or $40,000 per couple from your RRSPs for the purchase of a home. You must repay the amount you withdraw within fifteen years, repaying a minimum of one-fifteenth each year, or there will be a tax penalty.

You can only borrow from your RRSP if neither you nor your spouse has owned and lived in a home as your principal residence within the last four years. There are other restrictions on borrowing as well. For more information, speak to the institution that holds your RRSP, or go to Canada Customs and Revenue Agency's website at www.ccra-adrc.gc.ca and hunt for the Home Buyers' Plan.

Provincial Home Ownership Savings Plans

Some provinces have home ownership savings plans. You must meet certain requirements to be eligible. If you save for your down payment by depositing money into such a plan, you will receive a credit against your provincial income tax for the year. Ask your bank or trust company whether your province has a plan and what the details are.

MORTGAGES

A **mortgage** (a **hypothec** in Quebec) is a special kind of loan available to home purchasers or owners, and we talk a lot more about them (as we have mentioned) in Chapter 7.

An Affordable Monthly Payment Equals an Affordable Mortgage

When you take out a mortgage, you should borrow only the amount of money you can afford to repay. The amount you can afford to repay is governed by the monthly mortgage payments you can afford to make. The monthly mortgage payments for any mortgage depend on

- the amount borrowed (the **mortgage principal**)
- the mortgage **interest rate**

The larger the amount being borrowed and the higher the interest rate, the larger your monthly mortgage payments will be.

The first step in figuring out how much you can afford to borrow is to figure out how large a monthly mortgage payment you can afford. In order to know what mortgage payment you can afford to make, you have to calculate your net monthly income and then deduct all your monthly expenses to see what you have left for a mortgage.

TABLE 2: MONEY AVAILABLE FOR MORTGAGE PAYMENTS

Net monthly income	—	Monthly expenses (living expenses and non-mortgage housing expenses)	=	Money available for mortgage payments

What is Your Net Monthly Income?

Let's start this procedure by calculating your net monthly income.

What is Income?

Income is money that is earned. If you have a job, your salary or wages are your income. If you are self-employed, your income is the fees you collect for the goods or services you provide. Other forms of income include

- commissions
- tips
- interest
- dividends
- rent received

Gross Income and Net Income

If you are paid wages or a salary, your employer makes deductions from your pay cheque every pay period. Common deductions include income tax, Employment Insurance premiums, Canada Pension Plan or Quebec Pension Plan contributions, union dues, insurance payments, and private pension plan contributions. These amounts are deducted automatically. The amount you are paid before the deductions are made is called your **gross income**. The small amount you actually receive (after the deductions are made) is called your **net income**.

Since you can spend only the income you receive after deductions are made, you should use your net income rather than your gross income for the purposes of calculating what you can afford.

Calculating Your Monthly Income

Different people receive their income at different intervals. You may be paid weekly, every two weeks, bimonthly (twice monthly, but it's different from every two weeks—it's less frequent), or monthly. Self-employed people may receive their income at other less regular intervals.

Because mortgage payments are normally made monthly, it's necessary to see what your income is on a monthly basis, no matter when you are actually paid. To convert your net income to a monthly amount, use the following table:

TABLE 3: CALCULATING YOUR MONTHLY INCOME	
If you are paid:	Multiply the net amount of your pay cheque by:
weekly	4.33
every 2 weeks	2.165
bimonthly	2

If you are self-employed or can't accurately predict your income, you should estimate what your income will be for the current year and then divide that figure by 12 to give you an estimated monthly income. To be safe, make your estimate on the low side rather than on the high side. Let's call your newly calculated monthly income Figure A. Figure A = _____.

What Are Your Monthly Living Expenses?

Once you have determined your net monthly income, the next step is to deduct your monthly living expenses. Before you can deduct these expenses, you have to know what they are.

Identifying Your Living Expenses

Your living expenses are made up of all the money you spend on things other than housing, such as groceries, transportation, clothing, and entertainment. If you have receipts for the past year, go through them rather than relying on your memory of what you've spent. Table 4 on page 19 will help you identify your monthly living expenses.

Calculating Your Living Expenses on a Monthly Basis

Now that you've calculated your income on a monthly basis, you have to do the same for your expenses so you can subtract them from income.

CONVERTING YOUR EXPENSES: Some expenses are incurred on a weekly basis, the most common example being groceries. To calculate your monthly expenses for these items, estimate what you spend in an average week, then convert this weekly amount to a monthly one by multiplying it by 4.33. People are always tempted simply to multiply the weekly amount by 4, but that doesn't work because the average month has more than twenty-eight days in it. If you calculated every month as having only four weeks, you would end up with a year of forty-eight weeks instead of fifty-two. (Now you know exactly why bimonthly is not the same as every two weeks.)

Some expenses are incurred on a monthly basis, such as telephone and cable TV. Just use the amount from your monthly bill. Some expenses are incurred on a yearly basis, such as insurance premiums, car licence fees, and membership dues. To convert these annual amounts to monthly amounts, divide by 12. Finally, some expenses—car repairs, clothing, and vacations—are incurred on an irregular basis. The simplest way to deal with these is to estimate the total amount for the entire year (or add up what these things cost last year) and then divide by 12.

TOTALLING YOUR EXPENSES: After you have converted all of your expenses to a monthly figure, total them and deduct this total from your net monthly income (Figure A). What you have left out of your monthly income (if anything) is what you have to spend on mortgage payments *and* other housing expenses. This will probably be very depressing.

It is at this point that many people realize they will have to make some sacrifices in order to own a home. (There we go, sounding like your mother again.) So the next step is to go through your living expenses again and see where you can make cuts. It's very important to be realistic here, because the money you cut from your living expenses will end up being committed to mortgage payments. You won't be able to get it back if you decide you need it—at least not without paying off your mortgage first.

It's not a good idea to reduce basic expenses like groceries and child care. Be careful in reducing other expenses as well. Are you sure that you can live through a Canadian winter without a vacation in the sun? Do you want to go through the year with fewer new clothes or dinners out?

You can use the following table to help you figure out both the expenses you have now and the adjustments you would be willing to make in order to buy a home.

TABLE 4: MONTHLY LIVING EXPENSES

Expense	Actual monthly amount	Slash-and-burn monthly amount
Household expenses	$ _____	$ _____
Groceries	_____	_____
Household supplies	_____	_____
Household help	_____	_____
Telephone	_____	_____
Cable TV	_____	_____

Loan payments $ _____ $ _____
    Credit cards   _____   _____
    Bank loans   _____   _____
    Car loan   _____   _____
    Other   _____   _____

Transportation $ _____ $ _____
    Car insurance   _____   _____
    Licence fees   _____   _____
    Maintenance   _____   _____
    Gasoline   _____   _____
    Parking   _____   _____
    Public transit   _____   _____
    Other   _____   _____

Clothing $ _____ $ _____
    Self   _____   _____
    Spouse   _____   _____
    Children   _____   _____

Personal grooming $ _____ $ _____
    Haircuts   _____   _____
    Dry cleaning   _____   _____
    Other   _____   _____

Health $ _____ $ _____
    Insurance (health,
        disability, life)   _____   _____
    Uninsured medical services   _____   _____
    Drugs   _____   _____
    Dentist/orthodontist   _____   _____
    Other   _____   _____

Entertainment $ _____ $ _____
    Eating out   _____   _____
    Movies, plays, and
        sports events   _____   _____
    Newspapers, books,
        and magazines   _____   _____
    Club fees   _____   _____
    Vacation   _____   _____
    Sports equipment   _____   _____
    Gifts   _____   _____
    Other   _____   _____

Children's expenses	$ _____	$ _____
Day care	_____	_____
Babysitting	_____	_____
School fees	_____	_____
Lessons and activities	_____	_____
Summer camp	_____	_____
Other	_____	_____
Pets' Expenses	$ _____	$ _____
Food	_____	_____
Day care	_____	_____
Vet bills	_____	_____
Savings	$ _____	$ _____
Charitable Donations	$ _____	$ _____
Total (This is FIGURE B.)	$ _____	$ _____

Money Available for Monthly Non-Mortgage Housing Expenses

Now let's look at non-mortgage housing expenses for the home you want to buy, so we can deduct them from income too. We're inching closer to knowing what an affordable mortgage payment is.

The non-mortgage expenses of owning a home include

• property taxes
• utilities
• home insurance
• maintenance and repairs

What your monthly non-mortgage housing expenses will be will depend on the particular home you buy. Some homes have low property taxes, cost little to heat, and will require relatively little maintenance; others are very expensive to run on a monthly basis. Some of the expenses of running the home may be set out on the **feature sheet** prepared by the seller's real estate agent when a home is listed for sale. If all the information you'd like isn't there, ask your real estate agent to try to find out more. You may have to estimate some amounts, based on your own experience or on friends' experience.

As with your living expenses, you must figure out how much you will spend on non-mortgage housing expenses on a monthly basis. Use the following Table 5. The less you spend on these monthly expenses, the more money you will have available each month to pay your mortgage.

TABLE 5: ESTIMATED MONTHLY NON-MORTGAGE HOUSING EXPENSES

Expense	Monthly amount
Property taxes	$ _____
Water	_____
Electricity	_____
Natural gas	_____
Fuel oil	_____
Home insurance	_____
Repairs and maintenance	_____
Gardening	_____
Snow removal	_____
Condominium common expenses	_____
(if you're buying a condo, these replace some of the maintenance and repairs, and gardening and snow removal)	
Total (This is FIGURE C.)	$ _____

Money Available for Monthly Mortgage Payments

Now you're ready to calculate how much money you have available to make your monthly mortgage payments. Take the amounts from your previous calculations and insert them into the following table:

TABLE 6: MONEY AVAILABLE FOR MORTGAGE PAYMENTS

Net monthly income	$ _____	(Figure A)
less:		
Your monthly living expenses	$ _____	(Figure B)
Your monthly non-mortgage housing expenses	$ _____	(Figure C)
equals:		
Total available for mortgage payments	$ _____	(FIGURE D)

Calculating the Principal Amount of Your Affordable Mortgage

You now know how large a monthly mortgage payment you can afford—it's Figure D. The next step in working out how big a mortgage loan you can afford is to find out what your mortgage interest rate might be. Check your local newspaper's business or real estate section, or telephone some banks or trust companies for the current interest rates or look up mortgage interest rates on their websites. Call the most-quoted current interest rate FIGURE E. FIGURE E = _____ , and it's roughly the interest rate you'll pay if you take out a mortgage right now.

Using Figure D and Figure E, you can calculate how much mortgage principal you can afford to borrow. Go to Table 8 on page 25. It shows mortgage principal, based on different monthly payments and interest rates. Move down the left-hand column until you find the figure closest to your Figure D, then move across the page to the column that's under the interest rate closest to your Figure E. That amount will be approximately the mortgage principal you can afford to borrow.

THE MAXIMUM PRICE TO PAY FOR YOUR HOME

Add the amount of mortgage principal you can afford to borrow to the sum of money that you have for a down payment. The total is the maximum price you can afford to pay for a home, including the particular home you're looking at.

A Word of Warning

Think carefully before you spend the maximum amount you can afford. All the mortgage calculations you do in this chapter are based on current interest rates. However, as you will see in the chapter about mortgages, any mortgage you get will probably have to be renegotiated before you have paid it in full—perhaps several times. If interest rates have gone up at the time your mortgage comes due, your renegotiated mortgage will have a higher interest rate and your monthly payments will go up. You should leave yourself some leeway for such a possibility.

The Price Range of Homes You Should Be Looking At

The amount you can afford each month for your mortgage will depend on the particular home you buy. That's because non-mortgage housing expenses vary from home to home. So you might be asking yourself: How can I know what price range of homes I should be looking at? To figure out this price range roughly, fill out the following Table 7:

TABLE 7: TOTAL MONEY AVAILABLE FOR MORTGAGE AND NON-MORTGAGE HOUSING EXPENSES

Net monthly income	$ _____	(Figure A)
less:		
Monthly living expenses	$ _____	(Figure B)
Total available for mortgage and all housing expenses	$ _____	

Go to Table 8 to find out how much mortgage money you could afford to borrow if you could use this total amount of money to pay your mortgage. The amount you get from Table 8 will be quite a bit more than you can in fact afford, because you will also have to pay all non-mortgage housing expenses out of it. Take the amount of mortgage principal you calculated using Table 8 and add it to the money you have for a down payment. Start looking at houses below this price range.

Pre-Approved Mortgages

Many banks and trust companies will allow you to apply for a mortgage before you have found the home that you'd like to buy. Getting **pre-approval** for a mortgage lets you know in advance the maximum amount of money that will be available to you.

While the bank or trust company will not actually give you the money until you buy the home, they will commit themselves to lending you a maximum amount at a specified interest rate, so long as you buy a suitable home within a fixed period of time (usually no more than 60 days).

So now you've figured out what you can afford! You can start to think (rather than dream) about where you want to live and what kind of home you want.

TABLE 8: HOW MUCH MORTGAGE PRINCIPAL YOU CAN BORROW AT VARIOUS INTEREST RATES AND MONTHLY PAYMENT AMOUNTS

Interest Rate / Monthly Payment	4%	5%	6%	7%	8%	9%	10%	11%	12%	13%	14%	15%
$ 500	$ 95,050	$ 86,000	$ 78,125	$ 71,425	$65,525	$60,575	$55,875	$51,925	$48,450	$45,375	$42,125	$40,125
600	114,060	103,200	93,750	85,725	78,625	72,675	67,050	62,300	58,150	54,450	51,100	48,150
700	113,070	120,400	109,375	100,000	91,750	84,550	73,200	72,700	67,825	63,525	59,625	56,175
800	152,080	137,600	125,000	114,275	104,850	96,625	89,375	83,075	77,525	72,600	68,150	64,200
900	171,090	154,800	140,625	128,575	117,950	108,700	103,550	93,450	87,200	81,675	76,650	72,225
1000	190,100	172,000	156,250	142,850	131,050	120,775	111,725	103,850	96,900	90,750	85,175	80,250
1250	237,625	215,000	195,300	178,575	163,825	140,975	139,675	129,800	121,125	113,425	106,475	100,325
1500	285,150	258,000	234,375	214,275	196,600	181,150	167,600	156,775	145,350	136,125	127,775	120,375

Amortized over 25 years
Figures rounded off to the nearest $25

3 WHERE DO YOU WANT TO LIVE?

Now that you know what you can afford, you can start to think about where you want to live: what features you want in a home and what location. For some of you the size and appearance of a home are the most important things. For others, location is everything. For many of you, what you want may not be what you can afford. In the end, your choice of a home will probably involve a trade-off among price, features, and location.

THINK ABOUT WHAT YOU WANT

Before you start to look at homes, you should have an idea of the features and location you want. Make a wish list for your ideal home. Then have a preliminary look around to see whether or not what you want is available in your price range. You may have to make changes to your wish list to reflect what you can actually afford.

Location

When we talk about location, we don't mean where in Canada you want to live. We assume that you already know both the province and the general area. Within that general area, you still have a wide choice: Would you prefer to live right in the city, in a suburb, in a smaller town, or in the country? You should also think about the kind of community you want to live in, how close to your family and friends and place of work you want to be, and whether the services you want are nearby.

Features

When we talk about features, we mean the size and appearance of the home. How many bedrooms are there? Are there new bathrooms and kitchen? Is the place in move-in condition or is it a handyman's special? How large is the lot? When you list the features you want in a home, don't just think about whether a home meets your present needs. Think about your future needs as well.

The Wish List

To help you identify your wishes and needs for your new home, use the following checklists. Distinguish between the things that you absolutely must have and the things that you would merely like to have if you could.

HOME FEATURES

	Must have	Would like
Single-family detached		✓
Single-family semi-detached		
✕ Multiple family		
Townhouse		
Number of storeys		
✕ Apartment-style condo		
Exterior (brick, wood, siding)		
Number of bedrooms	3	4
Number of bathrooms	1	2
New bathrooms		
Master ensuite bathroom		
Large kitchen		✓
New kitchen		✓
Family room		✓

Separate dining-room	_____	_____
Sunroom	_____	_____
Fireplace(s)	_____	_____
Finished basement	_____	_____
Basement apartment	_____	_____
Nanny's quarters	_____	_____
Lots of closet space	_____	_____
Type of heating	_____	_____
Central air-conditioning	_____	_____
New plumbing	_____	_____
New electrical system	_____	_____
Municipal water and sewers	_____	_____
For a house or townhouse:		
Large property	_____	_____
Backyard with fence	_____	_____
Swimming pool	_____	_____
Trees and landscaping	_____	_____
Deck or patio	_____	_____
Finished basement	_____	_____
Attached garage	_____	_____
One- or two-car garage	_____	_____
Private drive	_____	_____
For an apartment-style condo:		
Recreational facilities	_____	_____
Large grounds	_____	_____
24-hour security	_____	_____
Ample visitor parking	_____	_____
Move-in condition	_____	_____
Other (list)	_____	_____

HOME LOCATION

	Must have	Would like
Type of location		
city	_____	_____
suburb	_____	_____
small town	_____	_____
country	_____	_____

Easy commuting
    close to work
    close to public transit
    snow plowing
    adequate parking

Character of the neighbourhood
    size and appearance of homes
    restrictions on activities
    quiet street
    compatible neighbours
    safety
    mature trees
    sidewalks
    wildlife

Services
    close to good schools
    close to shopping and other services
    nearby emergency services
    recreational facilities and programs
    close to parks
    sidewalk snow removal
    garbage pick-up
    mail delivery to door
    water and sewage systems

Low property taxes

Stable property values

Have a Preliminary Look Around

Once you have some idea of the features and location you'd like, you should have a look around to see whether what you want is available in your price range. You can do this the traditional way by looking at real estate ads, by driving around to see what homes are up for sale, and by going to open houses. If you see something, you can call the agent named in the ad or on the sign (or you can call any real estate agent) for more information.

More and more people are becoming less and less traditional when they take a preliminary look. Now instead of opening the paper or getting into the car they turn on the computer and check out homes for sale using the Internet.

Hunting for a Home on the Internet

The smart way to browse on the Internet is to go to one of the "gateway" sites that will give you access to many properties listed on the Multiple Listing Service. Try the Canadian Real Estate Association's site (www.mls.ca), or the local board in your target area such as the Toronto Real Estate Board (www.realestate.ca), or the Calgary Real Estate Board (www.creb.ab.ca). You can select neighbourhoods and homes by price range; and when you click on a home that looks interesting you should be able to get interior and exterior pictures of it as well as a description of its features. If you want more detailed information, or if you want to visit in person, there's a contact number for the vendor's real estate agent. Actually, you can contact any real estate agent, you don't have to work through the vendor's agent.

If you've seen a home advertised for sale, you may also be able to get pictures and information on a website set up by the listing agent or the agency named in the ad. Some websites give out property addresses so you can go to the street and walk or drive by even before you contact an agent. The agency's website may be mentioned on the "For sale" sign or in their ad or use a search engine to find out whether the agent or agency has a website.

If you're looking for information about an unfamiliar city or neighbourhood, many cities and towns have their own website with maps that will allow you to locate things like shopping centres and schools, and to download transit schedules.

Fine-Tune Your Wish List

After some preliminary looking around, you should have a realistic idea of what is out there. It's unlikely that you will have found an affordable home that fully satisfies your wish list.

You will have discovered that similar homes have different price tags depending on their location. Since what you can afford is fixed, you will probably find that you have to compromise either on features or location. Have another look at your wish list and change it if necessary.

At this stage you should have a good idea of what kind of home you can get for the price you can afford, and where. You have narrowed your choice of features and location. You are now ready to start serious house-hunting— with buying in mind.

GO HOUSE-HUNTING WITH A REAL ESTATE AGENT

Unless you are only interested in a home to be constructed in a new development or building, the best way to find homes is to look with the help of an experienced real estate agent. Now you probably want to know

- what a real estate agent can do for you
- the cost of a real estate agent
- how to find a real estate agent
- how to work with a real estate agent
- the legal relationship between you and your real estate agent

What a Real Estate Agent Can Do for You

A real estate agent can:

- help you fine-tune your wish list
- get special access to information about the many homes listed for sale
- screen those homes to choose the ones most likely to be of interest
- arrange appointments for you to view the selected homes
- get information about neighbourhoods
- help you evaluate the condition of homes you view
- help you decide how much you should pay for a particular home
- help you make up an offer to purchase, and negotiate with the vendor
- put you in contact with building inspectors, mortgage lenders, contractors, movers, and other useful people

You may think that you don't need a real estate agent to find and look at homes that are for sale. But you're wrong. For one thing, real estate agents are hard to avoid. Most vendors use a real estate agent, and if you want to view a home that's listed with an agent, you'll either have to deal with that agent or some other agent. For another thing, using a real estate agent will get you access to a lot more information than you could find on your own and will also save you a lot of time.

Most homes that are up for sale are put on a **multiple listing service** or **MLS**. Only real estate agents have full access to the information on the multiple listing service, which includes details about the price, location, and features of each home. So a real estate agent will know more about the homes that are on the market than you could ever find out on your own.

A real estate agent will review all the MLS information, zero in on the homes most likely to be of interest to you, and take you to see only those homes. You won't waste your time looking at the wrong properties.

Cost of a Real Estate Agent

The general rule is that there will be no cost to you as the purchaser for using a real estate agent's services. The real estate agent involved in a purchase of a home is usually paid a commission by the vendor.

How to Find a Real Estate Agent

You could be spending a lot of time with your real estate agent and you need the agent to know and understand what's important to you in a new home. So you want to find someone you like, trust, and feel comfortable with, maybe someone who is of a similar age, background, and stage in life.

You also want an agent who is professional, has time for you, and will work hard. So it's best to find someone who has experience and works full-time. Try to avoid an agent who has so many homes listed for sale or is working with so many purchasers that he or she won't have enough time to spend with you. Look for an agent who is knowledgeable about the neighbourhoods that interest you the most. Finally, choose someone with a pleasant personality. It will not only be easier for you to work together, but the agent will be a more successful negotiator on your behalf.

The best way to find a real estate agent is to ask for recommendations from people you know and trust. If family and friends don't have anyone to recommend, you might want to use a real estate agent you met at an open house or spoke to on the phone during your preliminary search. Feel free to interview several agents before making your choice. You can ask each one:

- How long he or she has been a real estate agent
- How familiar he or she is with the areas where you'd like to buy
- How much time he or she will have to spend with you ("I'm terribly busy" is not a good answer)
- How quickly he or she will be able to return your calls
- For references, if you didn't get the agent's name from someone you trust

If the real estate agent you choose turns out not to have enough time for you or does not seem to understand what it is that you're looking for, or if you simply feel uncomfortable with him or her, end the relationship and choose a new agent.

How to Work with a Real Estate Agent

Tell your agent what you want and let him or her do the work of finding homes. As you look at different homes, explain what you like or don't like about each one so that the agent will be able to focus the search on homes that should appeal to you. Focusing the search works best if you work with just one agent at a time.

When you view a home, you have to examine its condition very carefully. Your real estate agent has seen many homes and may be able to spot problems that you miss. If you have specific questions about repairs that have been made or the cost of maintaining the home, ask your agent to get the answers from the vendor.

When you find a home that interests you, make use of your agent's expertise in getting information about the neighbourhood and the neighbours. A good real estate agent should be able to give you information about such things as the local schools, property taxes, and even the names of people living on the street.

If you want to try to buy one of the homes you've looked at, your agent can check sale prices of similar homes in the area to help you decide how much you're willing to offer. The agent will help you draft the actual offer to purchase and may suggest that you include special clauses for your protection.

Once you've signed an offer, your real estate agent acts as a go-between, taking the offer to the vendor and bringing you back the vendor's answer. During the negotiations, you won't meet with the vendor face-to-face.

Even after you reach an agreement to buy a home, your agent can still be useful to you by helping you find mortgage money, building inspectors, renovators, and so on. Your agent can also arrange any inspections of the home before the sale closes.

The Legal Relationship Between You and the Real Estate Agent

The real estate agent who hosts an open house, or who is named in an advertisement or on a "For Sale" sign, is the vendor's real estate agent, and is also the vendor's agent in a special legal sense. The real estate agent has a legal relationship with the vendor called an **agency** relationship. In an agency relationship, the agent has a duty to look after the best interests of the person he or she is working for (in this case, the vendor). The agent also acts in place of the person he or she works for. That means that if the vendor's agent makes a statement about the property for sale, it is the same as if the vendor personally made the statement.

You may think that the real estate agent who has been finding homes for you to look at is "your" agent, in the legal sense of the word, but most of the time that is not the case. He or she is the agent of the vendor unless you've made a special arrangement (see below under "Buyer's Agent").

Generally speaking, the fact that "your" real estate agent is really the vendor's agent will not have any effect on your house-hunting activities. However, as the vendor's legal agent, your real estate agent has a duty to pass on to the vendor any information that would affect the vendor's decision to accept your offer to buy the home. So be a little careful when you are negotiating the price of a particular home. Don't tell your real estate agent the maximum price you are willing to pay, if it's higher than the price you've offered.

Buyer's Agent

If you think you would prefer to work with an agent who represents only *your* interests as buyer, you can hire your own agent by signing a **representation agreement** with a real estate agent. The agent becomes your legal agent and will represent you alone. In return, you agree to look for homes with that agent and no other for a stated period, usually 60 or 90 days. You also agree to pay a fee to the agent for his or her services (even if you cheat on your agent and buy a home with another agent during the 60 or 90 day period). But the agreement allows the agent to negotiate a fee from someone besides you. When you submit an offer on a home, your agent will probably be willing to agree to accept a share of the commission on the home deal (which the vendor pays) as payment of the fee under the representation agreement. In other words, you as buyer won't have to pay the buyer's agent.

Dual Agent

What if you sign a representation agreement and then your agent shows you a home on which he or she is the listing agent (the vendor's agent)? In that case, the agent is a **dual agent**. A dual agent must tell both the buyer and the vendor that he or she is an agent for both, and that he or she could potentially have a conflict of interest. A dual agent has to treat both buyer and vendor fairly, but just the same you shouldn't tell anything to a dual agent that you wouldn't tell to a vendor's agent.

Despite what we've told you here, don't get all hung up on this vendor's agent/buyer's agent/dual agent business. For the most part, the services, advice, and expertise that a real estate agent provides a buyer will be exactly the same no matter whose agent the real estate agent is.

HOMES FOR SALE BY THE VENDOR

What if you find a home that's being sold by a vendor who doesn't have a real estate agent? There could be an advantage to you in buying privately—namely, that the price may be lower. The vendor won't have to pay a real estate agent's commission and may be willing to share the saving with you. It is just as likely, however, that the vendor wants to keep that saving, in which case the price will not be any lower than if a real estate agent were involved. In fact, you may find that a vendor who wants to sell privately has an unrealistic idea about the value of the property and may want more than its market value.

There can also be disadvantages to buying privately. For example, the vendor may hover over you as you view the home (when you view homes being sold through an agent, the vendor has usually been persuaded not to be there). If you make an offer on the home, you may have to negotiate with the vendor face-to-face rather than through your agent.

If you decide to buy privately, be sure to research the home and local home prices thoroughly. If you're not sure that the asking price is fair, you can pay a fee to have a real estate agent give you an estimate of the home's market value.

HOMES THAT AREN'T FOR SALE

What if you've found a street that you really want to live on, or a condo building you'd really like to live in—but there aren't any homes up for sale? Choose several houses or units that you like. If you've got an agent, ask him or her to approach the owners to find out if they're interested in selling. If you don't have an agent, write a letter telling the owners that you are interested in buying, and hand-deliver it to the door of each home.

We've told you how to find homes to look at. In the next chapter, we tell you how to evaluate the homes you see so that you can decide which one you actually want to buy.

4 EVALUATING THE HOMES YOU SEE

In the course of house-hunting, you will probably see many different homes. Some you will be able to eliminate from consideration immediately. Others you will want to think about. You may end up evaluating several homes to see how they compare with your wish list (from Chapter 3) and with each other. In order to keep track of the homes you have looked at and are thinking about, use one or more of the following methods:

- Make a copy of your wish list for each home you view and check off its features and location.
- Take notes by hand or by using a tape recorder.
- Photograph or videotape the home, if the vendor will let you.
- Keep a copy of any "feature sheet" giving details about the home.
- Use the pre-printed evaluation form that your real estate agent may give you.

When you are evaluating the homes you see, think about the location of the property, its features, and its condition. Below we set out some specific things to consider.

LOCATION OF YOUR HOME-TO-BE

Some people fall in love with a place and buy it for its new kitchen and bathrooms, and they don't bother to look beyond the home itself. Once you're in love, it's hard to be objective. The fact that your garbage will only be picked up occasionally, or that the "nearest" school is not exactly near, will pale in importance as you look adoringly at the brand new cabinets and stove or the gleaming bathroom fixtures. But some day after you move in, when your love has started to fade, garbage pick-up and a school within walking distance will suddenly seem a lot more important. That's why we asked you to identify some things about the location of the home when you were creating the wish list.

Some of the "must haves" you identified on your location wish list will depend on the municipality that the property is located in. Each municipality has its own government, services—and taxes. The quality of the services, and their cost, can vary widely from municipality to municipality. Other "must haves" will depend on the neighbourhood. What a neighbourhood is varies from place to place: it can be a small town or a district within a city. Sometimes the choice of neighbourhood and the choice of municipality amount to the same thing. In large urban areas, however, there are so many different kinds of neighbourhoods that the choice of neighbourhood may be as important as, if not more important than, the choice of municipality.

Kind of Location

The kind of location means

- a city
- a suburb
- a small town
- the country

The decision about what kind of location is often a life-style choice, although the choice will also have an effect on the price of the home you buy.

Easy Commuting

Probably the question about location that concerns people most is: How long is it going to take to get to work? The only sure way of finding out is by making the trip at the usual time you travel, using whatever method of transportation you intend to use. The neighbourhood may have traffic restrictions in place designed to limit rush hour traffic. These restrictions may limit your ability to get in and out of the neighbourhood during those times, so don't forget to take them into account too.

If you or members of your family rely on public transit, you should check with the municipal transit authority for information on the nearest transit line, including

- the nearest stop
- when service is available (evenings, weekends, and holidays)
- the frequency of service
- transit routes
- transit fares

Whether you walk, drive, or take public transit, you will want to know how quickly the neighbourhood is plowed out following a snow storm. Call the municipality and ask what plowing priority the street and neighbouring streets have been given.

If the home you are looking at does not have a garage or private drive, check to see whether street parking is allowed and whether you need a municipal permit to park on the street.

Character of the Neighbourhood

The character and appearance of the neighbourhood are major factors in deciding where to buy. First impressions are very important, but remember that one look at a neighbourhood is not enough. You may have done your neighbourhood shopping on weekends or in the evening. What you saw then may not be the same as what you would see on a different day or at a different time. Go back to the neighbourhood or street or high-rise building you are looking at several times. You will see different things at different hours and on different days of the week. Get out of your car and walk around because there are things to hear and smell as well as to see.

Size and Appearance of Homes

Every neighbourhood has a character. Some neighbourhoods are very urban, with homes close together and close to the street, while others are suburban, with houses more widely separated and set back on large lawns. Some neighbourhoods are strictly residential, while others have some shops or light industry. Some neighbourhoods have only single-family homes, while others have multi-family homes or high-rises.

The character of neighbourhoods was once simply allowed to evolve by itself. Now, however, municipalities use **zoning by-laws** to control the look of a neighbourhood. Zoning by-laws can preserve the character of a neighborhood by restricting the rights of owners to change how their property looks, or they can allow the character to change by permitting owners to alter their property.

Municipal zoning by-laws may control

- the minimum size of the lots
- the size of the house on any lot
- the location of the house on any lot

If you like the present character of a neighbourhood and would like it to stay that way, you want to make sure that the zoning does not allow for any changes, such as

- your neighbour tearing down the house next door, which is just like yours, and replacing it with a monster home
- someone buying a neighbouring property and building two or three new homes on it

On the other hand, you may wish to

- build an addition to the existing house
- tear down the existing house and build a new one

If you want to be able to make changes, find out whether the existing zoning will allow you to do so. If it doesn't, you can apply for special permission from the municipality—but the application process can be long and expensive, and there is no guarantee that you will get the permission you're asking for.

Restrictions on Activities

Municipalities also use zoning by-laws to control the activities in the neighbourhood. Zoning by-laws may prevent the carrying on of a business and may also control such things as

- the number of unrelated people who can live in a home
- whether or not rooms or flats can be rented out in a home
- the number and kind of pets a household can have

If you like what's going on in the neighbourhood right now, you may want to contact the municipality to make sure that the zoning by-laws do not allow for changes such as

- a neighbouring property being used for a business
- a neighbouring home being converted into an apartment building or boarding house

But if you think you may want to change the way the property is used after you move in, for example, to carry on your business from your home or to add a basement apartment, you should check that the existing zoning will allow you to do so. Again, if it doesn't you can apply for permission, but getting permission is not a sure thing.

Quiet Street

If you're concerned about traffic noise, be sure to visit the area during morning and evening rush hour. Listen as well as look. While there may not be a lot of traffic on the street itself, there may still be a lot of noise if the neighbourhood is near a major street or highway. Check at other times of the day and night as well to see if noise will be a problem for you. If the street is near a place of worship or sports facilities, for example, there may be a traffic or parking problem at times.

Traffic may not be the only source of noise. Listen for noise from neighbours, airplanes, trains, and any surrounding bars, restaurants, or factories. You should also check for unpleasant smells that might come from restaurants, factories, or farms in the area, or from neighbourhood cooking.

Compatible Neighbours

You may want to know what kind of people live on the street or in the building: Do they look after their homes? Are they young or old? Are they families or single people? You will have to go back to the area at different times on different days to get a sense of who lives there. If you are house-hunting in the winter, you may get a sense that no one lives on the street at all!

If you want to know whether or not there are children in the area, make a visit at the beginning and end of the school day.

You can find out the names of people living in an area by checking a municipal directory that lists residents by address or by checking the municipal assessment rolls. Ask your real estate agent about directories and assessment rolls. Also, ask your agent whether homes in the immediate area are owner-occupied or rented. Owners often take better care of their property than renters.

Once you zero in on a particular home, pay attention to the next-door neighbours to see whether they're neat and quiet. These are the people whose garbage and noisy parties will affect you, and whom you'll have to deal with about fences and mutual drives.

Safety

Television and newspapers give a lot of coverage to violent crime and street prostitution, so you probably know what neighbourhoods have these problems. However, a lot of seemingly secure neighbourhoods have a high rate of burglaries and break-ins that you're not going to hear about in the media. You can find out the crime statistics of a neighbourhood by contacting the local police, a member of the local Neighbourhood Watch, if there is one, or by reading a community newspaper.

Mature Trees and Sidewalks

Are there sidewalks and mature trees? Sidewalks are handy for keeping small children from playing on the road and are safer if you enjoy taking walks or running. Mature trees can make a neighbourhood more attractive, and cooler in the summer, but they can be expensive to maintain and clean up after, and their root systems can cause problems.

Wildlife

Most people realize that if you buy a place in the country, you will have to share the neighbourhood with animals. Even in the city you may have to share your neighbourhood with raccoons, skunks, rabbits, and foxes—in some western areas even with cougars. Call the municipal animal control department to find out whether or not local wildlife is a problem in this neighbourhood.

While we're on the subject of our animal friends, there are urban areas in Canada where termites or carpenter ants are a concern. In such areas, whole neighbourhoods tend to be infested. Call the municipal building department to see whether the neighbourhood where you are house-hunting has been targeted for take-over by insects.

Services

Think about the kinds of services and facilities that you need to make your life safer and easier. Explore the surrounding area to make sure that the services that you'll rely on are readily available.

Schools

If you are a parent with school-aged children, one of the most important considerations when you choose a home is the schools in the area.

Call the municipal school board to find out the names of the elementary, middle, and high schools that serve the neighbourhood. If the local school is not within easy walking distance, ask the school board whether or not bussing is available. Get as much information as you can about the particular school from the school board, from people with children there, or from your real estate agent. You can also call the school and make an appointment for a tour and a meeting with the principal. Consider as king about

- the academic reputation of the school
- the availability of any special academic programs
- the availability of child care before and after school
- the availability of teams, clubs, and other extracurricular activities

While the local school is the most important consideration, there are good reasons to investigate the municipal school system as a whole. Call the school board associated with each municipality and ask them about the things that are important to you.

- If your child has special needs, is gifted, or simply does not thrive in the school nearest to your home, what programs are available and where are they?
- What is the board's policy about the integration of children with disabilities into the general school population?
- Are there specialized programs available at the elementary and secondary levels, such as French immersion or arts and drama, and where are they located?
- How many high schools are there within the school district, and will you have a choice among them?

If your children attend a private school, you may want to know whether or not there are other children in the neighbourhood who attend the school. You can usually get that information from the private school.

Shopping and Other Services

You should check the distance to the nearest stores, gas station, family doctor, place of worship, and other services you will need on a regular basis.

Nearby Emergency Services

Find out how close emergency services are.

- Is there a hospital within a short distance, and does it have a 24-hour emergency department?
- If there's no nearby hospital, is there an ambulance station with paramedics?
- How close is the nearest fire station, and how long would it take a fire crew to respond to a fire at your home?

• How close is the nearest police station, and what would their response time be to an emergency call from your home?

Recreational Facilities

You may want to drive or walk around the neighbourhood to see whether there are any nearby public

- parks
- playgrounds
- skating rinks
- tennis courts
- gyms
- swimming pools
- golf courses
- libraries

Some municipalities run instructional programs and sports leagues for both children and adults, and some do not. If the municipality has only a few facilities, you may find them crowded and the programs overbooked. Telephone the municipality and ask for information on community facilities and activities—and be sure to ask how difficult it is to register in programs. Will you have to line up at 6 a.m. to get your child into a swimming program, or can you just drop off an application and be assured of getting a spot?

Snow Removal

There are two kinds of municipalities when it comes to removing snow from the sidewalks: those that do and those that don't. But just because the municipality doesn't shovel your sidewalk doesn't mean that you don't have to. In fact, most municipalities have by-laws that require homeowners to remove the snow from the sidewalk in front of their house within a certain period of time after a snowfall. Some municipalities will remove your snow, if you don't, but will charge you for the service, usually by adding it to your tax bill. In addition, you may also be fined for not shovelling. Some municipalities, if requested to do so, will automatically shovel the sidewalks of homeowners who are elderly or disabled, usually at no charge or for a minimal charge.

Telephone the municipality and say that you would like information on snow removal.

Garbage Pick-up and Recycling

You put your garbage in the garbage can and leave it on the curb, and that's all there is to it, right? Wrong!

Every municipality has rules governing what garbage they will take, when they will take it, and how it must be packaged. While there are some municipalities that will pick up anything left at the curb that doesn't move (Beware, napping children and animals!), others will not pick up garbage if it is put out too long before pick-up, or in the wrong kind or size of container, or if it is not properly sorted into real garbage and recyclables. A homeowner we know, frustrated at having had her garbage rejected on several occasions, finally placed a big red bow on the garbage bag, with a note which read, "Will you accept this if it is gift-wrapped?"

There are some municipalities that do not pick up garbage at all, particularly in rural areas. Then it's up to you to take the garbage to the local dump, and you usually have to pay a fee for this privilege.

Telephone the municipality and ask for information on garbage removal and recycling. Some municipalities will provide you with written information and instructions.

Mail Delivery to Your Door

Most, but not all, Canadians have their mail delivered to their door. In many rural areas, Canada Post does not offer home mail delivery. Instead, mail is delivered to a local post office where it must be picked up. Even in some urban areas, usually in newer subdivisions or developments, home mail delivery is not available. In these areas, mail is delivered to community mailboxes. If you have any doubts about whether or not home delivery of mail is offered in the neighbourhood, call Canada Post's customer relations department.

Water and Sewage Systems

In most urban areas water supply and sewage disposal are provided by the municipality. While the municipal water supplies are usually safe, there are some places where there have been problems with water purity. Call the municipality to see whether or not there have been problems in recent memory. You don't want to cope with "boil water" orders as well as the more pedestrian troubles in life.

In most rural areas, each homeowner must rely on well water and must have a septic tank for waste disposal. If homes in the municipality rely on well water, the question is whether there is any groundwater contamination. Again, call the municipality for information.

Low Property Taxes

Property taxes vary widely from municipality to municipality. Strikingly similar homes in neighbouring municipalities can have very different tax bills. The factors that affect whether a municipality's taxes are high or low are many and complicated. Higher taxes do not necessarily mean that you will get more or better services. To get information about the general level of property taxes in a particular municipality, speak to a real estate agent familiar with that municipality.

Stable Property Values

When you buy a home, in addition to getting a place to live you are making a very large investment. The days of making huge profits on the sale of your home are probably over, but you hope that when it comes time to sell your home, you will make some money, or at least not lose any.

There are certain areas where homes tend to hold their value better, even if prices generally are falling. In these areas, home prices also seem to rise higher when prices are going up. No one can predict the future, but an experienced real estate agent can tell you about the history of prices in the area.

FEATURES OF THE HOME

House-hunting can be a bit of a chore, but it is also an adventure. It gives you a chance to see how other people live (and whether their furniture matches). Even if you decide that a particular home is not for you, you can get decorating or renovation ideas you'll be able to use in the home you do buy.

Now is the time that your wish list will be useful. Check how many of your "must haves" and "would likes" each home you visit has. But don't just focus on features. When you go through a home, try to picture how you would feel living there. Is there enough room for all of your family and possessions? Will you feel comfortable there? Will the home suit your needs five years from now?

CONDITION OF THE HOME

Once you've found a home that has the features you're looking for, go over it carefully to make sure that it doesn't also have problems you'd like to avoid. It's not enough just to look at the place; you also have to ask questions. And don't simply ask questions about specific things you may notice: ask the agent (or the vendor if present) if he or she is aware of any problems with the property.

The vendor and the vendor's real estate agent have a legal obligation to tell you about any problems they know about, whether or not you ask. In fact, if the vendor does not inform you about a defect that he or she knows about (whether or not you ask about it) you may be able to sue the vendor later. For more information about this see Chapter 10.

You may be thinking that you will have any home you buy professionally inspected, so why should you ask questions about it and go over it like a detective? While a professional home inspection should uncover any defects that the vendor is trying to hide, it is too expensive to do on every home you look at. You will only have one done only on a home you are serious about buying. We recommend that you ask questions and do an inspection yourself to eliminate homes that are in poor condition, so that you don't waste your time on them.

You can get a sense of the general condition of a home just by casually looking around. You'll notice right away if the house smells or if every room needs painting. But try to get a better idea of the potential repair and maintenance costs by focusing on the things in the following list:

EXTERIOR OF A HOUSE OR TOWNHOUSE

Roof
> Are shingles missing, cracked, or curled?
> How old is the roof? Even heavy-duty grade shingles only last 20 years.

Chimney
> Is it straight?
> Is the brick crumbling?

Eavestroughs and downspouts
> Are they rusted or corroded?
> Do they overflow?

Foundations
> Are there visible cracks or crumbling mortar?
> Is there soil erosion around downspouts?
> Do decks, patios, or the yard slope toward the house? If they do, you can expect water to run into the basement.

Brickwork
> Are there cracked or loose bricks? This may be caused by settlement in the foundation.

Is the mortar crumbling?

Are the bricks flaking (spalling)? The underlying cause may be poor-quality bricks and poor construction.

Is there white powder (efflorescence) on the bricks? This is an indication that moisture has penetrated the brick either from outside or inside the house.

Siding

Is vinyl siding buckling?

Is wood siding splitting, rotting, or buckling?

Is metal siding dented, pitted, corroded, or buckling?

Is stucco cracked, chipped, or loose?

Paint

Is paint peeling or flaking?

Concrete stairs and walkways

Are they uneven or cracked?

Wooden stairs, decks, and patios

Are they uneven, sagging, or rotting?

Are boards loose or missing?

Pool and equipment

Is the water cloudy or still? The pump may not work.

Is the pump noisy?

Are tiles loose?

Trees and landscaping

Are trees and shrubs overgrown or dying?

If house is exposed to the weather, are there trees to form a windbreak?

Fences and retaining walls

Are they leaning or rotting?

Next-door neighbours

Do they maintain their properties?

EXTERIOR OF AN APARTMENT-STYLE CONDO

Grounds
> Are they well kept? Are trees and shrubs healthy? Is there litter?
> Are there people you don't like the look of hanging around?

The Building
> Is brickwork discoloured or chipping or cracking?
> Are there cracks in the building's foundations?
> Is metal on doors, windows or balconies rusting?
> Can you hear noise (loud music, arguments, air conditioners) drifting out of the building?
> Is the security system working properly?
> Are entrance areas and corridors clean and well-lit?

Parking
> Is the parking area secure—well-lit and open, if outside; or accessible only by key or card, if inside?
> Do garage doors or barriers work properly?
> Are there security cameras?

INTERIOR OF ANY HOME

Kitchen
> Is there space for your refrigerator, dishwasher, and stove? Measure.
> What is the interior condition of cabinets?
> Are there signs of leakage under the sink?

Bathrooms
> Is there mildew or mould in bathtubs and showers?
> Is there adequate ventilation?
> Are there cracked or missing tiles?
> Are fixtures stained, cracked, or chipped?
> Is paint blistering or peeling or is plaster soft?
> Are there signs of leakage anywhere?
> Check the water pressure by turning on the taps and flushing toilets.

Walls
> Are walls straight?
> Are there cracks or holes?

Is plaster bulging?

Is paint chipping, flaking, or peeling? Most homes built before the 1960s have lead paint on the walls—if not as the surface coat of paint then somewhere below. Lead paint is not a health hazard as long as the paint is not flaking or chipping off the walls or woodwork. If it is, there is a danger of small children or pets eating paint flakes and suffering lead poisoning. (Removing lead paint should be done by professionals since the stripping process releases lead dust into the air.)

Is paint faded?

Is wallpaper peeling?

Ceilings

Are they stained, cracked, or warped? Is paint peeling? Any of these things may mean water leakage.

Floors and stairways

Are floors or stairs uneven?

Do floorboards squeak?

Are there hardwood floors under the carpeting (ask, or check for yourself by lifting loose carpet)?

Are floor tiles chipped, missing, uneven, or discoloured?

Is carpeting worn or stained?

Doors and windows

Are doors and windows unevenly hung?

Do doors and windows stick or scrape?

Are window panes broken or missing?

Are window frames rotting or stained?

Is caulking missing from window frames?

Air-conditioning

Is there central air-conditioning?

If not, is the heating system hot water? Not every hot-water heating system can accommodate a soft-duct cooling system.

Insects and other pests

Check for evidence of termites or carpenter ants: Is there sawdust around exposed wood? If so, tap the wood to see if it sounds hollow.

Check for evidence of insects or rodents by looking inside cupboards and closets for dead insects or mice, droppings, or traps and poison bait.

Neighbours

Can you hear them? Especially important if you're going to be sharing an interior wall, but noisy neighbours can make themselves known through open windows and even brick walls

INTERIOR OF A HOUSE

Basement

Are walls stained or damp? Are they crumbling or do they have white spots? These are signs of a damp basement.

Does the basement smell damp or musty?

Are there signs of drain backup?

Heating

How high are heating costs? Ask.

What kind of heating system is used and how old is it? Find out Then check with the manufacturer or its service representative how long such a furnace is designed to last. If the furnace is not natural gas but you would like to convert to natural gas, call the gas company to find out whether this kind of furnace can be converted.

Has the furnace been professionally serviced on a regular basis? Ask.

Do all the chimneys have liners? Ask.

Are furnace and pipes corroded?

Is there oil spillage around an oil furnace?

Is there a gas smell around a gas furnace?

Are there leaks around hot water radiators?

If the weather is cold while you're house-hunting, are there portable heaters around? Do you feel drafts in the house? Have doors and windows been left open to hide the fact that the house is cold even when the heat is on?

Electrical system

What kind of wiring is in the house? Copper wiring is safer than the aluminum wiring that is found in many older houses.

Check inside the control panel to see whether there are modern circuit breakers or older style fuse boxes.

Insulation

Has the attic been insulated and vented? Attic insulation is more important than exterior wall insulation. An attic vent will draw off moisture and will keep the house cooler in the summer.

What kind of insulation has been used? If urea formaldehyde foam insulation (UFFI) has been used, the resale value of the house will be affected, even though recent studies suggest that UFFI is not a health hazard.

WATERWORKS

Plumbing

Are there rust stains in the sinks and toilet?

Is the water pressure adequate? (Turn on taps and flush toilets.)

Septic systems and wells

How old is the well?

When was the septic tank last inspected and cleaned?

When was the well water last tested for purity, and what was the result?

What is the capacity of the well, and is there a cistern?

How many gallons per hour can the well pump handle?

SPECIAL CONSIDERATIONS FOR CONDOMINIUMS

If you're thinking about buying a condominium, there are special concerns that you should turn your mind to before buying a particular condominium unit.

What is Condominium Ownership?

Condominium ownership is different from ordinary home ownership, whether the condominium is an apartment in a high-rise or low-rise building, a duplex or a townhouse. If you buy into a condominium, you become the owner of a particular apartment or house. You also become an owner, along with all the other apartment or homeowners, of a share of the **common areas** of the condominium development such as the hallways, the elevators, the stairs, the lobby, the parking areas, the grounds, and recreational facilities. Common areas also include the exterior structure of the condominium buildings and all shared mechanical equipment such as heating, cooling, and water systems.

As an owner of the common areas you are required to pay a **monthly maintenance fee** for their repair and maintenance. The monthly mainte-nance fees are put into a fund out of which repairs and maintenance costs are paid. Part of the monthly fees are paid into a **contingency fund** or **reserve fund** which is set aside to cover costs if the condominium building needs major attention (for example if there are leaks in the walls or cracks in the foundation or serious problems with the heating system). When there's not enough money in the contingency fund to deal with a problem, all of the owners can be required to pay a **special assessment** to cover the repairs.

There are both advantages and disadvantages to condominium owner-ship. A major attraction of condominium ownership is that responsibility for actually doing maintenance and repairs belongs to the condominium corpo-ration. (That means that you won't have to worry about mowing the lawn or shovelling the snow—although you are responsible for the maintenance of the inside of your unit.) Also, some condominium developments offer facil-ities like tennis courts, exercise rooms, party rooms, and swimming pools. On the downside, condominiums have rules and by-laws that may limit your freedom to use your home as you wish.

Evaluating a Resale Condominium

If you're buying a condominium you should evaluate it the way you would any other type of home. But there are additional matters to consider.

Is the Condominium Corporation Financially Sound?

As a potential unit owner, you want to be reasonably sure that your month-ly maintenance fee will not change drastically, and that you will not be called upon to pay any special assessment. Asking the following questions before you decide to buy may keep you from buying into a condominium corporation that is not in good financial health.

WHAT IS THE CURRENT MAINTENANCE FEE AND IS IT REASONABLE? Find out what the current monthly maintenance fee is and make sure it is an amount you can afford. Does the maintenance fee include heat, electricity, and water, or are they extra? Ask the condominium manager whether the level of the month-ly maintenance fees throughout the condominium is high enough to cover the ongoing maintenance of the condominium and any expected repairs. If it is, fees probably won't rise too much after you buy.

ARE THE OTHER OWNERS UP TO DATE IN PAYING THEIR MAINTENANCE FEES? The condominium corporation may have set exactly the right monthly fees. But if many unit owners are not paying those fees, you could end up paying higher fees after you move in. You should ask the manager if all owners are up to date in their payments, and if not, how much has not been paid. While you're at it, ask what percentage of the units are occupied by owners. Owners who live in their units are more likely to continue to make their maintenance payments.

HOW LARGE IS THE CONTINGENCY FUND? Find out how much is presently in the contingency fund, and how much unit owners are required to contribute. If there's a fund of a reasonable size, your risk of paying a special assessment is reduced.

IS THE CONDOMINIUM PROPERLY MAINTAINED? If the condominium is properly maintained, the chance of a major unexpected repair is reduced. Ask the condominium manager whether any major repairs are being planned. If so, ask whether there is enough money on hand to pay for the repair. Also ask what major repairs have recently been done. Ask to look at the minutes of the condominium association's meetings for the past year—if there are problems in the building they'll likely have been brought up at a meeting. And you can arrange for a building inspection just as you arrange for a home inspection before you buy. Finally, if the building is still fairly new (less than 5 years old in most provinces), check with your provincial new home warranty plan to see if the building is covered under the plan. We talk about new home warranty plans at the end of this chapter.

How Well is the Condominium Managed?

The condominium manager looks after the maintenance of and repairs to the condominium. Ask other residents whether or not they are pleased with the present manager.

Features of the Unit

In addition to looking for the things you would look for in any home, make sure that your unit will not be too noisy by checking the soundproofing between your unit and neighbouring units. Also note how close the unit is to elevators, garbage chutes, recreational facilities, and other noisy common areas.

Facilities

Find out what facilities are included in your ownership. For example:

SECURITY: What kind of security is offered and does it seem adequate for your needs?

PARKING: Is a parking spot included with your ownership, and is there enough guest parking?

RECREATIONAL FACILITIES: What facilities are available? Are they well maintained? Is use of them included in your ownership or do you have to pay an additional fee? (If they're included—meaning that you're paying for them in your monthly fee—will you actually use the facilities or will you be spending money for a pool you never get wet in or a workout room you never raise a sweat in?) Are non-owners also allowed to use the facilities? Are the facilities over-crowded?

Restrictions

Find out from the condominium manager what restrictions there are in the by-laws and rules of the condominium corporation. For example:

- Can you rent out your unit?
- Can you have pets?
- Can you carry on a business in your unit?
- If you have a yard, can you garden? If you have windows or a balcony, can you put out plants?

Buying a Newly Constructed Condominium

Many of the issues we raised about resale condos apply to new condos as well (so read that section now if you didn't before).

If you buy a newly constructed condominium and the condominium is not **registered** at the closing date, you cannot become the legal owner until later. You will, however, probably have to make a cash payment. You will also be required to make monthly rental payments—but that's OK because you'll be able to move into the building as a tenant. Once the condominium corporation is registered, you will become the legal owner...and can stop paying rent and start paying your mortgage.

SPECIAL CONSIDERATIONS
FOR HOMES UNDER CONSTRUCTION

If you are buying a house or townhouse in a new development or an apartment in a new building, there are a number of special concerns.

Builder's Reputation

You are buying the services of the builder as well as the space your home will occupy, so it's important to buy from a reputable builder. You probably want to choose a builder who is registered in your province's new home warranty program. Check the builder's track record for building well and responding to complaints. Try to talk to owners of homes in developments or complexes by the same builder. Call your local Home Builders' Association or your provincial new home warranty program for information—especially whether there have been complaints—about the builder.

Picturing What Your Home Will Look Like

When you buy a house in a new development or an apartment in a new building, it is usually built *after* you buy it, so you have to imagine what it will look like. Sometimes the builder will have a model home or suite for you to look at, but other times you will have to buy from floor plans and sketches. It's important to make sure that the builder agrees to build the home you think you are getting.

In a development, your neighbours' houses will not usually be built either at the time you buy, so you will have to imagine what the street will look like as well as the house. You will probably pick the location of your house within the development from a site model or map. Look carefully at the model or map to see whether your street is likely to become a heavy-traffic route once the development is completed. Ask where shops, schools, and other sevices will be located, if it isn't clear from the model or map.

You should also go to a actual site of the house to check things like the view, the slope of the land and closeness to noisy highways. If the site you chose is located near the boundaries of the development, look at what is built on the neighbouring land. If there is nothing there, ask the builder what is going to be built.

Possible Inconvenience

When you buy a home that hasn't been built yet, there can be construction delays. You may not be able to move in when you planned. If you are selling your present home, you may end up having to find another place to stay until construction is finished.

Once you get into your new home, you may continue to live with the dust and noise of construction for quite some time. Roads may not be paved and landscaping completed until well after you move in.

New Home Warranties

All provinces in Canada have a new home warranty program, although in most provinces they're optional. If you deal with a builder who is registered under the provincial warranty program, your home will be covered against certain problems that may arise within a specified period of time after you buy. You will be given warranty documents, and your lawyer should go over them with you. You will probably have to make a detailed inspection of the home with the builder's representative before closing to make a note of any problems. The builder is supposed to fix them within a short time after closing. After closing you will be covered against things like major structural defects, defects in work and materials, water seepage through the foundation, defects in the electrical, plumbing and heating systems, and violations of the provincial building code. The warranty period, which depends on the province and the nature of the problem, can be from one to five years in most provinces (one to seven years in Ontario). As a rule the warranty kicks in only if the builder can't or won't fix the problems and the warranty plan administrators agree that the problems are covered under the plan. It may take time and possibly even a lawsuit to get a payout from the plan. In British Columbia the new home warranty plan went bankrupt when too many owners of leaky condos flooded the plan with claims. Having a new home warranty is not like having a fairy godmother.

5 MAKING AN OFFER TO PURCHASE

GETTING THE HOME YOU WANT (AT THE RIGHT PRICE)

Making an **offer to purchase** is how you tell a vendor that you want to buy his or her home and on what terms—particularly price. That sounds pretty simple, but sometimes it can take a bit of strategy to get a vendor to sell to you rather than someone else, and to sell at a price you like (or at least can afford). Your strategy will depend on what state the local real estate market is in.

In a Seller's Market

If you're buying in a **seller's market** (also known as a "hot" market), you really have to be on the ball to get what you want. While you're checking the plumbing upstairs another buyer could be getting his offer accepted downstairs, or the offer you put in could be topped by someone who just walked in off the street. Here are some of the suggestions experienced real estate agents make to help buyers in a hot market:

- Do all your homework beforehand—check out the neighbourhood for easy commuting, good services, low taxes, neighbours you'll have things in common with, and all the rest of it—before you start viewing homes.

- Be ready to view homes the second they come on to the market. If you wait until a time that's convenient for you, the "For Sale" sign will have been replaced by a "Sold" sign.

- Be ready to make an offer quickly—have your spouse and lawyer lined up for action, and get a pre-approved mortgage. (Note, though, that the mortgage lender will still want to inspect and appraise the property before actually giving you the mortgage money...just hope that the mortgage lender agrees with you about the home's value!) Have a home inspector at the ready too, although things may move too fast for you to have an inspection done before you make an offer. Some buyers even court disaster by putting in an offer before their spouses have seen the place.

- Offer the vendor's asking price or more—even though it's very common to offer less than the asking price and even though the majority of homes across Canada sell for about 95 per cent of asking price.

- Don't put any **conditions** (see below at page 66) in your offer, and be ready to agree to the vendor's terms such as closing date.

- Don't get caught in a bidding war. Set a cap on the price you'll offer and don't let yourself get drawn in to offering more. Run away and live to buy another day.

- If the market's just too hot for you, find a cooler area to buy in. A little further away from the action, similar homes may be selling for considerably less.

In a Buyer's Market

A **buyer's market** is also known as a "cool" market. Prices are already in the buyer's favour, but you may be able to get an even better deal.

- Do your research and know the value of homes in the area.

- Don't make a ridiculously low offer. You'll just irritate the seller, who may refuse to sell to you even if you make a more reasonable offer. Offer an amount only somewhat below the home's value.

- Look for a motivated seller, if there are similar homes for sale at similar prices. Someone who has to sell quickly will be more willing to accept a low offer than someone who's decided to hang on like grim death and wait for a good price.

In a New Development or New Building

Buyers often get a better price at the beginning of a project, when builders are still looking for bank financing or market build-up and need to sign up buyers to get them. Prices may rise as the houses or units are bought up—but prices may also fall on resale, so don't get carried away by any "almost sold out!" hype.

If the market for the homes on offer is slow, you may be able to negotiate a better deal with the builder. You may not be able to get a lower base purchase price, but you might be able to get a good price on upgrades (for example, hardwood flooring, more expensive carpeting, more luxurious bathroom fixtures).

MAKING YOUR OFFER

When you decide to make an offer on a home, your agent will discuss with you the price you want to pay and other matters relating to the deal (we discuss all of those matters below), and will then draw up the offer using a preprinted form. The form will be titled "**agreement of purchase and sale**" or, in Quebec, "**promise to purchase**." When the offer has been drawn up, you should have it reviewed by a lawyer before you sign it, if at all possible.

After you've signed the offer, your real estate agent will present it to the vendor, together with a cheque for the **deposit** (a deposit is a traditional way of showing that your offer is serious). You will have stated in the offer how long the vendor has to respond before the offer ends. The vendor may reject your offer, sign back a **counter-offer** (with new terms such as a higher price, or a different closing date), or accept your offer. If the vendor rejects your offer, there is no contract. You can either make another offer or walk away. If the vendor signs back a counter-offer, there is no contract. You can either accept the counter-offer, reject it, or make yet another counter-offer. If the vendor accepts your offer before it ends or you accept the vendor's counter-offer, you have a contract. The contract is called an **agreement of purchase and sale**.

THE NATURE OF THE AGREEMENT OF PURCHASE AND SALE

An agreement of purchase and sale is a contract in which you promise to pay the vendor an agreed amount of money in return for ownership of the property, and the vendor promises to transfer to you ownership of the property. Unless the agreement says otherwise, that ownership is to be unlimited and free of claims by anyone else.

The agreement of purchase and sale does not make you the owner of the property. The actual transfer of ownership and payment of the money take place at a later time that is called the **completion date** or **closing date**. You have a legal obligation under the agreement of purchase and sale to pay the promised amount of money (the **purchase price**) on the closing date, and the vendor has a legal obligation to transfer ownership to you on that date. If either one of you decides not to go through with the deal, that person can be sued.

By law, a contract to buy and sell land has to be in writing. If you make just an oral agreement with the vendor to buy the house, you won't be able to force the vendor to transfer ownership to you.

THE CONTENTS OF YOUR OFFER

The printed form of agreement of purchase and sale used by real estate agents varies from province to province, but the contents are similar. There are blank spaces to be filled in with the following:

- the names of the purchaser, the vendor, and the real estate agents
- a brief description of the property—its municipal address, lot measurements if it's a house, and maybe its lot and plan number
- the purchase price, the deposit, and the way in which you will pay the remainder of the purchase price (in cash, for example, or a combination of cash and a mortgage given back to the vendor)
- any chattels to be included in the sale (see below at page 65)
- the expiry date of your offer, the date by which your lawyer's investigation of title to the property must be completed, and the closing date

There are also a number of standard preprinted paragraphs, usually in very small print. Maybe it's just as well that the print is very small, because otherwise you might be tempted to try to read the paragraphs. These paragraphs are drafted by lawyers for lawyers and are very difficult to understand. The most important of these paragraphs deal with the title or ownership rights you will get when the deal closes and

- whether or not you agree to accept any limitations on your title or ownership rights
- the things your lawyer has to do to make sure you get the title or ownership rights you were promised by the vendor
- what happens if the vendor can't give you the title or ownership rights that were promised

The agreement of purchase and sale also has a place where you can insert custom-made clauses that cover matters of importance to you that are not mentioned in the standard preprinted clauses. Finally, the printed form has a place for you to sign and for the vendor to sign if your offer is accepted (once you've both signed, the offer becomes a contract).

Some of the things we've mentioned so far are fairly self-explanatory, like the names of the parties and real estate agents and the address of the property. But we think you need to know a bit more about some of the other things in an offer, so don't stop reading yet.

The Description of the Property

If you're buying a house, the dimensions of the land are set out. The vendor only has to sell you a property that is the size set out in the agreement. You want to make sure the property is the size that you think it is.

Any **easements** are also set out. An easement (**servitude** in Quebec) is a right that someone has to use or cross over another person's land. For example, if there is a shared driveway, the next-door neighbour has an easement over your half of the driveway, and you have an easement over the neighbour's half. If you are supposed to be getting an easement over a neighbouring property, you want to make sure that the description says so. If the description says that the property you're buying has an easement over it, you will have to take ownership of the property subject to that easement.

The Purchase Price and the Deposit

The purchase price is what you agree to pay the vendor for the home. The deposit comes out of the purchase price, and the amount of the deposit is deducted from the amount you pay the vendor on closing. As we mentioned in Chapter 2, the price may be **adjusted** (increased or decreased) before the closing in order to take account of such things as property taxes and utility payments made—or not made—by the vendor. The adjusted purchase price, not the purchase price in the agreement of purchase and sale, is the total amount you will pay the vendor.

When it comes time to pay, you'll put together the amount of the purchase price in up to three ways. The purchase price is made up of

- the deposit
- any mortgage that you take over from the vendor, or any mortgage in which the vendor acts as your mortgage lender (these are, respectively, an **assumed mortgage** and a **vendor take-back mortgage**, and we talk about them on page 64 and also in Chapter 7)
- the cash you pay on closing (calculated as the adjusted purchase price minus the deposit and minus the amount of any mortgage you take over from the vendor)

The Deposit

Your deposit—commonly equal to five per cent of the purchase price in most provinces—is handed over to the vendor with your offer. It will be cashed only if your offer is accepted, and the money doesn't become the vendor's until the closing date.

If you back out of the purchase without a legally valid reason, you may have to compensate the vendor for any losses he or she has as a result. Instead of suing you for the actual amount lost, the vendor can claim your deposit. So you stand to lose the amount of your deposit if you refuse to complete the purchase (that's why giving a deposit shows that you're serious about buying). The vendor will want a big deposit to make it less likely that you will refuse to complete the purchase. You can ask your real estate agent how large a deposit you should make. But the real estate agent also wants to make sure that you will complete the purchase (because otherwise he or she won't receive any commission), so the agent can't be totally objective.

When a real estate agent is involved, the deposit cheque is made payable to the vendor's real estate agent—not to the vendor. The real estate agent holds the deposit money in trust until the deal closes. During that time the money (which can be thousands of dollars) earns interest. If the money were sitting in your bank account, the interest would be yours. There is no reason why the real estate agent should be allowed to keep the interest, so have your agent put a clause into the offer that the vendor's agent will pay the interest to you.

Assumed Mortgages and Vendor Take-Back Mortgages

The vendor may already have a mortgage on the home. If the mortgage is in the right amount and has a favourable interest rate, you may want to **assume** this existing mortgage instead of or in addition to arranging a new one. If you assume an existing mortgage, you take over the vendor's mortgage payments and are given a credit against the purchase price equal to the outstanding balance of the mortgage. In other words, the amount of cash you have to pay on closing is reduced by the amount of the mortgage balance. If you want to assume an existing mortgage, you say so in your offer and set out the details of the mortgage (which are provided by the vendor's agent).

Sometimes the vendor may be willing to lend you some of the purchase price through a **vendor take-back mortgage**. The amount of any vendor take-back mortgage is deducted from what you have to pay in cash on closing. After the closing, you will make mortgage payments to the vendor. If you want the vendor to take back a mortgage, say so in your offer and set out details of the mortgage (this time the details are made up by you).

Cash on Closing

On closing you are required to pay the rest of the purchase price after deducting your deposit and the amount of any assumed mortgage or vendor take-back mortgage. This money is to be paid in cash or by certified cheque. You give the money to your lawyer for payment to the vendor's lawyer.

Chattels and Fixtures

In legal jargon, there are two kinds of property: real property and personal property. Land and a building on it are real property. Personal property is property you can move, like a sofa, a television, your clothing. Personal property can also be called **chattels** (**movables** in Quebec).

Personal property can become attached to real property. When this happens, the personal property becomes part of the real property, and then is called a **fixture**. You can go to a building store and buy wooden boards, which are personal property. If you use the wooden boards to make a built-in bookcase attached to the wall of your home, the bookcase is a fixture.

When you buy a home, fixtures are automatically included as part of it. Sometimes a vendor wants to take certain fixtures out of the house. In order for the vendor to do so, the agreement of purchase and sale must specifical ly state which fixtures. Chattels, on the other hand, for example washers and dryers, are not included with the home unless the agreement of purchase and sale says that they are.

It's often hard to know what is a chattel and what is a fixture. You can't always tell by looking at a bookcase whether it's attached to the wall or just standing there. If it's attached, it's a fixture and included with the house; but if it's not attached, it's a chattel and not included. So if you want something included in the purchase price, it's important to say so in your offer. If you don't, you may think it's included and staying while the vendor is planning to remove it.

Be sure to name specific things you want such as

- appliances
- light fixtures and ceiling fans
- carpets, drapes, and blinds
- bookcases and shelving systems, including closet shelves
- satellite dishes
- storage sheds
- garage door openers
- window air-conditioners

Dates

There are several places in the preprinted agreement of purchase and sale for dates to be inserted.

One date is called the **irrevocable date**, which is the date that your offer to purchase the home ends. The vendor has until that date to accept your offer. If the vendor does not accept by that date, your offer automatically expires. It is best to give the vendor only a short time, such as 24 or 48 hours, to decide whether to accept your offer. You don't want to have to wait too long to start looking at other homes if the vendor is not going to accept your offer.

Another date is the **closing date**, which is the date on which the purchase will be completed—the day you pay your money and become the owner of the home. Choose a closing date that gives you enough time to get the money you need to pay for the home and to get ready to move. Even if you're in a hurry, give your lawyer enough time to do the necessary legal work. In addition, the registry office (where most closings take place) is busier on some days than others. If you pick a busy day for your closing, there may be delays. Ask your real estate agent for advice about choosing a date. Your lawyer will check the date too when reviewing your offer.

The agreement of purchase and sale may also state a period of time in which or date by which your lawyer is to complete an investigation of the vendor's title to the property. This date is often known as the **requisition date**. Your real estate agent can give you some advice about the requisition date, and your lawyer should check this date as well before you sign the offer. Again, you want to make sure that your lawyer has enough time to do a proper investigation.

Custom-Made Clauses

In addition to the standard preprinted paragraphs in an agreement of purchase and sale, there is blank space to add custom-made clauses.

Conditions

You may want to be able to get out of the agreement of purchase and sale, even after the vendor has signed, for certain reasons:

- You can't sell your present home.
- You can't get mortgage financing.
- The vendor's mortgage lender won't allow you to assume the vendor's mortgage.
- A professional inspection of the home has turned up serious problems.

In order to be able to get out of the deal for any of these reasons, you must add a **condition**, a clause stating that the agreement is conditional upon the occurence of a certain event by a certain date. If the event does not happen by that date, the agreement is at an end and you can get your deposit back. If the event does happen by that date, the contract is binding and the deal goes ahead.

MAKING YOUR OFFER CONDITIONAL ON SELLING YOUR PRESENT HOME: If you already own a home, you may not have sold it yet. If you sign an unconditional agreement to buy this home, you will be legally bound to buy it, even if you can't find a buyer for your old home. To protect yourself, you can make your offer to purchase conditional on being able to sell your old home within a fixed period of time. If your offer to buy is accepted and you haven't sold your home before the end of that period, you don't have to go through with the deal. The vendor may not want to agree to a condition like this, especially if you're offering a lower price than the vendor would like.

MAKING YOUR OFFER CONDITIONAL ON GETTING MORTGAGE FINANCING: If you will need a mortgage to pay for your new home, you don't want to be legally bound to buy if you can't get a mortgage. If you make your offer conditional on getting satisfactory mortgage financing, you can choose not to complete the deal if you can't get a mortgage for the amount of money you need at a reasonable interest rate.

MAKING YOUR OFFER CONDITIONAL ON BEING ABLE TO ASSUME THE VENDOR'S MORTGAGE: The vendor may have a mortgage on the home that you'd like to take over. If the mortgage documents say that the mortgage lender's approval is necessary before the mortgage can be assumed, the offer should be conditional on getting that approval. Otherwise you'll have to go through with the deal even though you can't get the mortgage.

MAKING YOUR OFFER CONDITIONAL ON A SATISFACTORY HOME INSPECTION: Although you carefully looked over the home before you decided to make your offer, we strongly recommend that you make the offer conditional on a satisfactory inspection report from a qualified home inspector. A home inspector will examine the home and report to you on its age and condition, tell you whether repairs are necessary, and give you an estimate of repair costs. Ask your real estate agent or your lawyer for the name of a reliable inspector. If the inspector finds that the place is in bad shape for its age, you may be able to refuse to go ahead with the purchase.

Using a Condition to Pull Out

You can't just use a condition as an excuse to back out of the deal. You must make all reasonable efforts to satisfy the condition. If the agreement is conditional on selling your present home, you must list it for sale. If someone makes you a reasonable offer, you can't refuse it and then try to get out of the deal by saying you have not sold your home. If the agreement is conditional on your being able to get a mortgage or assume the vendor's mortgage, you must apply for the mortgage and provide all necessary information to the mortgage lender. You can't simply not apply and then try to get out of the deal by saying you have no mortgage. If the agreement is conditional on a satisfactory professional home inspection, you must arrange for the inspection. You won't be able to claim that the inspection is not satisfactory unless it reveals significant problems.

Other Special Clauses

You may wish to put in a clause that gives you the right to visit the home before the closing date so that you can take measurements for carpets and drapes or have a contractor give you an estimate for work to be done after closing.

You may also wish to add a clause giving you the right to inspect the property just before closing to make sure that it's in more or less the same condition it was in when you agreed to buy it.

If the property has a pool and you can't have it inspected because the pool isn't open for the summer, you may want to add a clause that the vendor **warrants** that the pool and equipment are in good working order, and that your lawyer can hold back part of the purchase price until you have had the pool inspected. If the inspection confirms that everything is all right, the money will then be paid to the vendor.

There may be other clauses that your lawyer or real estate agent will suggest that you should put into your offer.

The Vendor May Not Agree to All Your Terms

You can put anything you like into your offer, but it's entirely up to the vendor to accept it, reject it, or sign back a counter-offer. The things that the vendor is most likely to change are the purchase price and the amount of the deposit. The vendor may also want a different closing date, or may remove one or more of your special clauses. If the vendor makes any changes to your offer, then it's a counter-offer and you have to decide whether or not you want to accept it.

IT'S IMPORTANT TO HAVE A LAWYER REVIEW YOUR OFFER

You might wonder why you must have your lawyer review your offer when you have an experienced real estate agent to help you draft it.

Once your offer is accepted by the vendor, you have a binding contract. You are stuck with the deal! You will have to pay a lot of money when the deal closes, and you want to be sure that you'll get what you want in return. Your lawyer reviews the offer to make sure that it includes all the right clauses so that you will get what you expect.

In a hot real estate market, you have to move quickly to make an offer on a property before someone else snaps it up. You may think there is no time to have your lawyer review your offer, and you may be right. (You can ask your lawyer before you start house-hunting, for advice about clauses you should include in any offer you make.) On the other hand you may be wrong, so call your lawyer to see if he or she can review the offer quickly— by fax, for example. If not, ask your real estate agent to put a clause in the offer making the agreement conditional on satisfactory review by your lawyer within 24 to 48 hours. Or, finally, you can just put your offer in and hope for the best.

PRIVATE SALES

If you decide to make an offer to a vendor who is selling privately, you will not have the help of a real estate agent to draft your offer. The vendor may give you a printed form to use—the vendor may even try to fill it out for you. Your best bet is to have your lawyer draft the offer for you. However, if the offer is drafted by you or the vendor, it is absolutely essential to have your lawyer review it before you sign it.

THE RESPONSIBILITY TO CLOSE

Once you sign an agreement of purchase and sale, you are legally bound to pay for the property, and the vendor is legally bound to transfer ownership of the property to you and to give you possession of the house and property.

If the Purchaser Refuses to Close

On the day of closing, you have a legal obligation to pay for the home. If you refuse to close the deal without a valid reason, the vendor can claim your deposit, although he or she may have to sue to get it from the real estate agent.

Instead of claiming the deposit, in most provinces the vendor can sue you for **damages** (money compensation). If the vendor is successful, the damages you're ordered to pay by the court will amount to the difference between what you were supposed to pay to buy the home, and what the vendor actually receives after selling it to someone else. You may also be ordered to pay some of the vendor's legal fees.

If the Vendor Refuses to Close

On the day of closing, the vendor also has a legal obligation—to transfer the home to you and let you take possession of it. If the vendor has changed his or her mind about selling since you signed the agreement of purchase and sale, you can sue for **specific performance**. If you are successful, the court will order the vendor to hand over to you ownership and possession of the home on exactly the terms set out in the agreement of purchase and sale. The court may also order the vendor to pay you damages to compensate you for your trouble. The vendor will probably also be ordered to pay some of your legal fees.

While a court action is going on, there's a good chance you can prevent the vendor from selling the property to anyone else by registering notice of your lawsuit against the title to the home. Your lawyer will take care of that.

Obviously, you didn't sign an agreement to buy a home with the intention of backing out at the last minute. Neither did the vendor. It is very unusual for a vendor to refuse to close.

Once you have a signed agreement of purchase and sale, your house-hunting is over! Now it is time to turn things over to your lawyer.

6 THE PURCHASER'S LAWYER

DO YOU NEED A LAWYER?

We'll give you the bad news right up front: you're going to need a lawyer to buy a home, and it's going to cost at least several hundred dollars and maybe as much as several thousand dollars, depending on the cost of your home and how complicated the deal is. The following discussion of the role of the purchaser's lawyer should help you understand both why you need a lawyer and why lawyers charge as much as they do.

The Role of the Lawyer in Purchasing a Home

Before you decided to buy your home, you spent a lot of time and effort making sure it suited your needs and budget. You also carefully examined its physical condition and maybe even hired a professional home inspector to help you. But nothing in this process told you who actually owns the property and whether anyone other than the owner, such as a bank or mortgage company or unpaid creditor, has a claim to the property.

Before you hand money over to the vendor for the home (and you will pay tens if not hundreds of thousands of dollars), you will want to be sure that the vendor is in fact the owner and has the right to sell it free of any claims by anyone else. Put into legal jargon, you want to get not only the home but a **good and marketable title** to the property. If you buy a home that has a claim against it, such as a mortgage, builder's lien or judgment, you will get not only the home but the claim too! Even though the vendor is the one who owes the money, the creditor may be able to force you to sell the property in order to pay the claim.

Information about ownership of and claims against land is found in **land registry** records and in other records kept by the government. It takes professional training to find these records and then interpret them through a **title search**. A lawyer has that professional training and can ensure that you are getting a good and marketable title. A lawyer is also able to deal with the vendor (through his or her lawyer) to get claims against the property removed so that the title becomes good and marketable if it wasn't to begin with.

A number of documents must be prepared and signed in order to transfer ownership of the property to you. The change in ownership must be registered in the land registry office, and there are taxes and fees that must be paid at the same time. Your lawyer will look after all these things for you.

The Lawyer as Insurance Against Title Problems

When your lawyer finishes preparing and registering the documents that transfer **title** (ownership) to you, he or she will certify that you have a good and marketable title to your home. This certification is really what you are paying your lawyer for. If it turns out that the lawyer was wrong about the title, you may be able to claim money from the lawyer as compensation. Lawyers are required by law to carry enough professional liability insurance to pay claims like these, which, given the cost of real estate, can be quite high.

Title Insurance

Recently, **title insurance** has become available in Canada. In a real estate deal without title insurance, a lawyer certifies that the property has a good and marketable title. In a deal with title insurance, the title insurance policy takes the place of a lawyer's certification and compensates the purchaser if it later turns out that there is a problem with title. Title insurance has been used in real estate transactions in the United States for a long time. Canadians have got along without it because land registry records in Canada are more reliable and therefore contain fewer title problems, and also because Canadians have been content to rely on their lawyer's written certification— backed up by their lawyer's professional liability insurance—that there are no problems with the title to their new home.

Title insurance costs two or three hundred dollars or more. Some types allow your lawyer to reduce your legal fees because a full title search is not necessary.

Do you need title insurance when you're buying a home? It's useful if you're in a hurry to close your deal—it can speed the process up (by eliminating a lot of the title search) so that it takes as little as a week. If there's no rush but it turns out that your lawyer needs to do unexpectedly expensive searches for your transaction, sometimes title insurance can take the place of those searches and end up costing you less. For most people, though, it makes more sense to rely on your lawyer's certification that you're getting a problem-free title. But talk to your lawyer about whether you should get title insurance. Ask

- whether having title insurance will give you any greater protection against title problems than you already have without it
- the cost of different available types of title insurance
- whether using title insurance will reduce your legal fees

Compare the total cost of your real estate deal if you get insurance to the total cost of the deal if you don't. If it's cheaper with title insurance, get title insurance. If it's more expensive with title insurance, ask your lawyer whether the extra cost is worthwhile.

What About Paralegals and Other Non-Lawyers?

While you may be convinced that you need some kind of professional help in completing your property purchase, you may still be wondering why that help should come from a lawyer, as opposed to a **paralegal** or other non-lawyer who may seem knowledgeable about real estate and may offer a lower price.

The answer to your wonderings is that you have to have a lawyer, for two reasons.

The first reason is that in all provinces other than British Columbia and Quebec only lawyers are permitted by law to complete real estate deals. In Quebec real estate transactions are handled only by **notaries**, and they can be handled by notaries as well as lawyers in British Columbia. Any other non-lawyer who looks after an entire real estate transaction is breaking the law and can be prosecuted by the provincial government. (The law in this area may be changing in some provinces to allow paralegals to do real estate deals—but we still recommend you stick with a lawyer or notary.) The second reason is that only a lawyer's certification of title is certain to be backed up by insurance to protect you if problems arise.

WHAT DOES A LAWYER ACTUALLY DO?

It helps to understand what a lawyer does in order to decide which one you want to hire and how much you want to pay. Your lawyer will

- review the agreement of purchase and sale
- search the title to the home
- review the plan of survey of the property (if you're buying a house)
- advise you how to take title to the property
- prepare or review all the necessary documents
- explain the documents to you before you sign them
- close the transaction and register the documents
- notify utilities and government offices that you are now the owner
- provide you with a reporting letter and certification of title

Review of Agreement of Purchase and Sale

You may have asked your lawyer to review the terms of the agreement of purchase and sale before you signed it. If you did not, your lawyer will first become involved after receiving a copy of the signed agreement from you or your real estate agent. Either way your lawyer must review it now.

In the agreement of purchase and sale, the vendor promised to transfer ownership of the home to you on the closing date. Unless you agreed otherwise, that ownership is to be unlimited and free of claims by anyone else. Your lawyer will review the agreement to see whether or not you agreed to accept any limitations to your ownership. Between the date the lawyer receives the signed agreement and the date of closing, it is the lawyer's job to make sure that the ownership you get on the closing date is exactly the same as the ownership the vendor promised you.

Search of Title

To make sure that you get the ownership you were promised, your lawyer must search the records for the property in the land registry office to confirm that the vendor is the owner and to look for any claims against the property. He or she must also contact the utility companies (gas, electricity, water) to make sure that all charges have been paid by the vendor. Your lawyer must also confirm the amount of the municipal realty taxes, and that they have been paid. Finally, in most provinces your lawyer must make sure that the property satisfies all municipal requirements, including zoning. By the way—let your lawyer know if there are signs that the home was renovated. Then your lawyer will check whether or not the proper building permits were obtained when the renovation was done. If they weren't, the municipality could order the renovation to be undone because it was undertaken without permission and carried out without inspections that made sure it met provincial building code standards.

If your lawyer discovers any problem with ownership of the property, he or she will ask the vendor's lawyer to correct it by the closing date. If the vendor cannot correct the problem, you have the choice of going ahead with the purchase anyway (maybe at a reduced price) or, depending on how serious the problem is, ending the deal and getting your deposit money back. Your lawyer will give you advice about the best thing to do if a problem is found.

Review of Plan of Survey

If you are buying a house, there are certain questions that a lawyer will be able to answer only if there is an **up-to-date plan of survey** of the property. You only *think* you're buying a house. What you're really buying is land and any buildings that happen to be sitting on it. So you want to be certain that the house is in fact on the land you are buying. You need a plan of survey for this, and you also need a plan of survey to make sure that

- the house is totally on your land and not partly on your neighbour's land
- your neighbour's house is not on your land
- any fences between properties are on the lot line
- the size and location of the house and any other buildings satisfy zoning requirements

A plan of survey is a scale drawing of a property, prepared by a registered land surveyor. It shows the location of all boundaries of the property, and the location and size of the house, garage, sheds, fences, driveways, and any **rights of way** over the property as of the date the survey was made. If any changes have been made to the size, shape, or location of any of these things since the survey was made, the survey is no longer accurate and up to date, even if it was just recently made. For example, if an addition or a deck has been built or a swimming pool has been installed since the survey, the survey will no longer be accurate. If no changes have been made since the date of the last survey, it is still accurate and up to date even if it is very old.

If the vendor has a survey, he or she will generally be required to provide a copy. However, the survey the vendor has may not be up to date. If there is no up-to-date survey, or no survey at all, the vendor is not required to give you one unless that was agreed to in the agreement of purchase and sale. If you can't look to the vendor for a survey then your lawyer will ask your permission to arrange to have one done. A plan of survey costs up to a thousand dollars, and you have to pay the money up front. It's your choice, but if you don't have an up-to-date plan of survey, your lawyer will not be able to provide you with a complete certification of title. If you are financing your home purchase with a mortgage from a bank, trust company, or insurance company, the mortgage lender will almost certainly insist on an up-to-date survey at your expense.

Taking Title

Your lawyer will talk to you about who's going to be the **registered owner** of your home and, if there's more than one owner, what kind of ownership you want.

Who Will Be the Registered Owner?

A registered owner of property appears on all the legal documents as owner of the property. Registered owners have the right to sell the property or mortgage it or give it away, or to prevent another registered owner from doing these things. If you are a single person and are buying the property alone, you will be the registered owner. If you are married or living with a partner, or there are two or more of you buying the property, you have to decide, with your lawyer's help, who should be the registered owner(s).

Generally speaking, if two or more people are paying money for the purchase of the property, all of you will want to be shown as registered owners. That's to make sure that the property cannot be sold without your permission and that, if it is sold, you'll all get a share of the money. People who are living together but are not legally married do not have an automatic right to a share in property, or an automatic right to prevent property from being sold, unless they are registered owners of the property.

If homeowners are married to each other, a spouse who is not a registered owner has certain rights over the home. So it's not always as essential for a legally married couple both to be registered owners. In most provinces, both spouses have to give their permission before the property can be sold. In most provinces, both spouses are entitled to a share of each other's property if they separate or divorce (in some provinces, however, the size of the share is affected by whether only one spouse is named or both spouses are named as the registered owner(s)). Most husbands and wives who buy homes ask that both of them be shown as registered owners, even if they are not both paying for the home. But sometimes for business or other reasons it makes sense for only one spouse to be named as the registered owner. Talk to your lawyer about your business and financial situation to see whether it would be wise for only one of you to be named as the registered owner. Ask what rights over the home the spouse who is not a registered owner would have.

What Kind of Ownership?

If there are going to be two or more registered owners, you have to choose between two different kinds of ownership: **joint tenancy** and **tenancy-in-common**. (This does not apply in Quebec, where there is only tenancy-in-common.)

When two or more people own property in joint tenancy, each is an equal owner of the whole property. The most important feature of joint tenancy is the **right of survivorship**, which means that if one owner dies, that owner's interest in the property automatically passes to the surviving owner or owners, no matter what the dead owner's will says. Usually only people who are related or are living together as spouses want to own property as joint tenants.

If you want to own property in joint tenancy, the **deed** or **transfer** (the document that gives you ownership of the property) must clearly say so. If it doesn't specifically state that you are taking title in joint tenancy, you will own the property as tenants-in-common. Property shares of tenants-in-common do not have to be equal, and your co-owners will not automatically get your share of the property when you die. You can say in your will who will get your share when you die.

You and your lawyer should discuss which kind of ownership is best for you.

Co-ownership Agreements

If you are buying the property with another person, you should ask your lawyer whether or not you should have a **co-ownership agreement** to deal with such matters as

- acknowledgement of the contribution each owner made toward the purchase
- the responsibilities of each owner toward the maintenance and upkeep of the property
- what happens if one owner wants to sell the property
- how the proceeds of any sale should be divided

If you are married or living together as spouses, these matters can be dealt with in a **marriage contract** or **cohabitation agreement**.

Preparation, Review, and Explanation of Documents

There is a lot of paperwork involved in buying a home. Both you and the vendor have to sign documents. Your lawyer will prepare some of these documents, and the vendor's lawyer will prepare others. Your lawyer should explain all the documents to you before you sign them.

Your lawyer will also tell you exactly how much money you will have to pay on the closing date, and explain to you how that amount is calculated. The amount is almost always different from the amount in the agreement of purchase and sale. You already handed over some money as a deposit, but there are other items that must be taken into account that may increase or decrease what you pay when the deal closes, such as prepayments for utilities and property taxes (or arrears in payment) and interest on any mortgages you are assuming. These are called **adjustments**. It's your lawyer's job to check that the money you pay on closing is the correct amount. When your lawyer is satisfied that the amount is correct, he or she will ask you to bring this sum of money, in the form of a certified cheque, to the office a day or so before the closing.

Homeowner's Insurance

Your lawyer will advise you to arrange in advance for homeowner's insurance that will come into effect as soon as you become the legal owner of the property. Your mortgage lender requires insurance to be in place, and you want it for your own protection as well.

Preparing Mortgages Documents

If you are financing the purchase of your home with a mortgage from a bank, trust company, or insurance company, the mortgage lender may ask your lawyer to prepare the mortgage documents, and search the title for the mortgage as well. You'll end up paying for this, too.

Closing the Transaction

On the day of closing, your lawyer will arrange with the vendor's lawyer to pay the final purchase amount and to receive and register the **deed** or **transfer** transferring title in the property from the vendor to you.

The vendor's lawyer may give your lawyer the keys to your new home at the closing. If your lawyer's office is not easy for you to get to, before the closing date make an arrangement to have the keys left with someone who is closer, such as your real estate agent. The agent will give you the keys once your lawyer confirms that the deal has closed.

In some provinces, although you get possession of your home on the closing date, the payment of the purchase amount or registration of the deed or transfer may happen at a later time.

Notification of Utilities and Government Offices

After the closing, your lawyer will notify the utilities and government offices that you are now the owner of the property and will make sure that any outstanding matters with them (such as money still shown owing to them by the vendor) are cleared up.

Reporting Letter and Certification of Title

Your lawyer will send you a **reporting letter** giving the details of the entire transaction along with copies of documents, including the deed, the mortgage, if any, and the survey, if any. The most important aspect of the reporting letter is the lawyer's **certification of title** in which the lawyer states that you have good title to the property. If you bought the title insurance, your lawyer won't cerify title but will instead send you your title insurance policy.

HOW MUCH WILL A LAWYER COST?

Sorry to sound like lawyers, but it depends. Lawyers' fees vary from town to town and province to province. A lawyer's fee depends on a number of factors, including the price of the home, the complexity of the transaction, whether or not a mortgage is involved, and the level of service offered by the lawyer.

Most lawyers charge a flat fee for a real estate transaction. Some charge a fee based on the number of hours they actually spend on your transaction. Some lawyers quote a flat fee, but reserve the right to charge you an hourly rate if unexpected title problems arise. Ask the lawyer you are thinking of hiring what fee will be charged for your particular transaction.

In addition to the lawyer's fee, which pays for the lawyer's professional services, you will have to pay the lawyer's **disbursements**. These are payments made by the lawyer on your behalf for such things as a plan of survey, search fees, registration fees, long distance telephone charges, photocopy charges, mileage, and parking. These items, which do not vary a lot from lawyer to lawyer, can still add up to a substantial amount, so ask your lawyer for an estimate beforehand. If you buy title insurance you'll have to pay for the policy.

Some lawyers hire a person from outside their office to perform certain professional services, such as searching the records at the land registry office and closing the transaction. Confirm whether or not the fee the lawyer has quoted you will include such outside services. If not, ask how much extra you will be charged for them.

When comparing the fees of different lawyers, make sure you take disbursements and any extra charges into account.

HOW DO YOU CHOOSE A LAWYER?

Your home purchase is important to you, so you want to choose a lawyer who will do a thorough job at a reasonable price.

Get Several Recommendations

As with any other professional, the best way to choose a lawyer is to get several recommendations from people you know and trust. Ask friends or relatives who have bought a home who their lawyer was and whether they were happy with him or her. Or ask your real estate agent for a recommendation. If you have no one to ask, you can call your provincial law society for a list of real estate lawyers in your area.

Investigate the Possibilities

Once you have the names of several lawyers, you should do some investigating to decide which one is best for you.

Try to get some idea of the range of fees that each lawyer charges. The fee charged to your friend or relative may not be the same as the one quoted to you, because the lawyer's fee depends on a number of factors, as we have said, including the price of the home and the complexity of the transaction. You will find that there are expensive lawyers, cheap lawyers, and lawyers who are somewhere in the middle. While you don't need to hire the most expensive lawyer, it is probably not a good idea to hire the cheapest lawyer either. A lawyer who charges very low fees usually makes a profit because he or she processes a large number of transactions, and may not have a great deal of time to spend with you.

Find out where the lawyer's office is. Remember that you will have to go there, perhaps several times and most likely during normal business hours. Choose a lawyer whose location is not too inconvenient.

Speak to the Lawyer

Call the lawyer's office, or make an appointment to meet, to find out more about him or her.

Ask the lawyer how much experience he or she has in the real estate area. It is not necessary to hire a real estate specialist, but you probably don't want to be your lawyer's first real estate client. Ask how much the fee and estimated disbursements will be for your transaction and what services are included in the fee. Ask how much contact you can expect to have with the lawyer's office. Will your contact be primarily with the lawyer or with an assistant?

Try to get a sense of the lawyer's personality and style. Is this person someone you feel you can trust and communicate with comfortably and effectively? (If the lawyer uses an assistant, you may want to meet the assistant too.) The purchase of a home should be a happy occasion, and you will be spending a significant amount of money for legal services. So don't use a lawyer who makes you feel uncomfortable or whom you don't like!

Should You Use the Same Lawyer as the Vendor?

It is not a good idea for you and the vendor to use the same lawyer, even if it would save you money. What you want and what the vendor wants are not always the same, and you want your lawyer to represent your interests and your interests alone. In Quebec, however, it is customary for the notary to act for both parties.

You may be borrowing money by way of a mortgage to help pay for your home. If the mortgage lender is a bank, trust company or other financial institution it is customary for your lawyer to act for the mortgage lender as well.

☑ Choosing a Lawyer Checklist

Get several recommendations

❑ Ask friends, relatives, or your real estate agent.

❑ Call your provincial law society.

Investigate the possibilities

❑ Get some idea of the range of fees the lawyer will charge.

❑ Find out the location of the lawyer's office.

Speak to the lawyer before making your decision

❑ Find out how much experience the lawyer has.

❑ Confirm what the lawyer's fee and estimated disbursements will be for your transaction.

❑ Ask what the lawyer's fee includes.

❑ Ask how much contact you can expect to have with the lawyer.

❑ Decide whether you can work comfortably with this person.

7 MORTGAGES

There aren't many people who have enough money to pay the full cost of their new home in cash. It's difficult enough to accumulate the cash needed for a down payment, so most of us have to borrow in order to buy a home. When you borrow money to buy a home, you do it by getting a **mortgage** (known in some provinces as a **charge** and in Quebec as a **hypothec**). In this chapter we will tell you what a mortgage is, the strange language of mortgages that you need to know, where to get a mortgage, and the process you will have to go through to get one.

WHAT IS A MORTGAGE?

A mortgage is a contract by which a homeowner (or home buyer) borrows money. The lender of the money is called the **mortgagee**. The borrower is called the **mortgagor**. The amount of money borrowed is called the **principal**. **Interest** is the cost to the borrower of borrowing the money.

A mortgage has two parts. One part is a loan like any other kind of loan: the mortgagee (usually a bank or trust company) agrees to lend the mortgagor (you) money at a given interest rate, and you agree to repay the loan with interest. The other part of the contract gives the mortgagee a claim on your home as security to make sure that you repay the loan. If you don't repay the loan, in most provinces the mortgagee can choose to sue you on your promise to repay the loan, or take your home and use it to repay the loan, usually by selling it.

SPEAKING THE MORTGAGEE'S LANGUAGE

Most people go to a bank or trust company to get a mortgage. Some people go to a **mortgage broker**. Wherever you go, as soon as you walk in the door, people will start talking to you in a language that you don't understand. That's because a mortgage is a complicated legal and financial transaction. Mortgagees handle these transactions all the time and forget how complicated they are. They are also used to using legal and financial terms and forget that the rest of us don't have any idea of what they mean.

We've already told you what a mortgage is. Now we're going to tell you about other key words and concepts you need to be familiar with in order to understand what your mortgagee is saying.

First, Second, and Third Mortgages

If there is no mortgage on your home when you go to borrow the money you need, the mortgage you get is called a first mortgage. If you then decide to borrow more money under another mortgage, the next mortgage is called a second mortgage. The next mortgage after that is called a third mortgage. We could go on like this forever, but you've probably got the idea by now.

Each mortgage gives the mortgagee the right to take your home if you fail to repay the loan. Usually the mortgagee will sell your home and use any money that comes from the sale to repay the first mortgagee first, then the second, then the third, etc.

Because a first mortgagee gets paid first and therefore has a better chance of getting all of its money back if it has to sell your home, first mortgages have lower interest rates than second and third mortgages.

The Term of Your Mortgage and the Amortization Period

Every mortgage must be repaid in full by a fixed date. The length of time you have to repay your mortgage is the **term** of the mortgage. Most Canadian mortgages have terms of no more than five years. But mortgages are usually for many tens of thousands of dollars. The monthly payments would be very high if you had to repay such a large loan in equal monthly instalments in full by the end of a five-year term. In order to make the monthly payments lower, mortgagees usually calculate the payments as if the loan were being repaid over a longer period of time than the actual term of the mortgage. In most mortgages, the payment is calculated as if the mortgagor had twenty-five years to repay the mortgage. This make-believe period of time is called the **amortization period** of the mortgage.

When a mortgage with a term of five years has an amortization period of (is **amortized** over) twenty-five years, the mortgagor makes four years and eleven months' worth of monthly payments as if there were twenty-five years to repay the mortgage. These payments are much lower than if the loan payments were calculated based on the actual five-year term. But the last payment is a whopper! Most people don't have enough money to make it. They renew their mortgage when the term is up and continue making monthly payments amortized over a new twenty-five-year period.

The length of the amortization period makes quite a difference to your monthly payments:

- A $100,000 mortgage with an interest rate of 10 per cent and a term of five years, amortized over five years, would cost $2,147.70 each month.

- The same $100,000 mortgage with an interest rate of 10 per cent and a term of five years, amortized over a period of twenty-five years, would cost $894.49 each month.

You can also choose an amortization period somewhere in between five years and twenty-five years, for example fifteen years or twenty years. If your amortization period were twenty years, and you had the same $100,000 mortgage with an interest rate of 10 per cent, your monthly payments would be $969.03. Because you are making a slightly higher payment, your mortgage will be paid off five years earlier—and you will pay approximately $48,000 less in interest over the life of the mortgage. It makes sense to choose the shortest amortization period you can afford.

Blended Payments

As with any loan, you must repay not only the principal amount of the loan, you must also pay interest. Some of the payment you make each month is used to pay the interest on the loan, and the rest is used to pay down the principal. Payments which combine principal and interest in this way are called **blended payments**.

Every mortgage payment you make both pays back principal and pays interest. In most mortgages, the amount you pay every month remains the same (**equal monthly instalments**). As you make each payment, the principal of the loan is slowly (very slowly) reduced. As the principal is reduced, the amount of interest you must pay each month is also reduced, leaving more of your payment to pay down the principal amount of the loan.

At the early stages of your mortgage, almost all of your monthly payments go to pay interest on the loan. So don't be surprised to find out that, after several years and many thousands of dollars in mortgage payments, you still owe almost as much principal on your mortgage as when you first borrowed the money. Table 1 will give you nightmares. It shows you how much of a monthly payment of $894.49 goes towards principal and how much goes towards interest if you have a $100,000 mortgage at 10 per cent repayable over 25 years.

TABLE 1: BREAKDOWN OF PRINCIPAL AND INTEREST OF BLENDED PAYMENTS

Payment	Principal Repaid	Interest Paid	Balance Remaining to Pay
First of 1st year	$78.01	$816.48	$99,921.99
Last of 1st year	85.30	809.19	99,020.75
Last of 2nd year	94.05	800.44	97,941.12
Last of 3rd year	103.69	790.80	96,750.80
Last of 4th year	114.32	780.17	95,438.49
Last of 5th year	126.03	768.46	93,991.67
Last of 10th year	205.29	689.20	84,204.74
Last of 15th year	334.40	560.09	68,262.90
Last of 20th year	544.71	349.78	42,295.31
Last of 25th year	884.02	7.22	.00

Over the lifetime of the mortgage, you will have paid back the $100,000 principal—and you will also have paid $168,343.70 in interest.

Payment Frequency

Most mortgages are payable on a monthly basis, but some mortgagees give you the option of making your payments weekly or every two weeks. Paying weekly or every two weeks may make it easier for you to budget for your payments. However, it can also affect how fast you pay off your mortgage, depending on how the payment is calculated. Keep in mind that there are 4.33 weeks in each month. If you just divide your monthly payment by 4.33, you won't really pay your mortgage off any faster. But if you divide your monthly payment by four and pay that amount every week, you will significantly reduce the length of time it takes to pay off the mortgage.

Here's an example. A $100,000 mortgage with an interest rate of 10 per cent, amortized over twenty-five years, has a monthly payment of $894.49. If you divide the monthly payment by four, you get a weekly payment of

$223.62. If you pay that amount each week, you are in fact making monthly payments of $969.03. This is the equivalent of choosing a twenty-year amortization period—and a $48,000 saving in interest payments over the life of the mortgage.

Fixed and Variable Interest Rates

Interest rates change all the time. The interest rate for your mortgage is set at the time you apply to borrow the money. Most banks and trust companies offer different interest rates depending on the length of the term of the mortgage. Longer term mortgages usually have higher interest rates because the lender can't accurately predict whether interest rates will go up in the future. The lender bets that they will and sets a higher rate now so that it won't lose out later if interest rates do rise.

A mortgage with a **fixed interest rate** has the same rate of interest during the whole term of the mortgage.

If your mortgage has a **variable interest rate**, the interest rate starts in one place but it will go up and down over the term of the mortgage as general interest rates go up and down. If the interest rate goes down during the term of your mortgage, less of each monthly payment goes to pay the interest, and more of each monthly payment goes to pay down the principal. If the interest rate goes up, more of each monthly payment goes to pay the interest, and less of each monthly payment goes to pay down the principal. (It's enough to make you seasick, isn't it!) If the interest rate goes up so much that your monthly payment is not enough to cover the interest, your monthly payment may be increased by the mortgagee.

Different banks offer variations on the variable interest rate mortgage. Some banks allow you to set a maximum interest rate (or **cap**), or to convert to a fixed rate mortgage at any time. You may have to pay extra for these options.

Interest Calculated Semi-Annually Not in Advance

In most mortgages you'll see a term that the interest is calculated **semi-annually, not in advance**. We'll deal with the "not in advance" part first, because it's easier. Unlike rent, which is paid in advance on the first of each month, mortgage interest is paid "not in advance." When you make your June 1st rent payment, you are paying for the use of your apartment for the rest of June. When you make your June 1st mortgage payment, you are paying for the use of the money for the month of May.

Now for the "calculated semi-annually" business. This takes longer to explain, and we have to start the explanation with an explanation about interest. Interest can be either **simple** or **compound**. When you pay simple interest, you're just paying interest on the principal. When you pay compound interest, you're paying interest on the principal and you're also paying interest on the interest owing. That means you end up with a higher interest rate than the rate you're quoted (the **nominal interest rate**). The more often interest is **compounded** or **calculated** within a particular time period, the higher the real (the **effective**) interest rate. For example, if you're offered a mortgage interest rate of 10 per cent and interest is compounded semi-annually (twice a year), over a period of one year the real interest rate is 10.25 per cent. If interest is compounded monthly, over a period of one year the real interest rate is 10.47 per cent.

Interest can be calculated or compounded on any basis—daily, weekly, monthly, quarterly, semi-annually, annually. The more frequently the interest is compounded, the more interest you end up paying. Using the example of the $100,000 mortgage with an interest rate of 10 per cent and amortized over twenty-five years, if the interest is calculated monthly instead of semi-annually, the monthly payment will go up from $894.49 to $908.70. Over the life of the mortgage you would pay an extra $4000 in interest.

When you're shopping around for a good interest rate, make sure you note how often the interest is calculated or compounded.

Open and Closed Mortgages

Unless your mortgage specifically says so, you cannot repay the principal amount earlier than the end of the term (even if you win the lottery). The right to make payments of principal, over and above your regular monthly payments, is called a **pre-payment privilege**. A mortgage without any prepayment privileges is called a **closed** mortgage. A mortgage with pre-payment privileges is called an **open** mortgage.

Some mortgages are more open than others. A mortgage that allows you to repay any or all of the principal amount at any time and without payment of any financial penalty is called a **fully open** mortgage. Such mortgages are rare and seldom seen, and you will usually have to pay a higher interest rate for them. However, most mortgages from banks and trust companies allow for some limited prepayment of the mortgage principal. Either the mortgage will allow relatively small pre-payments without any financial penalty to you, or it will allow you to pre-pay a larger amount together with a financial penalty.

Portable Mortgages

You may be able to choose the option of having a **portable mortgage**. If your mortgage is portable, you can transfer it to a new home that you buy. There are two advantages to this. You won't have to pay a penalty to **discharge** (pay off) that mortgage if you sell your home to a buyer who does not want to assume the mortgage. In addition, if interest rates have gone up, you can keep the benefit of the lower interest rate even when you move to a new home.

CHOOSING THE MORTGAGE OPTIONS THAT ARE RIGHT FOR YOU

The interest rate you will be charged depends not only on the general interest rates in effect when you borrow, but also on which of the various mortgage options you choose. You will usually get the lowest interest rate for a short-term, fixed interest rate mortgage. You will usually be quoted a higher interest rate if you want pre-payment privileges, variable interest rates, or a longer mortgage term.

The lower the interest rate, the more money you can afford to borrow. So it is tempting to go for the lowest interest rate possible. Since that usually means a short-term mortgage, remember that you will soon have to renew the mortgage, quite possibly at a higher interest rate. If the interest rates go up, so will your monthly mortgage payments. If you have borrowed the maximum you can afford, you will find yourself in trouble. For example, if you borrow $100,000 at an interest rate of 10 per cent, amortized over twenty-five years, your monthly payment is $894.49 (are you beginning to wish we'd use a new example?). If the interest rate has gone up to 12 per cent when it comes time to renew your $100,000 mortgage, the monthly payment will rise to $1053.22. Adios vacation...maybe even adios home and mortgage.

WHERE TO GET A MORTGAGE

Mortgages are available from

- banks
- trust companies
- credit unions
- caisses populaires
- life insurance companies
- mortgage brokers
- private lenders
- your RRSP

Institutional Lenders

Banks, trust companies, credit unions, caisses populaires, and insurance companies are known as **institutional lenders**. While all institutional lenders tend to be competitive in the interest rates and types of mortgages they offer, there are some differences.

It is tempting simply to go to your own bank branch to apply for your mortgage, but it is a better idea to shop around first to compare what the different institutional lenders have to offer. Newspapers publish current mortgage interest rates in the business or real estate sections, or you can telephone or visit several institutional lenders or their websites.

Private Lenders and Mortgage Brokers

Institutional lenders are not the only mortgage lenders. There are also individuals who have money they want to invest, and who like the interest rates and security that a mortgage investment can give them.

Most people get their mortgages from an institutional lender if they can. Borrowers may go to private lenders when they have credit problems which make it difficult to get a mortgage from an institutional lender, or if they want to borrow more than 75 per cent of the purchase price and do not qualify with an institutional lender for a high ratio mortgage (see page 91).

Private lenders are also the most common source of second or subsequent mortgages. You may need a second mortgage for any number of reasons. For example, you may need extra money over and above your down payment and first mortgage in order to buy the home of your choice. Or you may need to borrow additional money after you have owned your home for a while, using your home as **security** to guarantee that the lender will be repaid. Second and subsequent mortgage interest rates are likely to be higher than first mortgage interest rates (whoever your lender is) because the second mortgagee's risk of losing money if you can't repay the loan is greater than a first mortgagee's. A first mortgagee gets paid first out of the sale proceeds if your home has to be sold to pay back the mortgage loan and interest, and a second mortgagee gets paid what's left.

Borrowing money under a mortgage from an individual is exactly the same as getting a mortgage from an institutional lender. The trick is knowing how to find these private lenders. Your real estate agent may be able to give you the name of a private lender. Or you can go to a **mortgage broker**.

A mortgage broker acts as a go-between, putting people who want to borrow mortgage money in touch with people or institutions who want to lend it. The broker may charge you a **brokerage fee** for this service, depending on your financial circumstances and credit-worthiness. Your real estate agent or lawyer can probably direct you to a mortgage broker.

Your RRSP

If you are lucky enough to have a **registered retirement savings plan** with as much money in it as you need to borrow for a mortgage loan, you may be able to get a mortgage from your own RRSP. You have to have a self-directed RRSP, the mortgage has to be administered by a trust company, and you have to be approved for the mortgage loan just as if you were trying to borrow someone else's money instead of your own. In addition, your RRSP must charge you a reasonable rate of interest on the mortgage. Oh well, you may not save any money on your monthly payments, but at least you will be paying interest to yourself. Speak to the institution that holds your RRSP to find out more about the applicable rules and regulations.

APPLYING FOR A MORTGAGE

Your mortgagee will have an application procedure for you to follow. The process of applying for a mortgage is designed to provide the mortgagee with enough information for it to decide whether or not it should risk lending you money. The mortgagee wants to make sure *first*, that you will make the mortgage payments every month; and *second*, that if you don't make the payments it can get enough money from the sale of your home to repay the loan.

Do You Qualify for a Conventional or a High Ratio Mortgage?

One of the first things an institutional lender decides is what type of mortgage you are eligible for, a **conventional** mortgage or a **high ratio mortgage**, because the mortgage type will determine the maximum amount you are eligible to borrow. These terms refer to the relationship between the amount of the mortgage and the amount of the purchase price of your home.

Conventional Mortgages

A conventional mortgage is a mortgage for no more than 75 per cent of the purchase price of your home. If you apply for a conventional mortgage, the maximum principal amount you can apply to borrow is three times the amount of your down payment.

High Ratio Mortgages

A high ratio mortgage is a mortgage for more than 75 per cent (up to a maximum of 95 per cent) of the purchase price. If a mortgage lender accepts your application for a high ratio mortgage, the maximum principal amount you can apply to borrow could be up to nineteen times the amount of your down payment.

It's the Canada Mortgage and Housing Corporation's (CMHC's) insurance program which makes it possible for people with as little as 5% of the purchase price in hand to buy a home. Until 1998, only first-time buyers were eligible for the "5% down" program, but now everyone is eligible. One of the restrictions under the program is that the maximum price of the home you can buy is capped—in the Toronto and Vancouver areas at $250,000, in other cities where home prices are on the high side and in northern areas at $175,000, and everywhere else in Canada at $125,000. There are some other restrictions and rules too. For more information, see CMHC's website at www.cmhc.ca or talk to your mortgage lender.

High Ratio Mortgages Cost More

If you don't repay your mortgage, the mortgagee can sell your home and use the money from the sale to pay itself the unpaid amount of your mortgage loan and interest. When the amount of the loan is for more than 75 per cent of the value of the house, there is a real risk that there will not be enough money from the sale to fully repay the debt. As a result of this greater risk, mortgagees generally charge higher interest rates for high ratio mortgages.

In addition, institutional lenders require a homeowner who takes out a high ratio mortgage to buy **mortgage insurance** from CMHC. This insurance pays the mortgagee if you can't make your payments and there is not enough money from the sale of your home to pay off the mortgage debt. The homeowner must pay a premium for this insurance, the cost of which depends on the value of the home and the size of the loan. The premium rate charged can be up to 4.25 per cent of the amount of the loan if the loan is for 95 per cent of the value of the home. So, for example, if you want to buy a home worth $175,000 and need a mortgage loan of $166,250 (95 per cent of the purchase price), you could be looking at a mortgage insurance premium of $7,065. You can either pay the premium up front when you take out the insurance or you can have it added to your mortgage loan and repay the mortgagee on a monthly basis.

What is the State of Your Personal Finances?

Any mortgagee is going to be very interested in your personal worth and trustworthiness. Even though the mortgage gives the mortgagee the right to take your home if you don't pay, the mortgagee's first choice is to have you repay your mortgage on time as you promised. So the mortgagee will want information about you to determine the likelihood that you'll pay up.

The mortgagee will want to know about

- your income and expenses
- your assets and debts
- your credit rating

Your Income and Expenses

In Chapter 2, we told you to calculate your income and expenses to figure out how large a monthly mortgage payment you can afford. Just as you don't want to borrow more money than you can afford to pay back, the mortgagee doesn't want to lend you more money than you can afford to pay back.

Mortgagees have formulas that they use to calculate how much they think you can afford to repay. These formulas are not as detailed and time-consuming as the calculations we took you through in the second chapter of this book—and if you're lucky, the mortgagee will serve you coffee while taking you through the process.

Mortgagees usually look at your gross income, not your net income; and while they look at your expenses, they usually only look at your debt payments. Most mortgagees do not want you to spend more than 30 to 35 per cent of your gross monthly income on your **shelter costs**—your monthly mortgage payment, property taxes, and heating costs, and condominium maintenance fees if your home is a condo (they call the relationship between your income and shelter costs your **gross debt service ratio**) or more than 40 per cent of your gross monthly income on shelter costs plus all your other debt payments (they call the relationship between your income and all your payments your **total debt service ratio**).

You may find that, based on its calculations, your mortgagee thinks you can afford to borrow more money than you think you can afford after sweating through your calculations in Chapter 2. Think long and hard before taking on a larger mortgage than your own calculations have shown you can comfortably carry.

As part of its application process, the mortgagee will want to see documents that confirm the amount of your income, such as

- a letter from your employer
- income tax returns
- financial statements, if you are self-employed

Your Assets and Debts

Mortgagees are very nervous people. Wouldn't you be nervous if you were lending a person like you as much money as you are trying to borrow? So they want to make sure that, if your income turns out not to be enough to repay the mortgage, you have cash and property other than your home that you can use to repay the mortgage.

In addition to proof of your income and expenses, the mortgagee will ask you about your **net worth**, which is the difference between the value of everything that you own and the amount of everything you owe (your **assets** minus your **debts**).

The mortgagee will ask you to list all of your assets and debts and to provide details of

- bank account numbers and balances
- RRSP account numbers and balances
- stocks and bonds
- other real estate
- vehicles such as cars and boats
- credit card accounts and balances
- any other debts

Your Credit Rating

One good indication of the likelihood that you will repay your mortgage loan is your past history of repaying loans. This history forms the basis of your **credit rating**. Your credit rating is also affected by the amount of your income, your assets, and your outstanding debts.

The mortgagee will want to know your credit rating and will ask you to sign a consent to allow it to get this information from your banks, your employer, your creditors, and credit rating agencies.

What is the Value of the Home You Are Buying?

Besides wanting to know about the state of your personal finances to find out whether you can repay the loan, the mortgagee wants to know the value of your home in case you can't. If you don't repay the mortgage loan, the mortgagee can take your home and sell it to satisfy the loan. Accordingly, the mortgagee wants to be certain that the home is worth enough to cover the loan, plus the expenses of selling the home.

While the price you pay for your home is a good indication of its value, most mortgagees, being very cautious and (as we have said) nervous creatures, will want additional proof of its value. They get this proof by having your home appraised. An appraisal involves an inspection by a real estate professional who decides what your home is worth by comparing it with similar homes. If your mortgagee wants an appraisal, *you* may have to pay for it. The mortgagee will arrange for the appraisal, which costs about $100 to $200.

INSURANCE WHEN YOU GET A MORTGAGE

When you take out a mortgage, any mortgagee will insist that you have adequate homeowner's insurance. When you borrow from an institutional lender, the mortgagee may discuss other kinds of insurance with you as well.

Mortgage Insurance

We've already talked about mortgage insurance above. Unlike most kinds of insurance you take out, mortgage insurance doesn't protect *you*—it protects your mortgage lender. If you don't pay your mortgage loan and your home has to be sold, mortgage insurance pays for the mortgagee's loss if there is not enough money from the sale of your home to repay the loan. Mortgage insurance is required if you are taking out a high-ratio mortgage, and may also be required by some institutional lenders if the home you are buying was ever insulated with urea formaldehyde foam insulation.

Other Kinds of Insurance

Often, banks and trust companies will suggest that you get various kinds of insurance that will help you repay your mortgage loan if, for instance,

- you die
- you cannot work because of illness or disability
- you lose your job

Life Insurance

Your mortgagee may suggest to you that you and your home co-owner(s) get insurance on each others' lives, which will help pay off the mortgage if one of you dies. Institutional mortgagees push something called **mortgage life insurance**. The amount payable if you die decreases as the principal of your mortgage is paid down. But any life insurance policy that pays out enough to cover your mortgage would serve the same purpose, so you can shop around for plain old ordinary term life insurance with the best premium rate.

Disability Insurance

Ordinary **disability insurance** pays you an income if you are unable to work because of illness or injury. It is possible to get **mortgage disability insurance** that will pay the amount of monthly mortgage payments, instead of paying you an income. But if you buy ordinary disability insurance, you get to choose what you spend the income on—it may turn out that your mortgage isn't your first priority.

Job Loss Insurance

Sometimes it may be possible to get insurance that will make your mortgage payments if you lose your job.

Where Can You Get Insurance?

The banks and trust companies may or may not provide any of this insurance themselves. They may recommend an insurance company and give you an application form to fill out. If you are interested in getting insurance to protect yourself against any of the misfortunes discussed above, you are not limited to the an insurance product recommended by your mortgagee. You may be able to get similar protection from other insurers at a better price, so you may want to speak to an insurance broker or check insurance websites to see what else is available before you make a decision.

MORTGAGES THROUGH THE VENDOR

Until now, we have talked about mortgages that you apply for and get from an institutional or private lender. Sometimes there's another way to get a mortgage—from the person who's selling you the property.

Assuming an Existing Mortgage

The vendor may have a mortgage on the home. If the mortgage is in the right amount and has a favourable interest rate, you may want to **assume** this existing mortgage instead of arranging a new one. If the mortgagee allows you to assume, you take over the vendor's mortgage loan and make the mortgage payments after closing.

Vendor Take-Back Mortgage

Your down payment and what you can borrow by way of a first mortgage may not give you enough to pay the vendor what he or she wants for the home. Sometimes the vendor is willing to lend you some of the purchase price by giving you a mortgage. This is called a **vendor take-back mortgage**. After closing, you make mortgage payments to the vendor. If you have enough income to make this additional mortgage payment, it's a simple way of getting the extra financing you need.

AN EYE TO THE FUTURE

Thinking about mortgages is not just a one-time exercise when you first buy your home. You may revisit the subject of mortgages if you want to

- use your home as a source of personal or business financing
- refinance your existing mortgage

Your Home as a Source of Financing

Whether or not you already have a mortgage on your home, you may be able to use your home as security to borrow money for other purposes. You can take out a mortgage (or a second mortgage) to

- get a lump sum of money, which you pay back by monthly mortgage payments
- secure a **line of credit** at your financial institution, which allows you to borrow money from time to time up to a maximum amount
- guarantee a loan made to your business

Some homeowners may also be able to get a **reverse mortgage** on their home that will provide them with a lump sum of money or an income. We talk about reverse mortgages in Chapter 16.

Refinancing Your Mortgage

You may want to **refinance** (renegotiate) your mortgage even though it is not yet up for renewal. Interest rates may be lower now than they were when you got your mortgage, or you may be concerned that interest rates will be higher than they are now when the time for renewal comes. Or you may want to pay off a chunk of the principal so you'll have a smaller mortgage debt to deal with.

When you renegotiate your mortgage, you are paying off your current mortgage and getting a new one. Unless your mortgage contains a pre-payment privilege, you will have to pay a penalty to refinance. The penalty is usually designed to compensate the bank for the loss of interest income, which is calculated on the difference between your current mortgage interest rate and your new rate. This penalty can be thousands of dollars. It makes sense to renegotiate and pay the penalty only if you think you're going to save more than the amount of the penalty in mortgage payments over the life of your new mortgage.

Some banks offer a "**blend-and-extend**" option that may help if you're looking for a lower interest rate. Under this option, you renew your mortgage now for a longer term than the one left on your current mortgage, and the bank gives you an interest rate that averages your old rate and the new rate. This is a good choice if you think that interest rates will be even higher than the blended rate when your current mortgage comes up for renewal.

PAYING OFF AND DISCHARGING YOUR MORTGAGE

You'll likely pay off your mortgage more than once in your lifetime (even though Table 1 in this chapter may have made you feel otherwise). You might find yourself paying it off when:

- you renegotiate the mortgage with the same mortgagee
- you negotiate a new mortgage with a different mortgagee, to take the place of your existing mortgage
- you sell your home
- you finally repay the principal and interest in full—after years of monthly payments, or if you come by a windfall that allows you to get rid of your mortgage

Before you pay off the mortgage, you find out exactly how much cash it will take to do so by asking the mortgagee for a **discharge statement**. It sets out the payment of principal and interest required to **discharge** (pay off and end) the mortgage as of a given date.

Getting a Discharge of Mortgage

Once you've made the payment that ends the mortgage, you want to get some legal proof that you've paid in full. Your proof is a standard legal document called, depending on the province, a "**Discharge of Mortgage**" or "**Discharge of Charge**" or "**Cessation of Charge**." Your mortgagee may prepare it automatically, or you may have to ask for it. Either way, it will cost you. Mortgagees pretty well always charge a **discharge fee** to provide this document, and it can be $150 to $250 or more. Institutional lenders usually take their time preparing the discharge—weeks or even months. But don't panic, it will eventually arrive. If you're dealing with a private mortgage lender, who might not be quite as reliable as a bank, you can make sure you get the discharge by having your own lawyer prepare the document and then taking it to the mortgagee to sign.

If you've paid off your mortgage and your mortgagee refuses to give you a discharge, you can apply to court to have the mortgage legally discharged. You'll have to prove how much was owing on the mortgage when you made the payment to discharge it, and that you paid the correct amount. The discharge statement is the best proof of what was owing and your cancelled cheque is the best proof that it was paid. You'll probably need a lawyer's help to take a mortgagee to court.

Registering the Discharge

The discharge document has to be **registered on the title** of your home at the provincial land registry office. Then anyone who is interested in your property (for example, someone who's buying your home, or a mortgage lender you've contacted for a new mortgage) will be able to see that that mortgagee no longer has any rights against your home. This is important because when you sell you normally promise the purchaser a title free and clear of any claims against it, including mortgages, and when you take out a mortgage the lender will give you a better interest rate and/or more money if no other mortgagee already has rights against your home.

If you discharge your mortgage as part of a renegotiation of your mortgage, or a negotiation for a new mortgage or a sale of your home, the lawyer acting for you will take care of registering the discharge document.

If you discharge your mortgage by making your final payment ever, you can have a lawyer handle the registration if you want. However, it's easy and usually cheaper to do it yourself. First, find the right local land registry office—you have to go to the one that covers property in the county or district where your home is located. For the address of the registry office, look at the ownership documents for your home, or contact your municipality or (if you have patience for recorded messages and some time on your hands) your provincial government. Or your lawyer's assistant or clerk may be willing and able to tell you. When you've identified the right registry office, call and ask what their procedure is for registering a discharge, what the fee is (it's probably around $50), and how it can be paid (cash, cheque, certified cheque). Ask when's the best time to come if you don't want to wait in line. You don't want to show up on the busiest real-estate-closing day of the month, often the last Friday. Next, make a photocopy of the discharge and any documents that your mortgagee sent to you with it, for your own records. Then take the original discharge and the other documents to the land registry office. You'll be directed where to pay your money and hand over the discharge. That's all you have to do.

8 HOMEOWNER'S INSURANCE

WHY YOU NEED INSURANCE

Buying a home is probably the biggest investment you'll ever make, and you want to make sure that your investment is protected from the moment that the home becomes yours. If anything happens to your home, you want to be able to repair it so that it doesn't lose any of its value (and, of course, so that the rain and snow don't fall on you in the living room). That's a major reason you need homeowner's insurance—to get the money you need to make repairs.

If you are borrowing money by way of a mortgage, the mortgage company has also made an investment in your home and is just as interested as you are in protecting it. In fact, they won't actually give you the mortgage money you need to buy your home unless you have homeowner's insurance in place to take effect upon transfer of ownership to you.

A HOMEOWNER'S POLICY

You need insurance to protect you against three different kinds of misfortunes that can happen to you as a homeowner:

- Your home can be damaged or destroyed.
- Your personal possessions can be stolen, damaged, or destroyed.
- Your guests, workers, or other visitors (or their property) can be harmed while at your home.

To get homeowner's insurance you have to apply to an insurance company. If the insurance company accepts your application, a **policy** of insurance will be issued. You pay for this policy by paying a **premium**. You are then said to be **insured** or **covered** against damage to your home, possessions, and guests.

Three In One

Homeowner's policies are really three policies of insurance in one to protect you against each of the three kinds of misfortunes mentioned above:

- If you own a house and land, **dwelling coverage** insures the house and other structures on the land against damage or destruction. The land itself is not insured. If you own a condominium unit, the condominium corporation is responsible for insuring most of the building you live in against damage and destruction. The unit owner doesn't have that much to insure because condo unit owners only own their homes "from the paint in and from the floor covering up." However, unit owners can buy **owner's improvements coverage** to insure upgrades and additions to the original unit, **supplemental coverage** for protection in case the corporation's insurance does not fully cover damage to the unit, and **loss assessment coverage** to pay any special assessment made by the condominium corporation in the event that its insurance does not fully cover the cost of repairs to common areas.

- **Contents coverage** insures your personal possessions (like furniture, clothing, and jewellery) against theft, damage, or destruction.

- **Third party liability coverage** insures *you* in the event that visitors to your home are injured.

Insurance is a Good Bet

When you buy insurance, you are betting that your home will be damaged, your belongings stolen, or your guests injured (even though you are hoping very hard that none of these things will happen). The insurance company, on the other hand, is betting that your home, belongings, and guests will stay safe and happy. By the law of averages, the insurance company is bound to be right most of the time. Nothing happens to most of the people who buy insurance. They simply pay their insurance premiums every year. The insurance company does not have to pay any money to them, and it invests their premiums and earns interest. These premiums and the interest are what the insurance company uses to help the few who do have something bad happen to them (and also to help the insurance company make a profit).

Shop Around

There's a lot of choice out there. There are many different insurance companies and types of policies. Your choice of company and of policy will affect how much you pay for insurance and what kind of insurance coverage you will get. We suggest that you shop around before you buy insurance. Leave yourself enough time to do comparison shopping—start at least one month before the closing date on your home purchase. You have to make arrangements in advance in order to have insurance protection in place when you become the owner of your new home.

When you go shopping for insurance, you will soon realize that there is a lot of gobbledygook and double-talk in the insurance business. The insurance companies know this and have been trying to simplify the language of insurance. Unfortunately, the concepts involved are very complex and confusing. No matter how simply you write about them, they're still hard to understand.

Because there are so many choices available and because you're bound to feel confused at some point, it's really important to get a good insurance agent or broker to help you choose the insurance coverage that's right for you. The purpose of this chapter is to help you know what information to give to your agent or broker, know what questions to ask, and understand the answers you get.

Your agent or broker will ask you questions such as:

• Do you want standard, broad, or comprehensive insurance?

• Do you want replacement cost insurance?

• What additional riders or endorsements do you want?

You may not have the foggiest idea what these questions mean—but the answers to these questions will affect

• what you insure

• which causes of damage you insure against

• how much your insurance will cost

• what you will get if you make a claim (and how easy or difficult it will be to get it)

In this chapter we'll explain homeowner's insurance to you so that you'll be able to have an actual discussion with your insurance agent or broker (instead of just saying "um" and "whatever") and make sensible choices about your insurance coverage.

WHAT CAN YOU INSURE?

Now we'll embark on a more detailed explanation of coverage under an ordinary homeowner's policy.

Your Home Itself

What you can insure (or even what you need to insure) depends on whether your home is a house and land or a condominium.

If Your Home is House and Land

Your house is insured under the dwelling coverage portion of your homeowner's policy. Dwelling coverage for a house and lot also covers structures on the lot such as a garage, carport or shed, and decks, swimming pools, and pool equipment. Your land is not insured, because it can't be destroyed. Even if your house is blown away by a tornado, your land will still be there. (Well, a major earthquake might dispose of your land.) Some things on the land which can be damaged are insured too, such as landscaping (trees and shrubs, but not grass) and fences.

If Your Home is a Condominium

The common areas of your building (building structure, plumbing, heating, electrical system, etc.) are insured by the condominium corporation and so are the original cabinets, countertops, built-in appliances, plumbing and electrical fixtures, and heating and air conditioning equipment in each unit. An ordinary condo owner's policy usually includes

- owner's improvements coverage to insure upgrades and additions to the original unit (such as upgraded bathroom fixtures or broadloom, or wood panelling or a built-in sound system)
- supplemental coverage in case the corporation doesn't have adequate coverage to repair damage to your unit that it is responsible for insuring, and
- loss assessment coverage in case the corporation's insurance doesn't fully cover damage to the common areas and the corporation makes a special assessment against units owners to cover the shortfall. If you have loss assessment coverage your insurer will pay you the cost of the special

assessment. However, you will probably not be able to get coverage for a special assessment made by the condominium corporation to cover the amount of any **deductible** that it had to pay under its own insurance. (Stay cool—we talk about deductibles later on in this chapter.)

Additional Living Expenses

While the primary purpose of coverage on your home is to get you money for repairs or (in the worst case scenario) to replace your home, the coverage also pays **additional living expenses** if you have to move out of your home because of damage. It may also allow you to make a claim for some of your lost wages if you miss work because of damage to your home.

Your Belongings

Under the contents coverage of your homeowner's policy, the contents of your home are insured against loss or damage. Contents are your personal property, such as your furniture and appliances, your clothing and jewellery, your television and stereo, your books and plants, your tools, a boat that you store on your premises, and so on. Your personal property is covered, to a certain extent, even when it is off your premises. For example, you are covered if leaking water damages a mahogany table in your condo storage locker, or if someone steals your watch at work. But personal property that is not usually kept at home is not covered—for example, your horse that normally lives in a stable elsewhere. Property that is being stored temporarily in your home for people who are not members of your household is not covered either.

Illegally acquired property is not covered. Attention cross-border shoppers! This can mean both stolen property AND imported property that was not declared to Canada Customs.

Your Rear End

The third party liability portion of your homeowner's policy insures you against claims made against you by third parties up to a maximum of $1,000,000. A **third party** is someone from outside your household. You are protected if you accidentally injure

- someone, either at your home or elsewhere
- someone's property, either at your home or elsewhere

You are covered if a visitor slips on the rug in your front hall, or if you unintentionally whack your neighbour's prize rose bushes with a hoe while you are enthusiastically working on your vegetable garden. You are also protected if, while on vacation in Florida, your young son, the budding baseball star hits a home run through the plate glass window of the hotel lobby.

NOTE: Your homeowner's insurance does NOT apply to any injury you cause while you are driving a car.

If someone makes a claim against you, your insurance company must defend any lawsuit against you. This means that the insurance company will pay your legal fees and will pay the amount of any settlement or court judgment. Because the insurance company is paying, it will probably choose the lawyer and will have the final say on how the matter is handled by the lawyer.

If your home is a condominium, the third-party liability portion of a condominium-owner's insurance is much the same as a house-owner's except that it takes into account the fact that your home is only the interior of your unit. The condominium corporation's insurance is intended to cover injuries that occur in common areas of the condominium property. Unit owners can also buy coverage against a special assessment made by the corporation in the event that the corporation's insurance is not enough to pay a claim made by a third party against the corporation. But you probably won't be able to get coverage for a special assessment made by the condominium corporation to cover the amount of any deductible that it had to pay under its own insurance.

WHAT CAUSES OF DAMAGE CAN YOU INSURE AGAINST?

No insurance company will insure you against damage caused in absolutely every way. There are only certain **perils**, or causes of damage, that an insurance company will agree to cover you against, no matter how much money you are prepared to pay.

What Causes of Damage Can You Insure Your Home and Belongings Against?

The perils that an insurance company is willing to insure you against are called **insurable perils** or **insured perils**.

Insurable or Insured Perils

The following are the only commonly insurable perils:

- fire
- lightning

- robbery, burglary, and theft
- riot
- windstorm or hail
- explosion
- water escape from (or rupture or freezing of)
    - plumbing
    - domestic appliances
    - heating systems
    - air-conditioning systems
    - sprinklers
    - pools
    - public water mains
- sudden release of smoke (excluding release of smoke from fireplaces)
- impact by aircraft or vehicle
- vandalism while the building is normally occupied
- glass breakage in a building that is normally occupied
- transportation of personal property (while it is temporarily removed from your home)
- falling objects, as long as they were not pushed by snowslide or movement of the earth (so if the earth moved for you, don't tell your insurance company!)

How many of these perils you are insured against depends on the kind of policy you buy. If you get a policy that insures you against all of the insured perils, it will state that you have **all risk coverage**. But keep in mind that "all risk coverage" only insures you against the risks in the insured perils list, not against all possible risks.

Additional Insurable or Insured Perils

In addition, you may be able to buy coverage against these other perils:

- earthquakes
- spills of furnace oil
- sewer backup

For these perils, you have to make special arrangements by paying a separate premium for a **rider** (also called an **endorsement** or **form**) to your policy.

Uninsurable Perils

There are certain perils that Canadian insurance companies will not insure anyone against. These include

- normal wear and tear on and normal deterioration of your property
- your own failure to maintain your property in good condition
- floods and waves
- melting snow and ice
- repeated or continuous water seepage
- leaky eavestroughs and downspouts
- sump pumps that malfunction
- freezing outside the home that causes damage
- explosion caused by vibrating pipes ("water hammer")
- direct damage from the intentional application of heat
- intentional damage by the insured
- criminal activity of the insured
- theft from a home that is not ready for occupancy
- contamination of property (by pollutants or toxins)
- war

Types of Homeowner's Policies

Homeowner's policies are often categorized according to the number of perils that they insure you against. The more perils, the more expensive the policy. The three types of policies offered in Canada are listed below, in order of least expensive to most expensive:

STANDARD COVERAGE provides coverage for your home and belongings against a package of some of the perils from the insured perils listed above. These perils are called **named perils** or **specified perils**. The package of perils is chosen by the insurance company. You should decide for yourself whether these are the only perils you want to be covered against.

BROAD COVERAGE provides coverage against all the perils from the insured perils list ("all risk coverage") on buildings, and coverage on contents against named perils only. Again, it is the insurance company that chooses the named perils in the package.

COMPREHENSIVE COVERAGE provides coverage on your home and contents against all the perils in the insured perils list.

A policy that only insures you against named or specified perils, instead of all perils, might cover burglary but not theft. A loss of personal property is considered burglary if there are signs of forcible entry to your home. If there are no signs of forcible entry to your home, a loss is considered theft.

As you can see, none of these policies provides coverage against any of the additional insurable perils. If you want to have insurance against any of those perils, you must have a rider added to your policy, which will involve the payment of an additional premium.

What Kinds of Third Party Claims Can You Insure Yourself Against?

Under your third party liability coverage, your insurance company pays claims made against you by other people. You are not covered for all types of claims made against you. You are mainly covered for claims for bodily harm or damage to property, and only if you harm the other person *accidentally*. Further, your homeowner's policy does not cover you against

- any injury you cause while driving your car
- most claims arising out of your work or business

A Special Concern for Condominium Owners

If you own a condominium unit and you get loss assessment coverage for special assessments made against you by the condominium corporation, you may wish to insure yourself against more perils than your condominium corporation is insured against. If the condominium corporation's common areas are damaged or the corporation is responsible for injury to a third party, insurance will only cover the corporation for perils named in the corporation's policy. If the peril is not insured against, the condominium will have to come up with the money through a special assessment against the unit owners. Special assessment coverage purchased by a unit owner will pay the cost of an assessment only if the cause of the damage is a peril that the unit owner paid to be insured against.

HOW MUCH INSURANCE COVERAGE SHOULD YOU HAVE?

A homeowner's insurance policy, as we have said, has three different parts: dwelling coverage—or for condo unit owners, owner's improvements coverage, supplemental coverage and loss assessment coverage; contents coverage;

and third party liability coverage. The amount of coverage is different in each part.

Coverage for Your Home Itself

Dwelling coverage is the coverage for a house. The amount of coverage you get depends on the value of your house and other structures on the property. Your land is not taken into account.

For condo unit owners, the amount of coverage you get depends on the value of your upgrades and additions, and on the completeness of the condominium corporation's coverage.

Replacement Cost Insurance

If your home or any part of it is damaged, you want your insurance policy to pay you enough money to repair it. If your home is destroyed, you want enough money to replace it. If your home were destroyed, it would probably cost you more to replace it than it was worth before. Even if your home were only damaged, the cost of repairs might be more than the home was worth.

If you want to get enough money to cover the actual cost of replacing what was damaged or destroyed, you should get **replacement cost insurance**. If you don't have replacement cost insurance, the insurance company does not have to pay you any more than your home was worth before it was damaged or destroyed. If you do have replacement cost insurance, the insurance company will pay you the full cost of replacing what was damaged or destroyed, even if the cost of doing so is higher than the actual value of the property, or even higher than the amount for which your property is insured. However, replacement cost insurance does not guarantee that your property will be replaced. Your insurance company will not pay to replace your home, or part of it, if it would be cheaper to repair it.

An insurance company will not issue replacement cost insurance unless you get their recommended amount of coverage. Also, you must increase the amount of coverage if, after you take out the original coverage, you make any improvements which increase the value of the property.

Houses: Insurable Value

The value of a house is fixed by the insurance company and is known as the **insurable value**.

If you want to insure your house for more than its insurable value, the insurance company will let you and will happily take the extra premium money you pay. But when the time comes for you to make a claim, the insurance company won't pay you any extra. This is why you get replacement cost insurance—instead of over-insuring your house.

If you want to insure your house for less than its insurable value, some insurance companies will refuse to insure you at all. Others will severely limit the perils that you are covered against. If you make a claim, you will be paid only a portion of your loss.

When you apply for insurance, your insurance broker or agent will ask you questions to help the insurance company calculate the insurable value of your property. If you have a mortgage on your house, the mortgagee will tell you how much insurance it wants you to have. Some mortgagees insist that you get coverage in the full amount of the mortgage, even if it is higher than the insurable value of your property. This extra coverage is useless for both of you, but try telling that to your mortgagee!

Houses: Limits on Structures on a Lot

If you own a house, your insurance policy will probably set a limit on the amount that it will pay for damage to structures on your lot other than the house, like a shed or detached garage. It will probably also set a limit on the amount it will pay for the replacement of trees, plants, or shrubs.

Find out from your insurance agent or broker what limits are contained in any policy he or she recommends. If you don't think the limited amounts would be enough, ask about making arrangements for additional coverage.

Contents Coverage

While the insurance company may assign a value to your home, it is strictly up to you to decide what your contents are worth.

Replacement Cost Insurance

If your contents are damaged, you want your insurance policy to pay you enough money to repair them. If they are lost or destroyed, you want enough money to replace them.

As you know, new things cost more to buy (often a lot more) than the old things they are replacing were worth. If you want to get enough money to cover the actual cost of replacing what you have lost, you should get replacement cost insurance. However, be aware that your insurance company will not pay to replace an item if it's cheaper to repair it, even if you have replacement cost coverage.

Without replacement cost insurance, if your possessions are lost or destroyed your insurance company will pay you only what they were worth immediately before the loss or destruction occurred. What your possessions were worth depends on their condition, resale value, and normal life expectancy. (Your policy may state that the value is calculated as "the cost of replacement less any depreciation or obsolescence," which means the same thing as we just said.)

Unlike replacement cost coverage on buildings, replacement cost coverage on contents does not give you the right to receive more from the insurance company than the face amount of insurance coverage you have bought. Be sure to value your belongings based on what it would cost to replace them new, and to get insurance coverage in that full amount.

Limits

For many kinds of property, your insurance company will pay only a limited amount for each stolen or damaged item—even if you buy replacement cost coverage. If you want to be paid more than the limit for any items, you must pay extra to get a rider to your policy specifically identifying them. Such items typically include jewellery, furs, silverware, and stamp collections.

Each insurance company sets different limits for these various items. Ask your agent or broker what the insurance company's policy limits are so you can decide whether you need a rider. Your insurance company will require a professional valuation in writing for each item before it will issue a rider.

There are other kinds of property which are also insured only to a limited amount, but for which you cannot get additional coverage, even with a rider. These kinds of property include pets, cash, and computer software.

Third Party Liability Coverage

Insurance companies offer a standard amount of coverage for claims that may be made against you because you have injured someone or damaged their property. This amount is $1,000,000.

One million dollars may seem like quite a bit of money, but if someone is badly hurt, the cost of care for the rest of his or her life can easily be several million dollars. You can buy **excess liability insurance** if you want to increase the amount of your third party liability coverage above $1,000,000.

HOW DO YOU GET INSURANCE?

If you are anything like the authors, you have spent a good part of your adult life trying to get away from insurance agents, not looking for them! Now is the time to call up that cousin, sister-in-law, or old friend from high school you've been avoiding like the plague all these years!

The Insurance Agent or Broker

There are two kinds of insurance professionals: **brokers** deal with a number of insurance companies; and **agents'**, although they are not employees of the insurance company, represent only one insurance company. Brokers can shop around to find the company with the best deal for you. An agent can only get you insurance from the one company he or she represents. So if you choose an agent, make sure that you have made some inquiries about the company as well as about the agent.

Finding an Agent or Broker

To find an agent or broker, ask for recommendations from family and friends, from your real estate agent, or from the agent or broker who deals with your car insurance. Or your employer or union or professional organization may have an arrangement with a particular agent, broker, or insurance company to provide insurance to you at a special discounted rate.

What the Insurance Agent or Broker Does

The role of an insurance agent or broker is to figure out your insurance needs and get you a policy that meets those needs. You will have to talk to him or her about the value of your home and contents, what perils you want to be insured against, what amount of coverage you would like to have, and what premium you can afford to pay. You want to find an agent or broker who is willing to discuss all of your concerns in detail.

You must be sure to tell the agent or broker exactly how you will be using your home, because that can affect the insurance you should get. For example, if you will be running a business from your home, or if you will be keeping other people's valuable possessions at your home, say so.

What are the Agent's or Broker's Responsibilities to You?

If you tell your agent or broker everything about what your property is worth, how you will use your property, the perils you want to be protected against, and the amount of coverage you want, he or she is responsible for getting you the right kind of coverage, within the budget you set. If it's not possible to get the coverage you want, or to get it at a price you can afford, your agent or broker must tell you so.

If you end up with a policy that doesn't cover you for a situation you should have been covered for, the agent or broker may be liable to you for the amount of money the right kind of insurance would have paid you. Ask your insurance agent or broker whether he or she is insured against making mistakes. Your provincial government may require agents and brokers to have such **errors and omissions insurance**.

Choosing an Insurance Company

Helping you to choose the right insurance company is really what you are hiring an insurance broker to do. The following information is useful if you want to make the choice yourself or if you want to discuss with your broker the reason for his or her choice.

There are many different companies that provide homeowner's insurance. Premium prices are usually competitive, but each company's policy will offer slightly different coverage. You want a policy that gives the best coverage you can get without having to pay extra for riders.

Each company has its own reputation for dealing well or badly with its clients. Ask acquaintances who have made a claim how their insurance company treated them. Some companies are very helpful and understanding and settle claims quickly; others resist paying claims and sometimes have to be sued. Keep in mind that some companies can afford to provide cheaper coverage because they don't pay very many claims.

What you want is an insurance company that treats its clients well and a policy that provides the best coverage for your particular needs, at the best price.

The Application Process

To get homeowner's insurance, you have to fill out the insurance company's standard application form. This form contains information that helps the insurance company to decide

- whether it wants to insure you at all
- how much insurance coverage you should have
- how much it will charge

It is very important to be absolutely honest in filling out the application form, because if you make any false statements the insurance company may have the right to refuse to pay if you make a claim.

Applying for Coverage for a House

If you own a house, the application form is designed to get from you the necessary details about the house that will help the insurance company to fix its insurable value. The questions on the form concern the size, age, and condition of the house and other structures on the property. The insurance company may require an inspection of your house.

If your house is in really bad condition, you may find it difficult to get insurance at all. The insurance company may consider your home too big a risk and will refuse to gamble with you that it will not be damaged or destroyed.

Applying for Contents Coverage

It's up to you to know what belongings you have and what they are worth. Before making your application for contents coverage, be sure to

- value your contents for what you believe it will cost you to replace them
- check with your agent or broker to see what kinds of possessions are subject to limits (so you can decide whether you need to buy a rider if it would cost more than the limit to replace your possessions)

Before you can put a dollar value on your contents, you must figure out what you own by making an **inventory**. This involves going through your home, room by room, and noting what you have and how much it originally cost. (If you are moving into a new home, you can make this inventory while you are packing). In the Appendix at the end of the book you will find sample inventory lists to help you.

Prepare a list of the contents of each room of the house and describe each item. You can make your inventory

- in writing, and then attach photographs
- on an audio cassette, by dictating the list and description (this works well for collections of things like books or stamps)
- on a video cassette (this is best for large items like furniture, equipment, and appliances which will show up well on film)

It is a good idea to attach to the inventory receipts from the purchase of expensive items.

Store a copy of the inventory off your premises, just in case a burglar takes your inventory along with your VCR. Your safety deposit box is a good place. You should update the inventory regularly as you get rid of and buy new possessions.

Does this sound like too much work? (If you think this is too much work, wait until you see the chapter on home safety!) If you can't bring yourself to do a thorough inventory of all your possessions, at least keep an inventory of expensive items that are likely to attract thieves, such as jewellery, TVs, stereos, CD players, and computer equipment.

HOW MUCH WILL YOUR INSURANCE COST?

The amount you have to pay for your insurance depends on different factors for each of the three different kinds of insurance coverage included in your homeowner's insurance. You will be billed a single amount as a premium for a package made up of all three kinds of insurance.

Coverage for Your Home Itself

How much you have to pay for coverage on your home depends (among other things) on

- how many perils you choose to be insured against (this is determined when you decide among standard, broad, and comprehensive policies, and when you buy a rider for any additional insured perils)
- whether or not you choose to have replacement cost insurance

If You Own A House

If you own a house, the cost of insurance coverage depends not only on the number of perils and whether you've chosen replacement cost insurance, but also on the insurable value of the house and other structures on the property, and on what **rating** is given by the insurance company. We've already talked about the value of your house; now let's talk about your house's rating. Your insurance company will give your house either a **standard rating** or a **preferred rating**. A preferred rating is given to houses less than ten years old and to older houses that have been updated to the standards of a new house. A standard rating is given to a house more than ten years old, unless you can show it has been updated. The insurance company is concerned about wiring, plumbing, the heating system, and the roof. It may have an inspection done to find out if an older house should be given a standard rating or qualifies for a preferred rating.

If You Own a Condominium Unit

If your home is a condo, the cost of owner's improvements coverage depends not only on the number of perils and whether you've chosen replacement cost insurance, but also on the value of your improvements. Similarly, the cost of supplemental coverage also depends on the value of your unit as originally constructed. The cost of loss assessment coverage depends on the number of perils you choose to be insured against, the extent of the condominium's insurance coverage, and your percentage share of ownership of the condominium.

Renovations

If extensive renovations are being carried out on your home, the insurance company may insist that you pay a higher premium during the renovation process because the risk of damage or destruction is greater during this time.

Discount on Your Premium

Your insurance company may give you a **discount** on your premium. For example, a discount will usually be given if fire alarms have been installed, and may be given if burglar alarms have been installed. Most insurers also offer a "claims-free" bonus to a homeowner who has not made a claim for three years or more. Ask your agent or broker what discounts you and your home are eligible for.

Contents Coverage

How much you have to pay for contents coverage depends on

- the number of perils you choose to be insured against (this is determined when you decide among standard, broad, and comprehensive policies, and if you buy a rider for additional insured perils)
- the value of your contents
- whether or not you choose to have replacement cost insurance
- what riders, if any, you buy for extra coverage on valuable items

If you are getting a discount on your home coverage for having fire or burglar alarms, or you are getting a "claims-free" bonus, the discount or bonus will also apply to your contents coverage.

Third Party Liability Coverage

Remember that all homeowner's policies provide $1,000,000 of third party liability coverage. So the amount of coverage is not an issue in determining the cost of the premium. The premium depends, rather, on things like the size of your property, any dangers that might be on it (such as a swimming pool), and whether there have been any claims against you in the past.

If you want coverage for more than $1,000,000, excess liability coverage can cost from under a hundred dollars to several hundred dollars for an additional $1,000,000 in coverage. Depending on the insurance company, you may have to buy a separate policy. Some companies don't offer excess liability insurance at all.

Payment Options

You will be billed a single amount for your policy premium, even though the policy is made up of a package of coverage for home and contents and for third-party liability. Most insurance companies offer different options for paying the premium, such as monthly payments instead of a single yearly payment. If you choose to make several payments instead of a single one, you may be charged some kind of service fee, and you may have to agree to automatic withdrawals from your bank account.

HOW DO YOU MAKE A CLAIM?

If your home is damaged or destroyed or your contents are damaged, destroyed, or stolen, you will want to make a claim under your insurance policy for compensation. As with so many things in life, this won't be as easy as you would like it to be. A little bit of knowledge should help you find your way through what can sometimes be a complicated and frustrating process.

Consider the following questions before you make a claim:

- Whose losses are covered under the policy?
- Is it worth my while to make a claim?
- What must I do to get my claim processed?
- How much money will be paid out, and who will get it?

Whose Losses are Covered Under the Policy?

Whose losses are covered depends on what has been lost, taken, damaged or destroyed.

If Your Home Itself is Damaged

STRUCTURES: As the owner of your home, you are the person who took out the insurance. The insurance policy is in your name (you're called the **named insured**). If your home is damaged or destroyed, you're the person who suffered a loss and are entitled to get the money to repair or replace the damaged or destroyed structure. If your property is mortgaged, the mortgage lender is also a named insured.

ADDITIONAL LIVING EXPENSES: If your home is so badly damaged that you cannot continue to live there, your insurance will pay not only your reasonable living expenses as the named insured, but also those of members of your household.

LOST WAGES: Your policy may allow you to make a claim for wages lost because of damage to your home. In that case, coverage is limited to the wages lost by the named insured and his or her wife or husband. If you're fortunate enough to have a child who has a job (but not fortunate enough for the child to have moved out), that child's lost wages are *not* covered.

Contents

Your belongings, and the belongings of members of your family who are living in the household with you, are covered under your contents insurance. Your family includes anyone under the age of 21 who is in your care. If you are living with someone but are not legally married, that someone's belongings are not necessarily covered. You have to have lived together in a marriage-like relationship for one year if you have a child and otherwise for three years before your significant other's belongings are covered by your insurance.

If anyone else's personal property is damaged or destroyed at your home, their loss is not covered under your contents insurance. It is covered, if at all, under your third party liability coverage.

Third Party Liability Insurance

If someone is accidentally injured on your property or their personal possessions are damaged, that person cannot make a claim under your insurance policy. Your third party liability does not cover the third party directly. It covers you and certain members of your household if the third party makes a claim against any of you. It pays on your behalf any compensation you are legally responsible for paying to that third party.

The members of your household who are also protected from third party claims under your liability insurance are the same people who are insured under contents coverage.

Is it Worth Your While to Make a Claim?

Before you make a claim to your insurance company, there are two things to consider:

- a deductible may apply, and if your claim is not large you may not actually collect anything from the insurance company
- when you make a claim under your homeowner's insurance policy, your premium may go up—the same way your car insurance premium rises when you make a claim.

Deductibles

Most insurance policies require an insured homeowner to pay a certain amount of each claim. This amount is called the **deductible**, and it ranges from about $200 to $500. If your premium is low, you will probably have a high deductible; if your premium is high, you will probably have a low deductible. For example, if you have a claim for $425 and a deductible of $500, your insurance company will pay nothing on the claim. If you have a claim for $1,500 and a deductible of $200, your insurance company will pay $1,300 on the claim.

Check with your insurance company about the amount of the deductible for the kind of claim you want to make. There is usually no deductible if you are making a claim under a rider.

If you will receive very little once the deductible is taken into account you may not want to bother making a claim.

Increase in Insurance Premium

Speak to your insurance company or agent before you make a claim to find out how much your premium is likely to rise if you do make that claim. Whatever the increase, it will usually last for three years. In some cases you may gain something from the insurance company now but lose it all back by paying increased premiums.

What Must You Do to Get Your Claim Processed?

While the claims process may vary from insurance company to insurance company, there are certain standard steps that are usually followed.

The Usual Procedure

Calculate what the money value of your loss might be, and contact your agent or insurance company to find out how much your deductible will be and what the effect of a claim will be on your premium.

If you decide to make a claim, the claims department of your insurance company will tell you what particular steps they want you to follow. One of them may be to call the police if criminal activity is involved or suspected.

For any insurance company, you will have to prove that you have suffered a loss and that you should be paid a certain amount of money in compensation as a result.

Proof of Loss Form

If you are making a claim under your contents coverage for an item that was damaged, you may have to fill out **proof of loss** form and provide a written estimate of the cost to repair the item. If the item was destroyed or stolen, you may have to provide an estimate of the cost to replace it. Get the written estimate from the place where you plan to buy the replacement or have the repair made. Your insurance company may direct you to stores or repair people they are used to dealing with, if you don't know anyone.

You should take care in completing the proof of loss form, because the information you provide will become the basis for what the insurance company pays you. You will be asked to:

- list all items you intend to make a claim for
- give the make, model, and serial number of any items that have them
- state the date and place of purchase if you can
- give the replacement cost for destroyed or stolen items (use the price of a comparable item if the identical item can no longer be found).

Insurance Adjusters

If your loss involves a house or condo unit, or contents worth a large sum of money, the insurance company will send an **insurance adjuster** to inspect the property and estimate the damage.

Independent Evidence of Loss

Keep in mind that the insurance company wants to pay as little as possible. Evidence you yourself gather may establish a higher loss figure than evidence gathered by the insurance company. If you have independent information about the value of your loss, you'll be in a better position to judge the fairness of the compensation that the insurance company offers you. And if you think the compensation isn't enough, you'll be in a position to negotiate for more.

There are a number of things you can do to support your claim if you think that the insurance company may not want to pay you what your loss is worth. It's up to you how much of this you choose to do. Your eagerness will probably depend on how much money is involved and your past experience with insurance companies.

- Photograph or video the damaged property. Keep one copy of the pictures for yourself and give one to the insurance company.

• Get independent replacement cost or repair estimates even if the insurance company has sent its adjuster to make an estimate.

• If you're not satisfied with what the insurance company offers you, even after you give them your own evidence, you can contact an **independent insurance adjuster**. An independent adjuster does not work for your insurance company, but is still an insurance professional whose opinion may be accepted by your insurance company.

• If you're unable to reach an agreement with your insurance company, you may have to hire a lawyer. You can ask the lawyer to negotiate for you or to sue the insurance company to force them to pay you what you think you're entitled to.

Should You Claim First or Pay First?

This decision will depend on how badly you need to replace what you've lost or fix what is broken. If you have water gushing from a broken pipe, you probably won't want to wait for the insurance company's cheque to have it repaired. If you've lost a bracelet you wear only once a year, you can probably wait to replace it.

If you do go ahead with repairs or replacement, get invoices and send a copy to the insurance company. Make sure you keep copies for yourself too.

If you can't live in your home, you will have to pay your own additional living expenses and make a claim for reimbusement later. Keep all your receipts and send copies to your insurance company.

Tell the insurance company what you are planning to do. You want to know that the expense in question is one that the insurance company is willing to pay you back.

How Much Will be Paid?

The amount you'll get from the insurance company depends on a number of factors which we have already told you about:

• the total amount of your coverage

• the amount of any deductible

• whether or not you have replacement cost insurance

• whether your property is replaced or only repaired

• if you are entitled to have property replaced, whether you actually replace it or choose to take a cash settlement

Who Will Get the Money?

PAYMENTS IN ADVANCE: If payment is made in advance to allow you to repair or replace property, the cheque from the insurance company will probably be made out jointly to you and the person who is making the repairs or selling you the replacement article. This is the insurance company's way of keeping tabs on both you and the person you are doing business with.

REIMBURSEMENT FOR PAYMENTS ALREADY MADE: If you've already made a payment with the approval of your insurance company, the reimbursement cheque will be made payable to you.

PAYMENT OF THIRD PARTY LIABILITY CLAIMS: These payments are generally made in settlement of a lawsuit, and will be paid to the third party, probably through his or her lawyer.

PAYMENTS TO OTHERS THAN THE NAMED INSURED: If the named insured can't or won't make a claim on behalf of anyone else covered under the policy, that other person can make the claim. For example, suppose your teenager's stereo is stolen from his bedroom in your home. Because you're annoyed with him for never cleaning his room, you refuse to make a claim. He could make the claim himself because he is insured under your contents policy as a member of your household.

9 MOVING TO YOUR NEW HOME

War is hell. Moving is worse.

Packing up everything you own, moving it to another place and then unpacking it, while you still need all the things you've either just packed or haven't unpacked yet, is a special kind of torture.

You probably haven't stopped to think about what's involved in getting yourself and all your belongings to your new home. Instead, you've no doubt spent many pleasant hours picturing what it will be like to live there. In your fantasy, all your furniture has been miraculously transported to your new home without any effort or inconvenience. Unfortunately, that's not the way it works.

Moving is chaotic, but with planning you'll at least have organized chaos instead of absolute chaos. And speaking of planning, there's more to moving than moving vans. In this chapter we tell you how to

- do some preliminary planning
- choose the right mover
- decide what the mover will do
- pack for the move
- live through moving day itself
- deal with the aftermath

Most of this chapter assumes that you're making a local move or discusses concerns that apply equally to local moves or long distance moves. There's a section at the end of the chapter about special concerns for a long distance move.

PRELIMINARY PLANNING

Preliminary planning for your move involves getting ready to look for a moving company. It also involves preparing yourself and your family for the move.

Get Ready to Talk to Movers

Start thinking about your move early enough that you will be able to book your move at least six to eight weeks before your planned moving date.

Before you talk to any movers, you have to give some thought to certain matters. Any mover you speak to will want to know where you are moving from, where you are moving to, when you are moving, and what you want the movers to move. The moving from and to questions are easy—you know your old address and your new one. The other questions may look easier than they are.

When Are You Moving?

When you are moving will depend to a large extent on your closing date. If you are selling a home as well as buying, you are probably doing both on the same day. You have to move out of your old home on the closing day and, unless you are storing your belongings, you'll want them moved to your new home. If you have been renting, you may choose to keep your apartment or house past the closing date. Doing so gives you more leeway to move gradually or to move later.

The mover will want to know not only what day you want to move but what time of day. You can ask for the **first move of the day**, which means that the movers arrive at your place at a fixed time, usually about 8:00 a.m. If you ask for the **second move of the day**, the mover won't be able to set a fixed time of arrival. In choosing between the two, keep in mind that you won't be able to get the keys to your new home and move your things in until your lawyer and the vendor's lawyer have finished closing your deal. This may not happen until the afternoon of the day of closing.

If you book the first move of the day and the movers finish loading the moving van quickly, you and they may end up waiting to get into the new home. You pay the movers by the hour, including any waiting time. On the other hand, if you book the second move of the day and you have a lot to move, you may not have to wait to get into the new home but you may still be moving in late into the night. In deciding between the two, ask your mover how long it is likely to take to load the van at your old home. If it will take a long time, you are probably better off booking the first move of the day.

What Do You Want the Movers to Move?

Keep in mind that the more the movers move, the more it will cost. The strategy then is to have them move less rather than more. There are ways to reduce the movers' load:

• Get rid of the stuff you don't need.

• Get things moved by others for free.

Get rid of anything you don't need by having a garage sale, by giving things to charity, or just by throwing things away. Many people hoard things they had no need for in their old home, let alone in their new home. If you are thinking about having furniture reupholstered or carpets, drapes, or furniture cleaned, schedule the work so that the items are picked up from your old home and delivered directly to your new home. Put off purchase, or at least delivery, of new furniture until you are in your new home.

You may want to move some of your belongings yourself, particularly smaller items that are fragile or valuable. Doing this won't reduce your moving bill noticeably, but it may give you some peace of mind.

Prepare Yourself and Your Family

There are a number of things that you should do to get yourself and your family ready for the move.

Arranging for Insurance on Your New Home

You will need to have homeowner's insurance in place as soon as you become the owner of your new home. You should start to make arrangements at least a month before the closing date of your home purchase. We talked about insurance in Chapter 8.

Notifying People of Your Change of Address

Unless you've gone into a witness protection program or are trying to escape from your creditors, you want people to be able to find you after you move. You want to continue receiving your magazines, and you want your friends to know where to bring their housewarming gifts.

Make a list of everyone who needs your address:

- friends and relatives
- credit card companies
- banks
- pension plans
- companies who pay you dividends
- insurance companies
- magazines and newspapers
- book and record clubs
- favourite charities
- clubs and organizations
- government departments, such as Canada Customs and Revenue Agency and the provincial department of motor vehicles

Notify each person on your list of your new address and your moving date. The credit card companies, magazine publishers, and government offices have change of address forms that you can send to them. For the others on your list, you can get change of address post cards from Canada Post. The post cards are free, but you have to pay the postage yourself.

In case you leave someone off your list, you should also go to the post office to arrange for Canada Post to redirect your mail to your new address. You have to fill in a form and pay a fee of about $30.00. Your mail will be redirected for six months, and you can pay for additional six-month periods. When you receive redirected mail at your new address, be sure to notify the sender that you've moved.

If you have the newspaper delivered to your door, call the subscription office to arrange for delivery to your new address.

Once you move into your new home, you must notify the motor vehicle licensing office immediately of your change of address. You will be issued a new driver's licence and vehicle permit showing your new address.

Helping Your Children Adjust to the Move

Moving can be hard on children of any age. Younger children can be frightened and confused by a change that they don't understand. Older children may be upset at the loss of friends and the prospect of a new school. How you help your child adjust depends on the child's age and personality.

Whatever the age of your children, tell them about the move as soon as possible and involve them in it as much as you can. Take them to see the new home, neighbourhood, and school, or if you can't do that, show them photographs or a videotape. Let them help in planning the decorating of their new bedrooms.

Let younger children know that their furniture, clothes, and toys will be moving with them. Have them help in the packing, and don't pack favourite items until the end. Encourage older children to make arrangements to stay in touch with their friends through visits, telephone calls, letters, and e-mail.

Transferring Utility Accounts

Telephone the water department and the gas, hydro, telephone, and cable TV companies to tell them of your move. In some cases your account and service will simply be transferred to your new address. In other cases, especially if you are moving out of the service area, your account will have to be closed, and you will have to contact the utility companies in your new neighbourhood to arrange for service. Every utility will charge you a fee for making account changes. Cancel any fuel oil delivery contract for your old home.

Making Arrangements with Your Lawyer

You will have to meet with your lawyer at least once just before closing to review and sign the necessary documents. You will also have to give your lawyer the money needed to complete your purchase—if you don't, you won't be moving. Some of this money may come from the sale of your old home, some may come from your mortgage. If your lawyer is handling the legal work involved in selling your home and preparing your mortgage, those funds will go directly to the lawyer. But there will always.be some amount of money that you have to take to the lawyer yourself. Leave yourself enough time to put your hands on the money, get it into the form of a certified cheque, and deliver it.

Ordinarily, the keys to your new home will be given to your lawyer at the closing, and you will have to pick them up from him or her. If your lawyer's office is not close to either your old or new home, it will be inconvenient for you. You should make arrangements through your lawyer to have the keys left at a more convenient location (such as your real estate agent's office) where you can pick them up after the closing.

Inspection Before Closing

If your agreement of purchase and sale gives you the right to inspect the home just before closing, make arrangements with your real estate agent to do so. You want to make sure that it's in more or less the same condition it was in when you agreed to buy it. If you see any problems, be sure to notify your lawyer immediately.

If you are buying a newly constructed home that is covered by your provincial new home warranty program, you will probably have to make a **pre-closing inspection**. The purpose of this inspection is to identify any problems in the home that the builder is required to fix. The builder will probably contact you to set up an appointment for this inspection. You might want to discuss the inspection with your lawyer beforehand, so that you know what to look for.

CHOOSING THE RIGHT MOVER

Before you choose a mover you should speak to three to five moving companies to get estimates and also a sense of the level of service and reliability each has to offer. Get names of moving companies from friends, your real estate agent, or the Yellow Pages.

Get Estimates

Ask each moving company for an estimate. For an accurate estimate of what your move will cost, the mover must come to your home and look at what you have to move. Each estimate should be in writing. In order to compare the different estimates, be sure that they all take into account the following:

• things to be moved
• packing, if any
• insurance
• any special charges
• taxes

Show the movers everything you want to move, including things in your attic, basement, or garage. Don't forget to tell the mover about anything stored elsewhere that you want them to pick up and take to your new home.

If you want the movers to do any packing for you, say so, and get an estimate from all the moving companies for the same items. Even if you don't want to pay for packing, you may have some items that the movers will suggest that you let them pack. If one mover makes such a suggestion, ask the others what they think.

Ask each moving company what insurance they recommend for your move and how much it will cost. (For more about insurance, see page 132.)

Ask each moving company if there will be any special charges, for example, for moving a piano or freezer, or because of the number of stairs at your old or new home.

Ask each company whether they offer any discounts or promotions. Let the different companies know that you are shopping around—it may encourage them to give you a better price.

To give you a rough idea, the cost of moving the contents of an average three-bedroom bungalow (without any packing) is about $1000, going up to about $1500 in peak times (the first and last weeks of the summer months).

Check Out the Mover's Reputation

Even if someone has recommended a mover to you, you should consider checking the following:

- how long the company has been in business
- size of the company
- how long the staff have been with the company
- whether the company is properly licensed
- whether the company can provide references from satisfied clients
- whether the local Better Business Bureau has any record of complaints about the company

Whatever the general reputation of the company, the success of your move will ultimately depend on the three or four people who show up with the truck. So try to find out if the people who will be doing your move have worked with the company for a while.

DECIDING WHAT YOU WANT THE MOVER TO DO

Once you decide which mover to use, you must decide exactly what services you want from them, and you must book the move and sign a contract. Be sure to book your move at least six or eight weeks before your moving day.

Packing and Boxes

You can arrange for the moving company to do all your packing for you. If you do, you don't have to pack anything. You don't have to live out of cartons for weeks before you move. You just go about your business until a day or two before the move, when the movers come with boxes and packing materials and pack your things. It sounds like heaven, doesn't it? Well, heaven is expensive. To have the movers pack an average three-bedroom bungalow would cost in the $800 to $1000 range (and more at peak times). If you want the movers to unpack at the other end, it would cost an additional

$400 to $500. As you can see, having the movers pack and unpack would more than double the cost of a local move.

The movers may recommend that you let them pack certain items. Usually these are large or expensive items that are easily damaged, like a marble table or a large mirror. The movers may tell you that they will not accept responsibility for damage to such things unless they pack them.

If you're doing any of your own packing, you need boxes, lots of boxes. You can buy or rent boxes from the moving company. If you don't get them from the moving company, your alternatives are to buy them from a store that specializes in boxes and other moving and packing materials, or to scrounge around in grocery and liquor stores. Liquor store and grocery boxes don't cost money, but what you don't pay in cash you may have to pay in self-respect because of the begging and pleading involved to get more than two boxes at a time. You should also know that these boxes may not be sturdy enough for moving. And they may have bugs in them. Check them carefully before you bring the boxes (and the bugs) into the house.

A Few Good Men

The hourly rate your mover charges depends on the number of men (and they probably *will* be men) they send, so you have to decide how many you want. It's not necessarily cheaper to have fewer men, because the move will take longer. If you've chosen a reputable mover, it's best to follow their advice about how many men you should have.

Storage

If you have to move out of your old home before the new one is ready for you, you will have to store your belongings. Your mover can arrange for **storage-in-transit**—you pay to have your goods moved out of your old home, into a warehouse for storage for up to sixty days, and then into your new home. You'll be charged a package rate that combines the moving and storage fees. If you need to store your things for more than sixty days, long-term storage arrangements must be made. If your goods are going to be stored in a warehouse, you may want to inspect it for cleanness and dryness.

If overnight storage turns out to be necessary during your move, for a fee some movers will simply store your possessions in the moving van.

Insurance

The standard moving contract limits the mover's liability for damage to your belongings to less than $1.00 per pound regardless of the actual value of the item. So if the movers destroyed your thirty-pound sound system, they would have to pay you less than $30.

Clearly, you need additional protection in case any of your things are lost, damaged, or destroyed in the move. You can buy insurance through your moving company which will provide greater protection. Ask your mover for a recommendation about how much insurance you should buy. But before you speak to your mover about this, contact your insurance company to find out whether the contents coverage in your existing homeowner's insurance will cover your belongings during your move.

The Contract with the Mover

Your contract with the moving company will set out

- the date and time of the move
- the number of men and type of truck
- the hourly rate
- any special materials or services to be provided, like boxes or packing

Because the bulk of the cost of moving is based on the number of hours that the movers actually spend on your move, the final cost is not set out in the contract. Only an estimated cost is given. You will probably have to pay a deposit when you book your move, and you will have to pay the balance of the price to the moving foreman when the move is completed. The moving company will tell you how they want to be paid—usually by cash, certified cheque, or credit card.

PACKING FOR YOUR MOVE

Your things can't be moved unless they are packed. If you hire the movers to do the packing for you, a crew will swoop in and do all your packing in a day or two. If you decide to do your own packing, the crew will consist of you and, if you're lucky, a helpful spouse and cooperative children. But even with their help, don't think you will be able to do it all in a day or two. You don't have the expertise, you won't have the manpower, and you still have the rest of your life to contend with.

There's no way around it. Unless you want to find yourself throwing things into green garbage bags as the movers are carrying your furniture out the door (as the husband of one of the authors does), you must start packing well in advance of moving day. As time passes, more and more of your belongings will be in boxes. You have to know what you can and can't live without so that you'll be able to decide what to pack first.

By now it should be clear to you (although it never did become clear to the above-mentioned husband) that packing for a move involves planning, one might even say militarily precise planning. You want to have a plan that allows you to

- pack what you need most last
- direct the boxes to the right room in your new home
- find what you need while things are still in the boxes
- pack things so they don't get broken and are easy to find

Don't forget that everything that's packed must be unpacked. Pack in haste and repent at leisure!

Decide the Order in Which You Will Pack

Walk through your home. On a room-by-room basis, identify in each room what you can live without until after moving day. Some rooms will have lots of things you can pack early, and these are the things you will pack first. For example, you won't miss too badly

- your off-season clothes
- books, records, tapes, and CDs
- silver, crystal, and fine china
- pictures
- knick-knacks
- personal files and records
- sports equipment, games, and some children's toys
- extra linens
- tools and off-season outdoor equipment

You can pack these and seal and pile up the boxes.

As moving day gets closer, you can pack some of the items you use more regularly but not daily. Kitchens and bathrooms are filled with this kind of stuff. Don't seal the boxes, and keep them where you can get into them easily. Don't pack things you must use on a daily basis until the last moment.

You should also pack a separate box of essential items that you will want to have as soon as you reach your new home; for example:

- toilet paper
- soap
- toothpaste and toothbrushes

- paper towels
- garbage bags
- paper plates, plastic cups, and utensils
- can opener
- screwdriver and pliers
- a flashlight
- some light bulbs
- snacks and drinks

Have an Inventory Plan

Having a proper inventory plan will help you to

- direct your boxes to the right room in your new home
- find things while they're still in the boxes
- make sure that all of your boxes have arrived at your new home

As you pack each box, assign it a number. Use a magic marker to write on each box the number and the room where the box is going. Write large enough for you and the movers to be able to read easily what you've written. This way the movers will know which room to take each box to without having to ask you about every box. Write the number on the top and each side of the box, so the number is visible no matter how the boxes are piled up. If you are planning to take any boxes in your car instead of sending them on the moving van, mark them clearly "Do Not Move."

Keep a list of every box you pack. Write down the number of each box, and next to each number write the room the box is to go to and a brief description of the contents of the box. It will be several days or more before all of your boxes are unpacked. If you need something from a box, you will be able to look through your list to find what box it is in and the room the box is located in, rather than climbing over piles of boxes and rummaging through them.

As you unpack each box, check it off against your inventory list. Then you'll know if any boxes did not get moved.

If you have a lot of furniture or a bad memory, you might want to list your furniture as well as your boxes on the inventory list. You can check off the furniture as it is moved out and in to make sure nothing has been forgotten.

How to Pack—Plan of Attack

Pick a room and start packing. When you've done all the packing you can in that room at that time, move on to another room. Don't mix things from different rooms in one box.

Boxes and Packing Materials

Make sure that your boxes are clean and sturdy. Tape the bottoms of the boxes to reinforce them. If you are assembling boxes, keep the bottom flaps flat and tape them, do not interlock them. Boxes should have either top flaps or a lid. The tops should also be sealed with tape. Use masking tape or special plastic moving tape.

Choose the right size box for what you are packing. Pack heavy items like books in small boxes. Use very large boxes only for light things like bedding and linens. Remember that some poor soul will have to lug around whatever you pack. Check that the box can hold the weight of what you've put in.

If you are packing breakable items, crumple up some paper to pad the bottom of the box and wrap each item individually. Anything really small should be packed in a small box and then placed in a larger box. If you put small things directly into a large box, you may lose them in the wrapping. Don't put heavy things on top of breakables.

If you use newspaper for wrapping, the ink can rub off. That's not a problem for some things, but a disaster for others. You can buy blank newsprint from your mover or from packing material stores.

Special Tips

CLOTHING: Movers have special wardrobe cartons you can rent. These have built-in rods, so you can just hang your clothes in them as you would in a closet. Your mover may say that you can leave clothing in dresser drawers. Keep in mind that the drawers will be taken out of the dresser.

PLANTS: Move plants in your car if you can. They may not survive a trip in the moving van if the weather is too hot or too cold or if the van is crowded. Speak to your local nursery to see if there is anything you can do to prepare your plants for the move.

LAMPS: Remove light bulbs before packing lamps. Pack table lamps in cartons. Pack the lampshades in separate cartons. Don't use newspaper to wrap lampshades. Don't forget to take down and pack any ceiling or wall lights that you're bringing with you.

COMPUTER EQUIPMENT: Before you pack your computer, be sure to back up any files on the hard drive. Move the computer yourself if you can, rather than putting it on the van. If you can't, keep the backup disks with you during the move. Check your owner's manual or with a computer store about packing your computer for a move.

CHINA: After padding the bottom of the carton, put heavier pieces in first. Stand flat pieces on their edge; do not stack them.

BOOKS, RECORDS AND CDS: Use small boxes, because these items are heavy. Pack books, records, and CDs on their edge; do not stack them.

APPLIANCES: Appliances with special connections, like air-conditioners, washers, dryers, dishwashers, and stoves, should be disconnected and prepared for moving by qualified service people. Refrigerators and freezers must be defrosted and emptied, and be completely dry before moving.

VALUABLES AND PERSONAL ITEMS: Don't send valuable or personal items such as money, jewellery, keys, or documents on the moving van. Pack them in a suitcase and take them in your car.

MOVING DAY

For the sanity of your children and your pets (not to mention your own sanity), it is best to arrange for them to spend moving day elsewhere. If it's a school day, let your children go to school. Your move may still be going on when school is over, so arrange for a friend or relative to pick them up and look after them until you can come and get them. Arrange to board your pets (with friends or at a boarding kennel) the night before your move. Pick them up the day after moving day. Don't let your pets outside except on a leash for some time after the move, or they may try to find their way back to the old home.

If you've packed and labelled everything properly, your move should go fairly smoothly, but you will still have to be around to supervise the loading of the truck. Control your desire to run away and hide when you see the van pull up outside your home.

When the movers arrive at your door, the **foreman** will go through your home to get an idea of what has to be moved and to note the condition of your belongings on an inventory list. Go with him to make sure that what he writes down is accurate. (Get a copy of this inventory once it's finished.) Give him any special instructions that you might have for any particular item.

You may want to put down mats or padding on banisters and doorways to protect the home from dirt or damage during the move.

Before the truck leaves for your new home, do a last minute check of all cupboards and closets, and basements, attic, and garage, if any, to make sure nothing has been forgotten.

You can't get into your new home or get the keys until your deal has closed. Stay in touch with your lawyer's office because it will be hard for your lawyer to find you on moving day unless you have a cell phone (and you remember to keep it with you and turned on). As soon as you have been notified that the deal has closed, you'll have to pick up the keys from wherever you arranged for them to be left.

When you arrive at your new home with the keys, you and the foreman should go through it so you can identify the rooms for him. This way he will know where your labelled boxes should go. Even though your boxes are labelled, you will have to be available to answer any questions the movers might have. So there's still no escape.

Before anything is moved in, put down mats and padding on banisters and doorways to protect your new home from dirt and damage.

As the movers are unloading the van, try to get a sense of whether all of your things have made it off the truck. Check off as much as you can on your inventory list, but don't expect to be able to check off each and every box and chair. Glance over your furniture and boxes to see if there is any obvious damage. Don't worry about doing a thorough inspection—you can do that as you unpack. If you do notice that something is damaged or missing, however, notify the foreman.

Although you are supposed to have **vacant possession** of your new home, you may find that the vendor has left behind the odd thing—like a huge freezer in the basement that stopped working in 1972. You may want to make an arrangement with the movers to take away large items like this before they leave.

When the move is finished, the foreman will give you the final bill for payment. It should be close to the estimate you were given, but it could be significantly higher if there was a delay getting to the new home or into it. If the amount of the bill is higher than the certified cheque the mover told you to have, they will accept cash, a credit card, and sometimes a personal cheque for the balance.

If you are pleased with the job the movers have done, you may tip them if you wish. Tipping is not required, but people sometimes give the foreman $15 or $20 for the crew.

AFTER YOUR MOVE

As you unpack, check to see if anything was damaged in the move. Check the foreman's inventory to make sure that the damage wasn't there before the move. If you discover damage, notify the moving company in writing. Take a photograph of the damage. If you're making a damage claim, don't throw out any documents relating to the move. You usually have a period of several months to make a damage claim, so you don't have to worry about checking everything you own instantly.

If you think you were overcharged for your move, write to the moving company immediately. Most reputable movers want their estimates to be reasonably accurate and will be concerned if that was not the case. The mover may be able to explain to your satisfaction why your move cost more than you expected or may give you a partial refund. If you are not satisfied with what the mover does, you can complain to the national moving line that the mover is associated with, the provincial body that licenses movers, or the Better Business Bureau.

If you can't get satisfaction from the moving company about damage or overcharging, you may want to consider suing. Unless there's a significant amount of money involved, a lawsuit is probably not worth your time, money, and aggravation.

LONG DISTANCE MOVES

If you are moving to another city or province, there are additional matters to plan for.

Relocation Concerns

When you get to your new location, you will have to find a new doctor and dentist and other professionals to serve you. You can ask for recommendations from your current doctor or dentist, or from your real estate agent or new employer. Get copies of your medical and dental records before you leave town if you don't want your new doctor and dentist to have to send for them.

If you have children, speak to their school about transferring their academic records to the new school. If you have pets, get a copy of their veterinary records.

Coordinating the Move

You and the moving van may not arrive at your new location at the same time. You may have to find somewhere else to stay until your belongings arrive or your home is ready. Tell the movers where you or your representative can be contacted. If the movers can't contact you, the unloading of the van may be delayed, which will increase the cost of the move. Except for delays like this, the cost of long distance moves is calculated on the basis of weight and distance, rather than on an hourly rate.

Shipping Pets

If you are sending pets by air, you have to talk to both your veterinarian and the airline. Check with the airline well ahead of time about regulations for shipping pets. Ask when is the best time to ship your pet, whether there are direct flights available, and what kind of special cage or carrier is needed. Also ask whether there are any weather conditions, such as extremely hot or cold weather, which would prevent them from accepting your pet for shipping. Find out what arrangements you have to make for pick up and delivery of your pet.

Speak to your vet about health risks of shipping your pet, the best kind of shipping cage, and whether the pet should be tranquillized.

Moving Cars

If you are shipping your car in the moving van, have it serviced beforehand to check that no oil or fluids are leaking which might damage other items on the van. Leave your gas tank no more than one-quarter full. Give the keys to the car to the van driver. If you are shipping the car during the winter, leave it in a heated garage for at least twenty-four hours before it is loaded onto the van to make sure that ice and snow have melted off and will not damage other items in the van.

TAX BREAKS

If you are moving for business reasons, you may be able to claim some of your moving expenses for tax purposes. Speak to your accountant or, if you dare, read your income tax guide. If you're moved at least 40 kilometres to be closer to a new place of work, you can deduct from your work-related income the following:

- transportation and storage costs
- your travelling expenses
- cost of selling your old home and buying a new one

If your employer is paying for your move, your moving expenses will not be deductible.

☑ Checklist for Moving

8 weeks before moving day

❑ Contact movers.
❑ Decide what can be sold, given away, or thrown out.
❑ If you're not buying boxes, start collecting them from stores.

6 weeks before moving day

❑ Make a list of people to notify that you are moving—and start notifying them.

4 weeks before moving day

❑ Contact utility companies to make arrangements to transfer service to your new home.
❑ Contact insurance companies to arrange for insurance on your new home.
❑ Start packing.

2 weeks before moving day

❑ Book elevators if you are moving out of or into a high-rise.
❑ Confirm arrangements with your mover.

The week before moving day

❑ Arrange with your real estate agent for a pre-closing inspection of your new home (if it's in your Agreement of Purchase and Sale).
❑ Make an appointment to see your lawyer and hand over a cheque.
❑ Confirm with your mortgage lender that your funds for closing are available.
❑ Arrange for service people to disconnect your major appliances.
❑ Defrost and dry out freezers.

Moving day

❑ Take a tranquillizer.

owning a home

10 | YOU'RE HOME. NOW WHAT?

Y ou're standing at the window watching the moving van pull away. Boxes are piled all around you, you're exhausted and you have every reason to be. If it's not the middle of the night, it's at least getting dark and you're probably dying for a stiff drink.

At the end of a long moving day, the job of organizing the chaos looks overwhelming. You think that you have to keep working until the kitchen is set up and a decent meal prepared for your family, the beds are made, and clothes have been hung up before they wrinkle any more. We're giving you permission not to worry about these things right now. Do the bare minimum that will let you sleep in your new home tonight. Then, either go out for dinner or order in a pizza. The boxes and the mess aren't going anywhere. They'll still be there waiting for you in the morning.

You've put a lot of energy into finding your new home and moving into it. Now you are a homeowner. Owning a home carries with it many special concerns and problems. In this chapter, we're going to discuss the matters you need to think about in the first days and weeks after you move in. In the next few chapters, we'll talk about some of the long-term concerns that homeowners have.

PRACTICAL MATTERS

The morning after moving day comes all too soon. Most of your time and energy over the next while is going to be spent unpacking and making your home liveable, and any time you have left over will be spent arguing with your spouse about where to hang pictures. Pressing as these matters are, there are other things that you have to turn what's left of your mind to.

Change the Locks

You should change your locks as soon as possible after you move into your new home. It seems a pity, having just received the keys to your new home, to render them useless. But you have no way of knowing that you've been given all the keys and, if you haven't, who might have one.

At the very least, you should have the tumblers changed in the locks so that the old keys won't work in them. If the existing locks don't seem adequate to you, this is a good time to upgrade them. See Chapter 12 on home security for more information about locks.

Get Connected

You should have contacted the water department and the gas, hydro, telephone, and cable TV companies before your moved to arrange for service in your new home. If you didn't, do it now—if you can find a telephone. If you have moved into an area serviced by different companies than you dealt with before, you may have to fill in an application form and provide credit references.

Get Useful Information

You should prepare a list of emergency phone numbers as soon as possible after you move in. In Chapter 13 on home safety, you will find a list to fill out.

You will have to pay your mortgage and your property taxes before you know it! Call your mortgagee and your municipality to find out when and where you have to make these payments. Don't wait for your lawyer to provide you with this information in the reporting letter because the payments may be due before the letter arrives.

After your move, you're going to have garbage—lots of it. Call the municipality to find out not only what your regular garbage pick-up and recycling days are, but also whether you need to make special arrangements for pick-up of large items and hazardous waste. You may have to pay a fee to have these things taken away.

Notify People of Your Change of Address

If you haven't already done so, make a list of everyone who needs your new address and notify them. Look at Chapter 9 on moving for suggestions about people to notify.

Don't forget to contact your provincial motor vehicle office to change the address on your licence and car ownership. All provinces have short time limits for doing this after you move. If you don't make the change, you may have to pay a fine. If you have to choose between notifying your mother and notifying the motor vehicle office, choose the motor vehicle office. Your mother may forgive your neglect but the motor vehicle office won't.

If you have young children, have them memorize their new address and telephone number right away. If they carry identification, change the address and phone number. Take your children for walks to familiarize them with the new neighbourhood so they won't get lost when you're not with them.

If you have pets and have moved to a new municipality, contact the animal licensing department and arrange to have your pets re-licensed. If your pets wear identification tags with your name, address, and telephone number on it (if they don't, they should!), don't forget to replace the tags with new ones. Don't let your cat or dog outside without a leash for a few weeks after the move, until they know their new home.

Collect the Interest on Your Deposit

In Chapter 5 we told you to put a clause into your offer requiring the vendor's real estate agent to pay you interest on the deposit you paid. Now it's time to find out how much money is owed to you, and to get your hands on it. Call your own real estate agent for information about when and how you will be paid. If you run into any problems collecting the interest, call your lawyer.

Have Your Home Inspected and Serviced

If you did not have a professional home inspection done before you bought the house, have the following inspected, and serviced if necessary, before you use them for the first time:

- heating
- air-conditioning
- fireplaces
- electrical system

PROBLEMS IN YOUR NEW HOME

Most people unpack their boxes and settle into their new home without too many problems. But sometimes, as you clear away the debris of your move, you'll be unpleasantly surprised. When you go to hang up your clothes, you may find the closets full of wire hangers—or worse, you may find that the beautiful closet organizers you thought were included in the purchase price are mysteriously gone. Later on, you may find that the air-conditioning doesn't work or that the roof leaks. What can you do when you find minor or major problems in your new home?

The Vendor's Responsibility to You

The bad news is that the vendor does not have very much responsibility to you for problems. Once you become the owner of a home, you also become the owner of its problems. If things break down, even if the breakdown happens right after you move in, generally you are the person who has to pay to fix them.

The Condition of the Home

The vendor has to hand over the home to you in the same condition it was in when the agreement of purchase and sale was signed, except for normal wear and tear. That doesn't mean, though, that you should be stuck with a problem that existed at that time if the vendor deliberately concealed it from you.

When you see the home for the first time without the vendor's furniture and pictures on the wall, you will probably see chipped paint, cracks, and little holes that you didn't notice before. If they were there when you signed the agreement, even though you did not notice them, you'll have to fix them and you won't be able to get any money from the vendor. The vendor may be legally responsible, however, for paying to fix major damage that he or she purposely concealed from you—for example, a gaping hole in the wall that the vendor covered with a poster.

What if you find something even more serious, like a broken pipe in a bathroom? If the pipe broke after you signed the agreement of purchase and sale, the vendor should have fixed it and in theory is responsible for fixing it now. If the pipe was already broken when you viewed the home, repairing it is your responsibility if the pipe was obviously broken and you should have been able to see it. The situation is different if the vendor hid the fact that the pipe was broken, for example, by turning off the water supply to that pipe and wallpapering over damage caused by the leak. Again, the vendor may be legally responsible for the cost of the repairs.

These possible problems show why it is so important to make a professional home inspection a condition of your agreement of purchase and sale. A good home inspector should find most of the serious problems, even if the vendor has tried to hide them. If the problem happened after the agreement was signed, the home inspection report will help to prove that and to pin responsibility on the vendor.

Fixtures and Chattels

We introduced you to chattels and fixtures in Chapter 5. The vendor has to leave behind all chattels that were included in the agreement of purchase and sale. If the vendor agreed to sell you the washer and dryer, they have to be there when you arrive. The vendor also has to leave behind any fixtures that the agreement of purchase and sale did not say could be removed. For example, unless the agreement of purchase and sale said so, the vendor cannot pull up the wall-to-wall carpets, leaving just the tacks behind.

The vendor only had to leave the chattels specifically promised to you in the agreement of purchase and sale, so it's not difficult to figure out whether the vendor fulfilled his or her agreement. The vendor also had to remove any chattels that weren't included in the agreement of purchase and sale and is still required to remove them if they were left in the home.

The question is more complicated when it comes to fixtures. That's because you and the vendor can have an honest difference of opinion about what was a fixture and what was not. You may think that anything that was bolted to the walls was a fixture and was to be left behind. The vendor, on the other hand, may never have intended to leave the item behind and knew that it could be easily unbolted without causing any damage to the wall or the item. This is why we told you in Chapter 5 that the agreement of purchase and sale should specifically mention any items you want left behind.

Any chattels or fixtures that were sold with the home should be in the same condition they were in at the time the agreement of purchase and sale was signed, except for normal wear and tear.

What Do You Do If There Are Problems?

We've told you what the vendor is legally responsible for, but there's a world of difference between legal responsibility and money in your hand. When you see the broken pipe in the bathroom, your first instinct may be to sue. But suing is expensive and aggravating, and the results are not guaranteed. Look upon suing as your last option, not your first.

To begin with, make a list of all your problems. Don't deal with just one problem at a time. After you have listed all the problems, collect evidence about each one:

- Get out any inspection reports.
- Speak to your real estate agent to find out what problems were disclosed by the vendor at the time of listing.
- Take pictures.
- Get estimates for repairs.

Get a sense of how much money all of the problems together are worth.

Contact the lawyer who acted for you on the purchase. Ask your lawyer whether the vendor is legally responsible for all, or any, of the problems. If your lawyer says yes, ask him or her to write a letter to the vendor's lawyer requesting payment. You may have to pay your lawyer to write this letter, although some lawyers consider a letter like this to be part of the home purchase. As a result of this letter, the vendor may agree to pay you some money, but if so, it probably won't be nearly as much as you think you're entitled to.

If the vendor won't pay you enough or won't pay you anything at all, your choices are either to sue or to forget the matter. What you decide will depend on the amount of money involved and your stomach for the stress and expense of a lawsuit. You can avoid some of the stress by having a lawyer handle your case, but you will have to pay legal fees. You've just had a taste of legal fees when you bought the home. Litigation is a lot more expensive. If the amount of money involved is only a few thousand dollars or less, you may be able to sue on your own in **small claims court** (call the small claims court office to find out what the monetary limit is in your province). You won't have any legal fees, but you have to put a lot of time and energy into preparing your case, and you'll have to present your case in court. When your case comes to trial, you may find that the vendor has hired a lawyer who's going to mop the floor with you. Here we'd like to share with you an old lawyers' saying that anyone who acts for himself has a fool for a client—and his lawyer's not too bright either.

This is our best advice to you: Avoid lawsuits whenever you can. Do this by being careful before you buy a home:

- If the vendor signed a disclosure statement, read it carefully.
- Examine the home like a hawk when you view it, and lots of questions if you suspect problems of any kind.
- Have the home professionally inspected for existing and potential problems.
- List in your offer the chattels and fixtures you want to buy with the home.
- Include a clause in your offer that all chattels not listed in the offer are to be removed by the vendor (legally this is unnecessary but it may remind the vendor to move the freezer out of the basement).

Special Rights for Buyers of Newly Constructed Homes

If you bought your home from a builder who is registered under the provincial new home warranty program, your home will be covered for certain problems that arise within a specified period of time after you buy. (A home that was registered when it was built may still be covered under the warranty, even if you bought it as a resale.) The length of the warranty period, which depends on the province and the nature of the problem, can be from one to five years (one to seven years in Ontario).

If your new home is covered by a warranty, you probably had to make a detailed inspection of the home before closing to make a note of any problems that you saw then. The builder is supposed to fix them within a short time after closing. After closing, you continue to be covered for things like major structural defects, defects in work and materials, water seepage through the foundation, defects in the electrical, plumbing, and heating systems, and violations of the provincial building code.

If you find a problem during the warranty period, you must notify the builder and also the home warranty program in writing. As a general rule, the warranty program won't pay to fix a problem unless the builder can't or won't fix it and the warranty administrators agree that the problem is covered under the warranty. All of the warranty programs have methods in place for resolving disputes between a homeowner and a builder without a lawsuit. But it's not unheard-of for homeowners to have to sue the warranty program to get a payment.

Have a look at your warranty documents. If you have any questions about what's covered or how to make a claim, contact the provincial warranty program or your lawyer.

11 REPAIRS AND RENOVATIONS

Some people buy a home knowing it will need a lot of work because they welcome the challenge of a handyman's special. Other people buy a home because it's in move-in condition and perfect for them—they don't want to do any work at all.

If you buy a home that you plan to fix up, you know before you move in that you are going to need to deal with general contractors, plumbers, and painters. But even if you buy a home you're not planning to lay a paint brush on, at some time something is going to break or something is going to need to be changed. So you can be sure that there are repairs (and maybe even renovations) somewhere in your future.

Whether you are building an addition or just painting your spare bedroom, whether you are putting on a new roof or simply having your drain unplugged, there are things you need to know about the legal and practical sides of hiring workers and having them in your home. If you go about repairing or renovating the wrong way, it will seem like a nightmare. If you do it the right way, it should seem no worse than a bad dream.

WHY ARE YOU DOING THIS TO YOURSELF?

You repair things because they are broken. Some things must be repaired if you want to continue to live in your home. Other things, if left unrepaired, won't drive you out of your home, but they will drive down your home's value.

Renovation and decorating are different from repairs because they are more voluntary. People renovate for various reasons. You may want more space—a bigger kitchen, another bathroom, or a family room addition. You may want to change the look of your home by taking out the wall between your living-room and dining-room or by putting in French doors to your patio. You may wish to make your home more energy efficient by installing a new furnace or putting in new windows. You may want to upgrade your home's infrastructure by replacing the plumbing or wiring.

Renovations always cost more, take longer, and are more of a disruption than you think, so there are a number of things to consider before you undertake a voluntary project. If you are renovating or redecorating, ask yourself the following questions:

- How can you pay for what you want to do?
- Is there a cheaper alternative to the work you think you want to do?
- Are there any obstacles that prevent you from doing what you want to do?
- Will the work you want to do increase the value of your home?
- Do you want to live through the mess and chaos?

How Can You Pay?

If you are moving into your new home with the intention of repairing or renovating or redecorating, you probably took the cost of your planned work into account when budgeting for your purchase and so already have the money set aside.

If you have been living in your home for a while, it may be that the carpets have worn and the paint has chipped, or your family has grown and you need a bigger kitchen or an extra bedroom. Some people set money aside each year so that they have a fund to draw on when they need to or want to spend money on their home. If you have money saved, you already know how much you have. Other people need to borrow the money.

If you need to borrow, you have to figure out how much you can afford to borrow. You can do this by reviewing your budget to see how large a monthly loan payment you can afford. Once you know this figure, you can calculate how much money you can afford to borrow. The calculations are pretty much the same as those set out in Chapter 2, which we made you do before we let you buy a home at all.

After you know how much you can afford to borrow, the next question is: Where can you get it? There are several different ways to borrow money for home renovations or major repairs:

- You can take out an additional mortgage on your home.
- You can increase the amount of your existing mortgage.
- You can take out a **personal loan** (the interest rate and monthly payments are usually higher than for a mortgage).
- You can get a **line of credit**—it gives you a maximum amount you can borrow, but you borrow only as much money as you need, when you need it (the line of credit can be in the form of a personal loan, or it can be secured by a mortgage on your home).
- You can use a credit card for small jobs (the interest rate will be very high, even compared to a personal loan).

Speak to your bank or mortgagee about financing the work you want done. As with your original mortgage, remember to shop around.

Is There Some Other (Cheaper) Way?

There may be a less costly way to achieve what you're trying to do.

Finding Extra Space

If you need more space, it may not be necessary to build an addition. You may be able to finish your basement to provide a family room, study, home office or extra bedroom.

A lot of new furniture on the market is designed specifically to make a home seem larger. Bunk bed systems allow children to share bedrooms and still have room to play and study. Hideaway beds and hideaway desks let one room do double duty as a bedroom or dining-room and an office. Closet units or closet organizers can help you find extra storage space.

Achieving Energy Efficiency

Before you undertake a major project to make your home more energy efficient, such as installing a new furnace or windows, think about simpler and cheaper ways to reduce your heating costs:

- Have your furnace inspected and serviced to make sure it's working efficiently.
- Turn down your thermostat at night and when you're away from home (you can get a timer for your thermostat to turn the heat up and down automatically).

- If there are drafts coming from windows or doors, weather-strip them and caulk gaps in the frames.
- Hang heavier drapes on windows.

Cooling Your Home

The installation of central air-conditioning in some houses is very expensive and difficult. As an alternative, consider installing a roof vent and ceiling fans, and supplement with individual room air-conditioners.

Improving Your Looks

If you're planning a renovation to make your home look better, you may be able to get a similar effect by simply redecorating. Instead of redoing your whole kitchen, consider painting the walls and cabinets and putting on new knobs and drawer handles. If your bathroom looks out of date, consider painting or wallpapering, re-enamelling the tub and sink, and buying a new shower curtain and towels. If your living room is dark, instead of installing new windows or a skylight, consider brightening up your colour scheme, getting rid of the heavy draperies we just told you to buy to keep out the breezes, and getting more lamps (especially lamps with halogen bulbs).

Are There Any Obstacles?

If your home is mortgaged, you must speak to your mortgagee before you start a renovation or a major repair that involves demolition of part of your home. Your mortgage may have a clause that allows the mortgagee to demand payment in full if you demolish any of your home.

If you live in a condominium, you may have to get the permission of the condominium corporation before you renovate. Check the condominium's by-laws.

Government regulations may be an obstacle to doing your repair or renovation exactly the way you want to do it. Provincial building codes set construction standards governing structural, electrical, plumbing, heating, and fire safety requirements.

Municipal zoning by-laws restrict the size, shape, and possibly the appearance of house renovations. If the work you are planning is not allowed under the current zoning, you can apply for a special exemption from the zoning (sometimes referred to as a **variance**). Your neighbours will be given notice of your application and will be given an opportunity to object. These applications can be very expensive and take a long time.

Will You Increase the Value of Your Home?

If your home needs repairs and you don't do them, you'll decrease the value of your home.

If you're renovating, it's not likely that you're doing it just to increase your home's value to a future purchaser. You're doing it for yourself. However, you should know that while some renovations increase the value of your home, others have no effect on its value; and still others actually decrease the value of your home. While knowing which renovations fall into which category may not affect your decision whether or not to renovate, it may affect how much you decide to spend.

The best return on your renovation dollar will come from a new kitchen or bathroom. Finishing a basement, building a wood deck, or putting in new windows will add something to the value of your home but probably not as much. A swimming pool will add nothing to the value of your home and may in fact make it harder to sell. For more information about renovations that make your home worth more on the market, speak to a real estate agent.

Any renovation that you do, no matter how little you spend, should look professional or it will lower the value of your home to a future purchaser. But while it's important to renovate to a reasonable quality, use luxury materials only if it's important to you personally. Most purchasers will not pay extra for them. Whatever kind of renovation you do, you also won't get your money back if you have over-improved for the home itself or for the neighbourhood (or building, if you live in an apartment-style condo).

Whether you have money already set aside or whether you're borrowing, there may be an additional long-term cost of renovating for you to consider. If you increase the value of your property (which is probably your sincerest wish), your property taxes may go up.

Can You Live Through It?

All renovations and major repairs are a pain to live through, but some are worse than others. It's not just a matter of noise, inconvenience, and dirt; sometimes it's a matter of your family's health.

Throughout the process, you will have to put up with workers traipsing through your home, usually starting at an ungodly hour. You must be around on a regular basis to supervise the work and to be available to make decisions and give instructions. Unless you pack fragile items away, they may be broken. Your furniture and clothes may get dust-covered unless you protect them.

Even if the ordinary level of inconvenience doesn't drive you screaming from your home, there may be particular times during a renovation or major repair that you will want to consider moving out. If you are adding on a second storey, you may have to live without a roof for a while. (Try not to make it during January, February, or March! The contractor can keep rain and snow out, but it's a lot harder to keep the heat in.) If you're putting in a new kitchen, there will be a time when you can't cook because your old kitchen will be gone and your new one won't be installed yet. During these times you have a choice between moving out and toughing it out.

Any renovation or repair that involves tearing down walls or cutting through cement floors will create a tremendous amount of dust. If your home is insulated with asbestos or has lead paint on the walls, the dust can be very dangerous. When floors are being refinished, there may be toxic fumes. For some people, the fumes from paint or carpet glue can be dangerous. As a matter of health and safety, you may have no choice but to move out for a while.

It's important to go into a renovation with your eyes open so that you can either make arrangements to go somewhere else (even if only for part of the time) or be braced for the ordeal if you decide to stay and live through it.

PRELIMINARY PLANNING FOR A RENOVATION OR MAJOR REPAIR

If you've decided to renovate or repair, you've got some idea of what you want to do, for example, put in a new furnace or build a family room addition or update your master bathroom. But, before you do anything at all, proper planning is essential.

Your first and most important step is to decide the maximum amount that you want to spend. There's no point in telling an architect or contractor what you want unless you also say exactly how much you have to spend on it. The plans they prepare will be useless to you if you have only half the money necessary to carry them out.

Next, you have to think about time, both when and how long. Do you have an absolute deadline by which the renovation or repair has to be done—like your baby's delivery date if you are making a nursery? Do you have a particular time of year when you want the work to be done—during your vacation when you are there to supervise the workers, or during the warmer months if you are having your roof removed? Do you have a maximum length of time that you want the work to take?

Then, decide whether or not you are willing to move out of your home for any part of the work. If you can't or won't, that may limit the kinds of work you can have done to your home. Some jobs are just too disruptive or dangerous for you to stay in the home.

Finally, consider whether you're going to do the work yourself or hire professionals. You can have someone do the whole job for you, from design to completion. You may already have a design that you want someone else to build. You may want someone to do the work for you while you supervise. You may want to do some or all of the work yourself.

Before you can decide who will do the work, or before you do any more planning or preparation, you have to know what work has to be done.

WHAT'S INVOLVED IN A RENOVATION OR MAJOR REPAIR?

There's more to a project than the construction work—it's just one of several stages. Someone must

- develop a design for the project, taking into account zoning and building code requirements
- find out whether a building permit or other permit or approval is required for the planned work, and if so, apply for the permit or approval
- arrange for any necessary municipal inspections
- hire contractors and workers, and select and buy materials
- pay the contractors and workers
- supervise the work

Designing the Project

However small your home improvement project, you will need some kind of design. Even if you are only having your house painted, you need to know what rooms you are painting, what colours, and how many coats of paint. If you are having a new roof put on, you need to know what quality of roofing you want and the colour.

Designing a Renovation

If you are doing a complicated renovation like a new bathroom, new kitchen, or an addition, designing your project will include the preparation of detailed drawings, including a floor plan, side elevations, and structural drawings.

The design stage starts with your ideal of what you want your renovation to look like and what you want it to do. Your ideal may come from pictures you've seen in a magazine or from other homes you've seen.

Next, you might develop preliminary sketches. Although they are more concerned with the look of your renovation than with technical specifications, the purpose of these sketches is to modify your ideal to take into account your budget, as well as building code requirements and zoning requirements.

Once you've settled on a design, the next stage is to prepare **working drawings** and **specifications**, which are used to get building permits and estimates for material and labour costs. If you hire someone to do the work for you, these drawings will be incorporated into the contract to define the work being done. The drawings will be used throughout the construction as a detailed guide for every step of the work.

Building Permits

Unless you're doing a small job like reshingling your roof or repainting, you may well need a **building permit**. A building permit is your municipality's formal permission for you to carry out your renovation. Any change to your plumbing, heating, air-conditioning, ventilation, or electrical wiring systems, or to the structure of the home will probably require either a municipal permit or municipal approval. You may even need a permit to build a deck or to remove a garage.

Contact your municipal building department to find out whether or not you need a permit for the particular work you are planning to do. If a permit is required, the municipality will tell you how to apply. You will have to submit technical plans and pay a fee—which can be several hundred dollars or more for a large project.

The building department will review your plans to make sure that they comply with municipal zoning requirements, the provincial building code, and any other relevant provincial or municipal regulations. If your plans are approved, you will get your permit. For some projects you can get approval in one day, but for others the approval process can take several months.

Getting a building permit sounds like a lot of trouble, doesn't it? But it doesn't compare to the trouble you'll get into if you do work that requires a building permit without getting one. It is illegal to start construction before getting a permit. You can be charged with an offence, you can be ordered to stop work, or you can even be ordered to tear down work you have already done.

You may think the municipality will never find out that you have done work without a permit. But after several weeks of being woken up by your contractors or looking at your dumpster, a neighbour may phone the building department to complain—at which point you'll be found out. Even if you safely make it to the end of your project, you may be found out when you try to sell your home and the purchaser checks to see whether or not your home complies with all municipal requirements.

Building Inspections

When you do a renovation or repair under a building permit, various municipal building inspectors will check your work at key stages of the construction to make sure that it is being carried out in accordance with the plans you submitted and the requirements of the provincial building code. It is your responsibility to know when the various inspections are required and to contact the building department to arrange for inspections at the right time.

A building inspector will probably need some notice to come out and inspect. If you don't schedule the inspection at the right time, you may have to stop the work until the inspector comes because the inspector must be able to see the area to be inspected. For example, if you put up drywall before wiring has been inspected, the building department can make you rip out the walls so that it can be inspected. In addition to scheduled inspections, a building inspector can visit the site at any time.

Workers and Materials

Unless you are doing all of the actual construction work yourself, you will have to hire people to do all or some of it for you. Even if you want to do it all yourself, you may not be able to. In some provinces, certain kinds of work, usually electrical, plumbing, and heating, must be done by licensed tradespeople. Even if you are allowed to do the work yourself, your work must meet all municipal and provincial requirements and pass building inspections.

There are building supply stores where you can get materials for your renovation or repair. However, there may be some materials that are only available to professional contractors or that are available to them at a better price.

Paying the Workers

If you do all the work yourself, there is no one to pay. If you hire someone who personally does the work for you, you pay that person directly. If you hire a contractor who has other people do the work, you pay the contractor...but things are in fact a bit more complicated than that.

Construction, Mechanics', or Builders' Liens

Every province has laws to make sure that people who work for contractors will get paid even if the contractor doesn't pay them.

For example, you may hire a contractor to put in a new bathroom for you, for $5,000. The contractor hires someone to tile the bathroom for

$1,000 and someone else to put in the plumbing for $2,000. (These people are sometimes called **sub-contractors**.) When the work is done, you pay the contractor his $5,000. What if, instead of paying the sub-contractors, the contractor pockets the whole $5,000? The tiler and the plumber can sue the contractor for what they are owed. You may think that's exactly what they should do and leave you out of it.

Unfortunately for you (although fortunately for the tiler and the plumber), the law provides otherwise. Provincial statutes give the sub-contractors the right not only to sue the contractor but also to make a claim directly against you and to enforce that claim by registering a **construction lien** (known in some provinces as a **mechanics' lien** or a **builders' lien**) against your home. This right exists even though you paid everything you owed under your contract with the contractor. Not only the tiler and the plumber are protected. Workers for the contractor or for sub-contractors and people who supply materials also have the same right to register a lien against your home.

Limitations on Your Liability to Sub-Contractors

Now you've heard the bad news about your relationship with contractors and sub-contractors. There really is no good news, although there is a limit to the bad news. In all provinces other than Quebec, the law limits the amount you have to pay the sub-contractors (when you have already paid the contractor). In Quebec, you as the homeowner would owe the sub-contractors the full amount that the contractor was supposed to pay them. However, in the other provinces, you only owe a percentage of what the sub-contractors were supposed to be paid:

- In Manitoba, you would owe the sub-contractors 7.5 per cent of the full amount of your contract with the contractor.

- In Newfoundland, Nova Scotia, Ontario, Saskatchewan, and British Columbia, you would owe the sub-contractors 10 per cent of the full amount of your contract with the contractor.

- In Alberta, you would owe the sub-contractors 15 per cent of the full amount of your contract with the contractor.

- In Prince Edward Island and New Brunswick, you would owe the sub-contractors 15 per cent of the full amount of your contract with the contractor for a contract of $15,000 or less and 20 per cent for contracts over $15,000.

No matter how many sub-contractors (and workers and suppliers) there are and how much they are owed by the contractor, the total amount you owe to all of them is limited to the percentages set out above.

Holdbacks

There is a way to avoid being put in the position of having to pay twice. Instead of paying the contractor the full amount you owe at any given time, you can—and you should—hold back some of the money you owe the contractor. The amount of the **holdback** is the percentage mentioned above for your province. Every time you make a payment to the contractor, whether you pay once at the end of the contract or in instalments, you should hold back that percentage.

Back to our tiler and plumber. Let's assume that you live in British Columbia where the holdback is 10 per cent. If you are required to pay the contractor two instalments of $2,500 each, you would hold back 10 per cent or $250 from each instalment.

Substantial Completion

You're probably asking yourself what you are supposed to do with the holdback. That's an excellent question. First of all, you hold it back. Remember we told you that sub-contractors can register a lien against your home. In each province, the sub-contractors are given only a limited period of time after **substantial performance** or **substantial completion** of the contract to register a lien:

- In Newfoundland and Quebec, the time period is 30 days.
- In British Columbia, Manitoba, and Saskatchewan, the time period is 40 days.
- In Alberta, Nova Scotia, and Ontario, the time period is 45 days.
- In New Brunswick and Prince Edward Island, the time period is 60 days.

You hold your money back for that period of time after substantial completion or performance of the contract. If your contract is payable in several instalments, you continue to hang on to all of the holdbacks until the end of the contract plus the lien registration period. If no liens are registered in the allowed period, at the end of the period you pay the holdback to the contractor.

If a Lien is Registered

It is very important to get legal advice if a lien has been registered against your home. If you don't do the right thing, you could end up paying twice for the same work.

When a lien has been registered, you must not release the holdback to the contractor. In some provinces, you will know if a lien has been registered because you must be given notice; in other provinces you wouldn't know unless you searched the title to your home in the provincial land registry office. In many provinces, if you receive notice of a lien, not only must you not release the holdback, you must not pay any additional money to the contractor either until the matter has been settled. If you receive notice of a lien, call your lawyer.

Is it safe for you to release the holdback if the work has been completed, the lien registration period has passed, and you haven't received any notice of a lien? In some provinces you are safe if you haven't received notice of a lien, but in others you have to go to the land registry office to see if a lien has been registered on the title to your home before you release the holdback. Speak to your lawyer before you release the holdback, to find out whether a visit to the registry office is necessary.

Supervising the Work

A project requires supervision so that the work moves at a reasonable pace and is completed to your satisfaction. Someone must make sure that the quality of the work is satisfactory—that the work is being completed in a **good and workmanlike manner** (the legal lingo). In addition, the work site should be relatively neat both for your sanity and for the safety of your family and the workers. Someone must decide in what order the work will be done. You may think that the sequence of the work is fixed, and it probably is if you're working in only one part of the house. But what if you're putting in a bathroom in the basement and also painting your kitchen? It makes sense to drill through the basement floor and stir up all the dust before you paint, rather than have the dust descend on the still-wet paint in the kitchen.

If more than one trade is involved, you have to worry about when the various tradespeople come and the order they come in. You want the electrician to do the wiring before the drywaller puts up the wall. You want the carpet laid after the painting and not before. If the electrician doesn't come on time, the whole project can come to a stop. You also have to make sure that municipal building inspections are properly scheduled.

In some renovation or repair contracts, instalments are paid when certain stages of the work have been completed. Someone has to make sure that the stages have been satisfactorily completed before the instalments are paid.

WHO WILL DO THE WORK?

Your choice is to do all the work yourself, some of the work yourself, or none of the work yourself.

Do-It-Yourself

There are several factors to consider before you decide to do the job yourself.

- Do you have the time to do the work yourself?
- Do you have the ability to do the work yourself?
- Will it be cheaper to do it yourself than to hire skilled help?
- Will you enjoy doing the work yourself?

Doing some of the work yourself may save you money and give you personal enjoyment, if you have the time and ability. (Remember that in some provinces ability is not enough—you have to be licensed to do certain work.) You may have vacation time that you can devote to your home improvement project, and you may have experience in home repairs and renovation. Even if you don't have experience, there are how-to books and magazine articles that give you step-by-step instructions on home projects. Keep in mind, however, that do-it-yourself projects are often more difficult than they look in the magazines and may take longer than you think.

What you're saving by doing any of the work yourself is the cost of labour. You have to decide for yourself how much your leisure time is worth. In any event, you may pay in the cost of materials and tools what you save in labour costs. Contractors can usually buy materials for less than you can. Also, you may not have the tools you need to do the job and will either have to buy or rent them.

Ask yourself whether doing it yourself will be a positive experience for you. Do you enjoy working with your hands, or does the thought of smashing nails with a hammer frighten you? Do you love the smell of freshly sawn wood, or does sawdust make you sneeze? Living through any renovation or repair is stressful. Doing it yourself usually means that the project (and the stress) lasts longer—and worse, you have nobody but yourself to blame for delays and mistakes.

Do Some of It Yourself

Of course, doing it yourself is not an all or nothing proposition. You can choose to do part of the work and hire professionals or tradespeople to do the rest.

The idea of physical labour may not appeal to you, but you may want to prepare the design for your project. There are even computer software programs to help you. But unless you are familiar with municipal by-laws and building code requirements, your design should be reviewed by an experienced contractor or architect. You need plans that will pass the building department's review process before you will be issued a building permit.

You may not want to do the physical labour yourself, but you may want to supervise the work, by acting as your own general contractor. You get your own materials and hire and organize the different sub-contractors and tradespeople to carry out the work. Acting as your own general contractor can take a lot of time. If you don't know what you're doing, there may be delays and the workmanship may be shoddy.

You may want to do some of the physical labour yourself. It's simpler to do finishing work, like painting or wallpapering, than to do skilled work like plumbing. (Again, remember that you may need a licence to do some kinds of work yourself.)

The other extreme from doing it yourself is to have all the work done for you. For example, if you're putting on an addition, you can have an architect do the design work for you and hire a contractor to do the building, or you can have a design-and-build company do it all for you.

Hire an Architect

You may want an **architect** to design your project. You choose to hire a particular architect because his or her work appeals to you. Many design-and-build firms use architects to design their projects, so you may not need to deal with an architect alone to get an architect's design.

There is another reason to use an architect's services. In addition to designing a project, an architect can help you choose a general contractor. An architect can also stay on to supervise the project, checking to see that the work is being properly completed, and advising you when the contractor is entitled to receive instalment payments. Unlike an architect who works with a design-and-build company, this architect is independent from the people who actually do the construction and can give you an objective opinion about the quality of the work.

Licensed architects are required by law to have professional liability insurance. So if you have to sue the architect because of damage to your home caused by mistakes in the design or in the supervision of your project, you know that there will be insurance money to pay your claim if you are successful.

Even when you use an architect to supervise the project, you still have to keep an eye on what's happening. You shouldn't hand over all responsibility to the architect, because you're the one who's paying the bills and you're the one who has to live with the renovation after it's done.

Hire a Contractor

If you're fixing your roof, you hire a roofing contractor. If you're painting your living-room, you hire a painting contractor. Pretty simple. But your renovation may involve several different kinds of work. If you're putting on an addition, you need someone to dig and pour the foundation, someone to frame the walls, someone to do the brickwork, someone to put on the roof, someone to do the plumbing, someone to put in the wiring, someone to drywall, and someone to paint. If you have all of this work to do, you hire a **general contractor**.

A general contractor is responsible to you for getting all the work involved in your project done, either personally, through employees, or by using sub-contractors. Sub-contractors are hired by the general contractor to do specific work that the contractor or the contractor's employees can't do. The general contractor is also responsible for supervising and coordinating all the different workers.

Contractors are not always required by law to carry insurance. If they have insurance it will probably only cover injuries to people or damage to property caused by their negligence while they are working in your home. They probably won't have insurance against defects in design and workmanship that show up after the job is finished. If a contractor does not have insurance, you may find it difficult, if not impossible, to get any compensation. Many contractors carry on business as corporations, and corporations often—deliberately—have little money or property to pay your claim.

You can act as your own general contractor, hiring and supervising the different tradespeople yourself. If you have problems, there's no one person you can complain to. You have to deal with each of the trades individually.

Use a Design-and-Build Company

A **design-and-build company** will design your project, prepare the plans and drawings, get the necessary permits, order materials and hire and supervise the people who do the work. A flat fee covers all services and materials from design to completion.

There are companies that specialize in one kind of project like kitchens, bathrooms or sunrooms and others that do general construction. In some companies the designs come from stock plans, and in others an architect or designer will prepare a custom design.

If the design was prepared by an architect, the architect's professional insurance may cover any damage to your home caused by design flaws. If no architect is involved, there is probably no insurance coverage for design flaws. The construction work itself may or may not be covered by insurance. As with a contractor, any insurance a design-and-build company has probably only covers injuries to people or damage to property caused by their negligence while they are working in your home.

HOW DO YOU FIND THE HELP YOU NEED?

If you have decided not to do the entire project yourself, you will have to hire others to do the work. Leaving aside the question of psychiatric help, which you won't need until your project is well underway, here are the things to consider when you're hiring a contractor, an architect or a design-and-build firm.

Contractors

You want a contractor who does high quality work for a reasonable price and who is honest and reliable.

Get Some Names

Get the names of several contractors from:

- family, friends and neighbours who have had similar work done recently
- your architect if you are using one
- your real estate agent
- local building supply and hardware stores
- your local home builders' association

Check Them Out

You should check out two or three contractors before hiring one of them. Get on the phone to the contractors and others and ask some questions. You want a contractor who

- has been in business in your area for a number of years
- is properly licensed to do the work—get the contractor's licence number and confirm with the local licensing office
- has third party liability and property damage insurance—get the name of the contractor's insurance company and call to confirm that the insurance is in force

- can give you references from satisfied clients in your area—ask for names and telephone numbers and call the references (make sure they're not relatives of the contractor!)
- has not been the subject of complaints—check with the local Better Business Bureau and the local homebuilders' association
- is available to do the work when you want it done—has reliable access to skilled workers and tradespeople and doesn't have too many jobs on the go
- will come back after the job is done to honour any warranties given

The Contractor You Don't Want

Avoid contractors who

- call you or come to your door offering to do work at a special price
- quote a price for the work without even looking at your home
- don't have an address, only a phone number
- tell you that you don't need a written contract for the work

Interview the Contractors

Once you have the names of several contractors who sound promising, arrange to meet with them individually at your home. Ask them about any of the matters in the list above that you don't already have an answer to. Also ask if they have pictures of finished jobs.

This is a good time for you to find out who will actually be doing the work. Is it the person you're talking to or somebody else? You don't have to meet every last person who will be working at your home, but you do want to meet the person who is going to be supervising your particular job, and perhaps anybody else who will be coming to your home on a daily basis. You don't want your home invaded by people who give you the creeps.

Check References

The most important thing you can do is to speak to people who have had similar jobs done by the contractor. Ask if you can look at the contractor's work (even if you've already seen photographs). Whether you can or can't see it, ask lots of questions, such as:

- Was the work started and completed on time?
- Did the work come in on budget?
- Were there any disagreements between them and the contractor on price, workmanship or materials?

- Were they satisfied with the quality of the workmanship?
- Has the work held up over time?
- Did the contractor work neatly and clean up when the job was finished?
- Did the contractor try to make the project as easy to live through as possible?
- Were they comfortable having the contractor and the contractor's workers in their home?
- Did the contractor come back when the job was finished to fix problems?

Get Estimates

Arrange to get estimates from the two or three contractors you have chosen. If you've had plans prepared by an architect, the contractors will base their estimate on the specifications in the plans. Otherwise, write down a detailed description of the work you want done so that the contractors know what they're giving an estimate on, and so that they are all giving an estimate for exactly the same work. Whether you provide the contractors with plans or a written description of the work to be done, each one should inspect your home before giving you an estimate.

If you haven't had plans and specifications prepared for you, you may not know in detail the exact nature of the work you will have done until you have talked to one or more contractors. The contractors may have different ideas about how to approach the job. Before you compare prices among the different contractors, you may have to talk to each one several times to help you decide on the approach you want to take. To be able to compare their estimates properly, make sure that they are all quoting a price on exactly the same work.

In addition to the price, you want the estimate to set out a description of the work to be done and the materials to be used. (If the estimate is based on an architect's plans, both the work to be done and the materials to be used are specified in the plans, and the estimate can just refer to those plans.)

If there is a significant difference in the prices you are quoted, ask the various contractors to explain. Price is a very important consideration when you are choosing a contractor, but the lowest price isn't necessarily the best deal. If one contractor's estimate is much lower than the others for exactly the same work, it may mean that the contractor has underestimated the job. The contractor may have miscalculated the scope or cost of the work or may have allowed himself a very narrow profit margin. If a contractor realizes in the middle of the job that he is not going to make any money (or may even lose money) he may be tempted to walk off the job.

In any event, price shouldn't be your only consideration. Also take into account what you have found out about each contractor's reliability and the quality of workmanship.

Architects

You base your choice of an architect on different considerations than you do your choice of a contractor. You want your architect to be honest and reliable and to charge reasonable fees, but your main reason for choosing a particular architect is that you like that architect's work.

An architect's main reference is the work you have seen. If you see a home or a building you admire, find out who the architect was. You can ask people you know for names of architects, and addresses or pictures of projects they have done. If you don't like what you see of the architect's work, there's no point going any further.

If you are interested in a particular architect, check with your provincial association of architects to make sure he or she is properly registered. Also check with people who have had the architect do work for them to see if they were happy.

Architects charge for their work on an hourly basis or a flat fee basis. If you are using the architect to supervise your project as well as design it, the architect may instead charge a fee equal to a percentage of the total contract price.

Design-and-Build Firms

In choosing a design-and-build firm you must take into account everything you would if you were choosing a contractor. In addition, you've got to like the designs the firm produces. It may be difficult to compare estimates from different design-and-build firms if their estimates are based on different designs and materials.

THE REPAIR OR RENOVATION CONTRACT

A renovation or repair contract is your agreement with the renovator or repairer about what work will be done and how much you will pay for it.

The Importance of a Written Contract

You should always have a written contract for any repair or renovation project. It doesn't matter whether you use, a contractor architect or design-and-build firm, it doesn't matter how highly recommended the person is, it doesn't even matter whether you're paying in cash—*put it in writing*. Both you and the contractor or architect or firm should get a signed copy of the agreement.

A contract is simply an agreement between two parties. In a repair or renovation contract, the basic agreement is that the contractor or renovator will do the work and that you will pay. But that's just the basic agreement. In order for your contract to be useful, it has to have a lot more detail than that. And whenever you get into details, there's room for confusion and misunderstanding. Putting the agreement into writing forces everyone to define the details, and that's when you find out whether everyone really *is* in agreement. When you leave out the details, you may think everyone shares the same idea but in fact each person has a different idea of what the agreement is.

When you have a detailed written contract, you have a written record of what everyone agreed to if there's a dispute later about what work is to be done and how much it costs. You don't have to rely on your own memory or someone else's—which is good since people tend to remember what's in their interest and to forget what's not. If you end up suing your contractor, the written contract is there for the court to look at too.

No reputable architect, contractor or design-and-build firm will be offended if you ask for a written contract. In fact, they will want the contract in writing as well.

Cash Deals

Your contractor may offer to do the work for a lower price if you pay in cash. Or you may ask the contractor if you'll get a better price if you pay cash. The obvious reason for paying cash is to let the contractor avoid paying taxes. You hope he or she will pass on some of the savings to you. Legally it is the responsibility of the contractor to collect and pay to the government any provincial sales tax and GST or HST on the work. It is illegal for the contractor to avoid paying taxes, and it is also illegal for you to conspire with the contractor to allow him or her to avoid paying taxes.

If you do pay cash, it doesn't mean you can't have a written contract. There's no connection between a written contract and the contractor's intention (or lack of intention) to pay taxes. The contract doesn't get sent straight to the GST office to be compared with the contractor's GST returns. However, the contractor may say to you, "Cash deal, no written contract." If you agree to a repair or renovation without a written contract, you are giving up all of the protection a written contract offers—particularly evidence of what your deal was if you have to sue the contractor. Think about whether you're saving enough money to give up that protection. Then think about whether you want to get involved with this contractor.

What Your Contract Should Contain

A contract for a renovation or major repair is a complex legal document with a lot of money riding on it. So you should probably have the contract reviewed by a lawyer before you sign it. The contract should contain the following things:

- names, addresses and telephone numbers of the contractor and the home-owner
- list of contract documents
- description of the work to be done
- description of any excluded work
- **extras** and **deletions** (don't worry, we talk about these strange terms below)
- description of materials to be used
- removal of material from the worksite
- use of other contractors
- who obtains permits
- timing
- contract price and payment schedule
- quality of the work and warranties
- insurance

A contract for a more limited project like installing a roof or painting the interior of your home does not need to be as long. It may just consist of the written estimate. But it should contain at least the following:

- names, addresses and telephone numbers of the contractor and the home-owner
- description of the work to be done
- description of the materials to be used
- timing
- contract price and payment schedule
- quality of the work and warranties

An architect's contract will probably be in a standard form prepared by the provincial architects' association. If it's for a substantial amount of money, you might still wish to have your lawyer review it before you sign it.

Names, Addresses and Telephone Numbers

It's important to identify the person or company responsible for doing your work. The name on the contract should be the same as the name of the person or company you have been dealing with. The agreement should also set out the name of an individual person who will be your contact, with a telephone number where that person can be reached. There should be an address and it should not simply be a post office box number.

List of Contract Documents

The contract for a renovation or major repair should list all the documents that will make up the contract, such as:

• the written agreement itself
• drawings (which should be either listed in the contract or attached to it)
• specifications (which should be either listed or attached)
• additional documents signed by both parties during the course of the project

Description of the Work

Your contract should contain a complete and detailed description of all of the work you want done. The written description of the work can take up several pages, or it can be very short if the work is well-defined (refinishing the floors, for example) or if the drawings and specifications are very detailed and are attached to the contract. The description for a major project should include:

• site preparation such as tearing down walls
• structural details such as framing, subfloors, insulation and electrical and plumbing hook-ups
• size and location of doors, windows and closets
• how the work will match such things as the existing roof-line, paint, trim and flooring of your home

Extras and Deletions

You may want to make changes to the contract as the work progresses. Any change to the contract is a new contract and has to be agreed to by both parties. You may want to have additional work done (an **extra**) or to cancel some of the work originally requested (a **deletion**). All changes should be in writing. This written **change order** should describe the change and set out the price for the change, and should be signed by the parties and attached to the original contract. The change orders will then form part of the contract as well. The contract may contain a clause setting out how the price for an extra or the credit for a deletion will be calculated if changes are made.

Changes are a common reason why renovations end up costing more and taking longer than originally planned, so think twice before you ask for anything to be changed after the work has started. Sometimes, though, changes can't be avoided. Just make sure that everyone is clear about what the change is and how much it will cost. And put it in writing. Then accept the fact that making the change will probably add time to the project.

Description of Any Excluded Work

The contract should state any work that the contractor is *not* responsible for because you or another contractor will be doing it instead, such as:

- painting
- wallpapering
- carpeting
- landscaping or repairs to landscaping

Description of the Materials

The contract should say who is to supply the materials, you or the contractor.

If the contractor is supplying the materials, they should be described in detail, including brand names and styles for furnaces, plumbing fixtures, windows, flooring, paint, etc. The contract should also state what **warranties** the contractor is giving for the materials supplied. Materials may come with a manufacturer's warranty, but you should be able to deal with your contractor if there's a problem, rather than having to go to the manufacturer. Just in case, make sure that the contractor gives you copies of any manufacturer's warranties.

Some contracts will say that materials costing up to a stated maximum price will be supplied by the contractor and that you get to choose them. This arrangement is commonly used for things like bathroom tiles and fixtures. The contractor will send you to a supplier. If you choose materials that cost more than the stated maximum price, it will be up to you to pay the extra cost.

Removal of Materials

If you want the contractor to salvage anything from an area that is demolished (for example, bathroom fixtures, broadloom or wood panelling) the contract must say so and must also say what you want done with the items. You may want the contractor to use the salvaged material elsewhere in the project, or you may simply wish to keep something for your own use later on.

The contract should state who is responsible for the removal of all other debris. Keep in mind that there is a cost attached to garbage removal whether you do it or the contractor does it. One way or another you'll have to pay for the actual removal of the garbage, and perhaps for a dumpster.

Use of Other Contractors

If you want a different contractor to do some of the work, the contract must say so. Your contractor may wish to charge you an administrative fee for coordinating that work with the rest of the project. If this is the case, the contract must say so, setting out what the fee will be.

Permits

Building and other permits may be required for your renovation or repair, depending on the nature of the work involved. The contract should list any permits required (the contractor will usually be the source of this information) and whether it is your responsibility or the contractor's to get the permits.

Timing

The contract should state the date on which the work will commence, and a date by which it should be substantially completed. If the work can be broken down into distinct stages, the contract may set out a completion date for each stage.

If you want to discourage your contractor from starting the work late or taking too long to complete it, put a clause into the contract that allows you to end the contract or pay the contractor less if she's late. Keep in mind, however, that the dates in the contract are estimates and not guarantees. You should be prepared to accept a reasonable amount of delay in starting or finishing the job.

Whether or not the contractor is penalized for lateness, it is usual for the contract to allow the contractor extra time to finish the work without penalty for any of the following reasons:

- changes you make to the work you want done
- unforeseen problems with the structure or systems (electrical, heating, plumbing, air conditioning, etc.) of your home
- reasons beyond the contractor's control, such as:
    - disputes
    - unavailability of materials
    - fire and natural disasters
    - court orders
    - delays caused by work you were responsible to do

The contract should set out the days of the week and hours that you want the contractor to work. If you don't want the contractor to work evenings or weekends, or to start too early in the morning, put it in the contract.

Contract Price and Payment Schedule

THE CONTRACT PRICE: The contract price should be the same as the estimate that the contractor gave you.

DEPOSITS: For a small job a deposit may or may not be requested when you sign the contract. The entire contract price is often payable when the job is finished. On a larger project it is not unusual for the contractor to ask you for a deposit at the time that the contract is signed. The deposit should be no more than 5 to 15 per cent of the total contract price. If the contractor must order custom-made products for your job, the contract will probably require you to pay the contractor for them when they are ordered. The contractor may also ask you to pay another chunk of the contract price when the work begins, and this amount should not be more than 20 to 25 per cent of the total price.

INSTALMENT PAYMENTS: The balance of the contract price may be payable on completion, or if the project has distinct stages the contractor may ask you to make **progress payments** after specific work has been finished. It is reasonable for you to agree to progress payments of this kind, but do not agree to progress payments that are linked simply to dates and not to completed work.

   If your contract is being paid in instalments rather than when the job is finished, you have to take care in calculating how much you should pay as you go along. On the one hand, you want the contractor to have enough money to cover expenses—and maybe even make some profit—as the work proceeds. On the other hand, you don't want the contractor to have so much money that it's to his or her financial advantage to walk away from the job without doing another lick of work.

PAYMENTS ON COMPLETION: If payments are tied to the completion of specific work, don't make the payments unless the work has been completed—and to your satisfaction. This goes double (if not triple or more) for the final payment, otherwise you may never see your contractor again. Having an architect supervise your project comes in handy here. The architect will certify that the work has been satisfactorily completed.

AND DON'T FORGET: Whenever you make any payments under your contract, always be sure to get a receipt. And don't forget to hang onto the lien holdback!

Quality of Work and Warranties

In the contract, the contractor should agree to

- be **diligent** in doing the work and to complete the work in a **good and workmanlike manner**
- complete the work in compliance with all provincial and municipal requirements, such as the provincial building code and municipal regulations and inspections.
- protect your home from construction damage and to complete the work with as little inconvenience to you as possible (which is still a lot of inconvenience)
- keep the project site safe and in reasonable order at all times
- restore your home to a reasonable state of order and cleanliness at the end of the job

The contractor should give a minimum one-year warranty on workmanship and materials. Unfortunately, the warranty is worthless unless the contractor will actually come back to honour it. That's why it's important to check a contractor's past performance in this area before you decide to use that contractor.

Insurance

You definitely want the contractor to have insurance...and the contractor may want to make sure you have insurance too.

THE CONTRACTOR'S INSURANCE: The contract should require the contractor to provide proof of the following insurance:

- workers' compensation coverage as required by provincial law
- third party liability coverage of at least $2 million

YOUR INSURANCE: The contract may require you to have certain insurance as well, usually fire, comprehensive, and third party liability. This is the kind of coverage already provided by your homeowner's insurance. But the renovation contract may require you to have more than the usual amount of third party liability coverage.

The contract may require you to notify your insurance company of the renovation or repair, but even if it doesn't you should speak to your insurance company before any work starts to make sure that

- you have the coverage required of you by the contract
- your insurance will remain in force during the project
- your coverage is adjusted to take into the account the increased value of your home when the project is finished

TIPS FOR SURVIVING YOUR RENOVATION OR MAJOR REPAIR

There are things you can do both before and during the project to make it easier on you.

Advance Preparation

The project will go more smoothly if you prepare in advance:

- Remove everything that can be removed from the work area.
- Protect anything that can't be removed from the work area.
- Expect dust everywhere, and protect your belongings accordingly.
- Decide where you want to put a dumpster (it will look nice behind your peonies).
- Decide where you want the workers to
    - keep their tools
    - come in and out of your home
    - eat
    - pee
- Tell your neighbours what's up before work starts—it may help to reduce complaints about noise, dirt, and your dumpster.

As the Work Progresses

If you want your project to come in on time and on budget, and not be *too* nerve-wracking, here are some of the things you should do:

- Find out who the supervisor on your project is if it's not the contractor you've dealt with—you should direct any questions or comments about the work to the supervisor and not to the workers themselves.
- Speak to the supervisor on a daily basis about how the project is going.
- Bring any problems you notice to the supervisor's or contractor's attention immediately.
- Be visible so that everyone knows you're keeping an eye on things, but don't follow the workers around obsessively.
- Keep your children away from the work area.
- Keep an eye on pets, especially cats—we know of some who ended up (temporarily) behind the new drywall.
- Get out for a while if the noise and dirt start to drive you crazy.
- Try to be present whenever an inspector is scheduled to visit.
- Be pleasant to the workers so that they'll *want* to do a good job for you.
- Don't make changes.
- But if you do make changes, put them in writing.

WHEN PROBLEMS ARISE

It goes without saying that there will be problems with your renovation or major repair. When you're trying to schedule different tradespeople who are working on other projects at the same time, there are bound to be some delays and mix-ups. There may even be problems worse than delays and mix-ups.

The Problems

Here are some of the problems you may run into:

- Your contractor never shows up in the first place.
- Your contractor abandons the job.
- Your contractor *doesn't* abandon the job, but you'd like to abandon the contractor because of delays or rotten workmanship.
- Your contractor charges you for changes that were not ordered in writing—or that were not ordered at all.

- A subcontractor, labourer or supplier files a lien against your home.
- The contractor refuses to finish the job after you've paid in full.
- The contractor refuses to honour the warranty.

The Solutions

The best solution to almost all of these problems is to avoid them in the first place by choosing your contractor carefully, drawing up a detailed written contract, and being sensible about how much you pay and when you pay it. But if things go wrong anyway, there may still be solutions.

The Contractor Who Doesn't Show Up

If your contractor doesn't show up when the work is supposed to start, call and find out when he or she is coming. If the delay drags on, write a letter saying that if the contractor hasn't shown up by a specified date you will consider the contract **abandoned**—you will want your deposit back and will hire someone else. This letter may be just the encouragement your contractor needs. If it isn't, you may have to sue to get your deposit back.

The Contractor Who Abandons

If you contractor abandons the job and it's clear he's never coming back, there's really nothing you can do to make him come back. If you set up your payment schedule properly, you'll only have paid for work that has actually been done. While you're left with a half-finished job, you should also be left with about half your money—which you will use to have the job finished by another contractor. Even so, it will probably cost you more than you have left over from the first contract to have the job finished, especially if the work that *was* done was badly done.

You can think about suing. But generally a contractor who abandons a job is in such deep financial trouble that he won't care about another lawsuit (and won't have any money to pay, either).

The Contractor You'd Like to Abandon

If you realize part-way through the job that the workmanship is poor, start by speaking to the contractor. If the contractor disagrees, you can call in the building inspector or some other third party for an objective opinion. (Be careful about calling in the building inspector—if the workmanship is bad enough, you may end up with a **work order** from the municipality forcing *you* to fix it whether the contractor agrees or not.) The contractor may have a change of mind and be willing to fix the work if a third party agrees with you. Or you can report the contractor to her licensing body or the local home builders' association or the Better Business Bureau.

If you want to get rid of the contractor, have your lawyer write a letter to the contractor stating that you consider the contractor to be in breach of the contract, ordering the contractor off the job, and saying that you consider your damages to be equal to whatever you haven't yet paid the contractor (if not more—more is better). The contractor may end up suing you, but at least the next time you see her it will be in court and not in your kitchen. Again, you'll have to find someone else to finish the job and it will probably end up costing you more than you set aside for the original contract.

If you're not happy with work that's been done, don't pay. You may technically be breaching your contract, but you'd rather be sued for money you owe than have to sue the contractor to get back money you've paid for work that hasn't been done right. Walk through the project before you pay at any stage to see whether you're satisfied with the work.

Your contractor may have several jobs on the go, and you only see him one or two days a week. If you're thinking of getting rid of the contractor because it's taking too long to finish the job, get an estimate from someone else on how much it will cost to finish the job. If it's no more than the unpaid balance of the contract, write a letter to the contractor (or have your lawyer write the letter) giving a fixed number of days to complete the work. Say that if the contractor does not finish the work within that time, you will find someone else to do so and you will subtract the cost from what's still owed to the contractor.

Charges for Changes

If the contractor presents you with a bill for changes that were not in writing, what do you do? If the contract says that all changes had to be in writing, legally you can refuse to pay for changes that were not. If you in fact asked for the changes and they were in fact done, legally speaking you may or may not have an obligation to pay but morally speaking you should pay something even if you dispute the amount. If you didn't ask for the changes, don't pay for them.

Liens

If a lien is filed against your home, do not pay the holdback to the contractor. Call a lawyer. Your liability should be limited to the amount of the holdback.

The Contractor Who Won't Come Back to Finish

You paid the contractor in full even though there were a few little things still left to be done. And the contractor never came back. Didn't we tell you not to pay until the job was finished! There's nothing you can do to force the contractor to come back. You can vent your feelings by complaining to the provincial or municipal licensing agencies, the provincial consumer protection branch, the Better Business Bureau or the local home builders' association. You can sue for the cost of the unfinished work, but it's probably not worth your while if it's only a small amount of work.

The Contractor Who Won't Honour the Warranty

Some time after the work is finished—and paid for—problems may arise. How you handle the situation will depend on whether or not the problems are urgent. If the problems are not urgent, make a list of them as you notice them. Call the contractor when you have collected several problems instead of calling each time you find a problem. If it's a major problem or one that needs attention fast (like no heat, or crackling noises when you turn on a light switch), call the contractor immediately. With luck, your contractor will honour the warranty in the contract and send someone to fix the problems.

If the contractor does not honour the warranty, it's up to you to decide whether you want the work done. Then you'll have to find someone else to do it. And then you'll have to decide whether or not to sue the contractor for the cost of the work.

HOME SECURITY

There are hundreds of break-ins across Canada every day—but if you take reasonable precautions, you can reduce the chance of *your* home being targeted by burglars. The things you do to prevent break-ins don't have to be fancy or expensive.

It's more effective to make your home look like a bad bet to burglars than it is to install a burglar alarm. You can discourage burglars by getting rid of places outside your home where a burglar can hide and work in peace, by getting homeowners in your neighbourhood or buildings to keep an eye on each other's place, by making it tough for a break-in artist to open your doors and windows, and by warning burglars that they'll have trouble selling your property. In this chapter we'll give you some guidance on the fine art of turning off burglars.

We'll also talk to you about the dangers of turning your home into a burglar-proof fortress. You don't want to make it so difficult for burglars to get in that it's also impossible for you to get out if there's a fire.

These should be your main goals when you set about reducing the chance that your home will be broken into:

• You don't want to attract the attention of potential burglars to your home.

- You do want your neighbours to pay attention to your home.
- You don't want to make it easy for burglars to enter your home.
- You do want to make it difficult for burglars to dispose of your belongings.

NEIGHBOURHOOD WATCH

One of the best protections against break-ins is neighbours who keep an eye on each other's homes. You should get to know who your neighbours are, when they come and go, and when suspicious-looking people are loitering, walking, driving, or parking around your neighbours' homes. You want your neighbours to take the same interest in you. Exchange phone numbers with neighbours whose homes can be seen from yours. Have an agreement to report suspicious activity directly to your neighbours or to the police.

You can make these arrangements informally or you may be able to join a community organization such as Neighbourhood Watch or Block Watch. If there's not a Neighbourhood Watch in your neighbourhood, you can be the one to set it up. To find out about joining or starting up a Neighbourhood Watch, contact your local police department.

If you live in an apartment-style condominium, get to know the neighbours in your building, don't let people into your building if you don't know them, and notify whoever's in charge of building security if you see strangers hanging around.

OUTSIDE YOUR HOME

You want your home to look nice, but if security is your concern, you don't want your home to be so nice-looking that it attracts the attention of burglars. Don't go out of your way to have the best-looking house on the block, with the most expensive car in the driveway. That can lead potential burglars to believe that you also have the best stereo, computer equipment, jewellery, etc.

Be Visible

Make sure that your doors and windows are visible from the street or from neighbouring homes by trimming back or cutting down tall shrubs around entrances and windows. You don't want to give a burglar privacy to break into your home, or an intruder a place to hide when you're opening your door.

If you are going to fence your property, remember that a privacy fence not only blocks your neighbour's view of your home, it also blocks their view of your burglars. On the other hand, although a burglar may be able to get into your property over a high fence, he'll have a bit of trouble getting your sound system and television out over the fence. If you fence your property, check that the gate is solidly hinged and keep it locked.

Don't Provide Burglary Tools

Don't leave tools in your yard or unlocked garage. A burglar will really appreciate it if you set out a ladder, hammer, axe, metal-cutter, or saw to help him enter your premises. Cut back any tree limbs that come close to a second-storey window and could be used as a ladder to the window.

Turn on the Lights

At night, light entrances and ground-floor windows so that burglars won't have a safe, dark place to work. These lights can be motion-sensor lights, which are triggered by anyone prowling around, or they can be light-sensor lights, which come on at dusk and turn off automatically at dawn. Install exterior lights high up, beyond normal reach, or put vandal-proof light covers on them so they cannot easily be unscrewed or broken.

Don't get completely carried away with lighting up your home, or you will attract attention to it and make burglars think you must have something to protect. To avoid annoying your neighbours, make sure your lights don't shine brightly into their homes.

Set up the Cameras

If you live in a condominium complex with a parking lot or garage, or with facilities, or even with a common entrance, there should be security cameras around the complex. If there aren't, lobby the condominium corporation to install them. The cameras don't have to be monitored by a security guard or doorman, if your building doesn't have either of those. The pictures can be relayed to the TV sets of the residents in the building. Added bonus: You've got your own reality television programming!

You can also set up security cameras at entrances to a house. Burglars will be absolutely positive that you have something worth stealing, but they'll probably feel extremely shy about having their pictures taken.

WHEN YOU'RE AWAY

You don't have to be gone for a week to be at risk for a break-in. If someone is watching your home with the intention of breaking into it, they may make their move while you're at the convenience store or walking your dog, or even working in your garden or chatting with your neighbour down the hall. Lock all doors and windows every time you go out, even for a few minutes. If you have an alarm system, turn it on. Take particular precautions around Christmas, when burglars know that homes are full of presents and homeowners are likely to be out partying.

Display Your Dogs and Warning Signs

Let potential burglars know that breaking into your home is not worth the effort. Get a big dog that barks at strangers. If you don't have a dog, you can still post a "Beware of the Dog" sign (although a burglar who has been watching your place won't be fooled, merely amused). If you have an alarm system, post stickers that say so. Even if you don't have an alarm, you can still post stickers that say that you do.

Turn on Lights and Timers

When you're out, leave lights on inside (but not always the same lights), and leave a radio playing (tuned to an all-news station, or a station that has talk rather than music). Also leave some lights on outside.

If you're going to be gone for more than a day or two, put several inside lights and the radio on automatic timers. Set the timers so that lights go on and off in different parts of your home at different times. Have the bedroom lights come on after the living area lights have turned off, and have the bedroom lights turn off at usual bedtimes to make it more difficult for a watching burglar to be sure that you are away. (If you are using lamps with a shade, take the shade off to reduce the risk of fire.)

You should also notify your immediate neighbours and ask them to keep an eye on your home. But be cautious about telling too many other people about your absence. Your teenager or the local delivery kid may have acquaintances who might take advantage of this information.

Carry on with Outside Maintenance

When you're away, ask someone to pick up your newspaper and mail daily. If you expect to be away for more than several days, stop delivery of your newspaper. If you live in a house, make sure that your grass is mowed regularly, or your driveway snowplowed and your walks shovelled after each snowfall. Have an agreement with a neighbour that you will do these things for each other if either is away, or hire a neighbour's child to do them, or contract with a gardening and snowplowing company to look after your premises. In snowy weather, ask a relative or neighbour to drive into your driveway to leave tire marks to make it look like you've been coming and going.

DOORS AND WINDOWS

To reduce the chance of a break-in, pay special attention to your doors and windows.

Doors and Locks

When most people think about protecting the entrances to their home, they think about installing proper locks. However, any locksmith will tell you that a lock is only as strong as the door and frame to which it is attached. Entrance doors and door frames should be solid wood, metal, or laminated wood core construction. Door hinges should be on the inside, not the outside, and they should be attached with heavy-duty screws that go right through to the framing stud.

Pay particular attention to doors leading from a garage to a house. A person who succeeds in getting into your garage will have lots of time and privacy to work on these doors. Lock your garage door as well as your house doors to reduce the risk of this happening.

Don't rely on locks that are part of the doorknob because they can easily be forced or removed. You should install **single-cylinder deadbolt** locks on exterior doors, including doors from the garage into the house.

Double-cylinder deadbolt locks must be unlocked by a key from the inside as well as the outside. These locks are often used if there is a glass panel in or beside the door—to prevent someone from breaking the glass and simply reaching in to unlock the door. The down side to this type of lock is that it may be difficult to get out the door in the event of a fire or other emergency. Keep a key near the door (but out of reach from the outside) and make sure that all members of your household know where the key is located. Instead of installing a double-cylinder deadbolt, you can replace glass windows with break-resistant plexiglass or you can leave the glass in and protect it with metal grillwork.

Keys

If you keep a spare key somewhere outside your home (just in case you lock yourself out), here are some places NOT to keep it, because they are places that burglars know all about: under the door mat, in a planter, above a ledge or door frame, in the mailbox. Take in all hidden spare keys before you go away on a trip.

Do not carry identification on a key ring. If someone gets hold of your home or car keys, there's no reason to let them know exactly what door the keys fit. Be sure to have your locks changed immediately if your keys are stolen or lost.

Peepholes

Install a wide-angle peephole in your front door so you can see who's out-side without having to open the door. If you have a mail slot that opens directly into your hall, make sure that it does not open wide enough for someone to reach in and unlock the door.

Sliding Doors

Sliding glass doors can be jimmied off their tracks. To prevent this, put a wooden broom handle or hockey-stick handle in the floor track when the door is closed. The stick should be exactly the length of the track for a snug fit. Or have a metal "patio bar" installed half-way up the door (they're avail-able at the hardware store).

Windows

Secure windows that slide to one side the same way you secure sliding doors, with a broom handle or other piece of wood in the track. Double-hung win-dows (windows whose lower or upper panel, or both, can be raised and low-ered) are usually fastened by a crescent latch, but crescent latches can be opened from the outside by slipping a knife between the sashes. Secure dou-ble-hung windows by putting on a better lock (ask your local hardware store for advice).

If you mount an air-conditioner in a window, it should be bolted to the window frame so that it cannot be lifted out. Keep the window from being opened further by blocking either a sliding window or a double-hung win-dow with a length of wood.

You may want to make basement windows burglar-proof by replacing the glass with plexiglass or by putting up security bars. Discuss with the con-tractor who does the work for you, or the building supply store that sells you the materials, how to make sure that it will still be easy to get out through the basement windows if there is a fire.

ALARM SYSTEMS

Alarm systems make your home a less attractive target to a potential burglar. This is recognized by home insurance companies, which usually offer lower premiums to homeowners with approved alarm systems. If you are consider-ing installing an alarm system, find out from your insurance company what kind of system they'll give you a discount for.

The least expensive alarm systems simply set off a siren if someone enters your house through a wired door or window. Then it's up to you to get help. The more expensive ones are connected through your telephone line to a friend or relative's phone, or to the alarm company's own switchboard. (If you have this kind of alarm, check whether your alarm is designed to go off if someone cuts the phone line.) It may be possible in your area to have your alarm connected to the local police station—but considering that there are far more false alarms than true alarms, you may not wish to have a direct connection with the police. If you have a history of false alarms with the police, they probably won't respond to a true alarm. And after they give you a freebie or two, they'll charge you for responding to false alarms. If you pay a service fee to be connected to the alarm company switchboard, an operator at the company will notify police or company security personnel that your alarm has gone off. Usually the operator will first call your home to find out if the alarm is false. You may have to provide the operator with an identification number to prove that it's the homeowner and not the burglar answering the phone. Keep the number in a place where you and family members can find it when your nerves are jangled from sirens going off...but not in a place where an intruder would also easily find it.

To find out what kinds of alarms are available, ask in your local hardware store, call some alarm companies, or call your local police department. If you choose a system that is connected to an alarm company's switchboard, make sure that the company is well-established and reliable. If they go out of business, your alarm will go out of business too.

An alarm system only works if it's turned on. Turn it on every time your home is going to be empty, even if it's only for a few minutes.

PROTECTION FOR YOUR VALUABLES

There are two steps to protecting your valuables. The first is to keep them in a safe place. The second is to identify them permanently to increase the chance that you'll get them back if they're stolen—and to decrease the chance that a burglar will be able to sell them.

Safekeeping

Expensive jewellery is best left in a safety deposit box at the bank. If you do so, you may be able to arrange to pay for insurance on these items only when they are out of the safety deposit box. Contact your insurance agent about this possibility. It's also a good idea not to keep large amounts of cash in your home.

If you want to keep your cash and jewellery close by so you can cuddle it whenever you feel like it, consider installing a burglar-proof and fire-proof safe in your home. For a lot less money and less security, you can also buy containers for hiding valuables that are disguised as beer or soft drink cans or other kinds of cans, or you can buy hollowed-out books. If you decide to try this method of hiding things, remember that quite a lot of people have accidentally thrown out what they thought was a can . . . and then found out that it was really a jewellery collection.

If you simply want to hide your valuables, here are some places that *burglars will be sure to look:* in the refrigerator and the freezer, under your bed or your mattress, under the bathroom or kitchen sink, in, under, and behind drawers. It is a good idea to leave some costume jewellery in your jewellery box to make a burglar think that she has found everything you have. If you really use your imagination to hide valuables, be careful not to be so creative that you can't find them later.

Identification

Professional burglars are usually more interested in selling what they've stolen than in keeping it themselves. If a thief knows he will have trouble selling your possessions, he's less likely to spend time stealing them. **Operation Identification** is a national program set up through police departments to identify personal property so that it's hard to sell if it has been stolen, and so that burglars know before they break in that your property is identified.

Contact your local police department or your insurance agent to find out about Operation Identification. Identifying your belongings involves engraving a **personal identification number** on them and placing an Operation Identification sticker in your window to let potential burglars know that you have done so. The police may loan you an engraving pencil or tell you where you can borrow or buy one (hardware stores carry them).

The engraving pencil will not work on some things such as jewellery, silver, china, fur coats, paintings, and papers (for example, stock certificates or bonds). Paintings and paper can be marked using a non-toxic invisible marking pen. Fur coats can be marked by lifting up the lining at the bottom of the back and writing your last name and/or your personal identification number in BIG letters across the skins of the back of the coat. Use an indelible pen if the fur is dark or an ordinary ball-point pen if the fur is light (an identifying number or name on the lining is of no use because the lining can be removed).

IN THE EVENT OF A BURGLARY

If you come home and find that a door or window has been forced open, don't go in (or if you're already in, leave immediately). Call the police from a neighbour's or from a cell phone. The burglar may still be inside and might attack you in order to escape or to prevent being identified. Do not clean up your home until the police have looked it over for evidence, but do look around outside to see if there are any suspicious vehicles or people. If there are, note licence numbers and descriptions.

If your home is broken into once, it may be broken into a second time shortly afterwards. That's because the burglar expects you to have contents insurance and to replace everything that was stolen. After a first break-in do a general security check of your premises. Take the burglary as a hint to upgrade your locks, doors, and alarm system, and to identify all your possessions (new and old) with your personal identification number. You will be pleased to know that many homeowner's insurance policies will help pay for new locks following a burglary.

☑ Home Security Checklist

Neighbourhood Watch

❑ Join or organize a Neighbourhood Watch in your community.
❑ Arrange with neighbours to keep an eye on each other's homes.

Outside

❑ Make sure your doors and windows are visible from the street or neighbouring homes.
❑ Don't leave tools that a burglar might find useful in your yard or unlocked garage.
❑ At night, light your entrances and ground-floor windows.
❑ Pressure the condominium corporation of your apartment-style building to install security cameras at entrances, in parking lots or garages, etc.

When you're away, make it look like you're still home

❑ Make arrangements with your neighbours to keep an eye on each other's homes.
❑ Use timers or sensors to turn on inside and outside lights at night and turn them off during the day.
❑ Leave a radio playing, tuned to an all-talk station.
❑ Stop delivery of newspapers.
❑ Have a neighbour pick up your mail.

❑ Have your walks or driveway shovelled of snow in the winter, and your grass mowed in the summer.
❑ Have a neighbour park in your driveway from time to time.

Doors and windows

❑ Entrance doors and their frames should be of solid construction, with hinges on the inside.
❑ Install deadbolt locks.
❑ Keep your doors locked, including doors leading from garage to house.
❑ Don't leave a spare key in an obvious place such as the mailbox, under the door mat, above the door frame, or in a planter.
❑ To prevent sliding glass doors and windows from being jimmied open, insert a stick snugly in the track.
❑ Consider installing an alarm system.
❑ Display a sticker stating that you have an alarm system (whether you do or not!).

Protecting your valuables

❑ Keep cash or valuable jewellery in a bank or home vault.
❑ Don't hide your valuables in obvious places such as in, under, or behind drawers, under the bed or mattress, in the refrigerator or freezer, or under the bathroom or kitchen sink.
❑ If you've chosen a hiding place that is not obvious, don't forget where it is!
❑ Make your belongings harder to sell, and therefore less attractive to a thief, by identifying them permanently.

In the event of a break-in

❑ If you're inside, get out. If you're out, don't go in. For your personal safety, it is best not to confront a burglar.
❑ Thieves often return after a break-in, so review your home security to avoid a second break-in.

☑ "To Do" List

❑ Get acquainted with immediate neighbours you don't already know.
❑ Light up your ground floor entrances.

❑ Install deadbolt locks on exterior doors.

❑ Put a wooden stick in the track of any sliding glass doors or windows.

❑ Install a peephole in exterior doors.

❑ Make sure any outside hiding place for your keys is a safe one.

❑ Permanently identify your valuables and put an "Operation Identification" sticker in your windows.

❑ Find a secret place to hide your valuables.

Things Not To Do

• Don't burglar-proof your home so well that you can't get out if there's a fire.

• Don't leave your doors unlocked or windows open while you are out.

• Don't enter your home when there are signs of a break-in.

• Don't confront a burglar or intruder in your home.

13 HOME SAFETY AND ACCIDENT PREVENTION

WARNING: This is a chapter full of warnings. The first warning is that reading too much about safety at one time can be harmful to your mental health. If you read this chapter in one sitting, you may wish to take to your bed and pull the covers over your head. But if you do, make sure that you haven't left the car running in the garage or oil heating on the stove.

Another warning: Being safe involves a lot of cleaning. Worried already? This is just the beginning!

Safety is an area of major concern to homeowners, even though accidents are unpleasant to think about. So that you don't have to face all of your fears at once, we've organized this chapter by categories. That will allow you to have a panic attack one evening about your home catching on fire, another evening about being overcome by carbon monoxide, and so on. Under each major heading, we have provided a checklist of the most important things to do to keep your family safe. Following each checklist is a more detailed discussion about what you should do and why.

FIRE SAFETY

There are stories in the news almost daily about the loss of life and property caused by home fires. Many people's greatest terror is of a fire breaking out in their home. But most fires are preventable, and, even if a fire does break out, proper fire planning can at least prevent loss of life. The following checklist sets out the key fire safety and planning matters of which every homeowner should be aware.

☑ Fire Safety Checklist

Smoke alarms

❑ Place a smoke alarm on each floor of your home.
❑ Test smoke alarms and the batteries once a month.
❑ Clean smoke alarms once a month.

Plan ahead

❑ Plan an escape route out of your home. If your home is in an apartment-style building, plan an escape route out of the building as well as out of your unit.
❑ Plan two ways out of every bedroom—door and window.
❑ Plan a meeting place outside the home.

In the event of fire

❑ Getting out is more important than fighting the fire or calling the fire department.
❑ Stay near the ground where the air is best.
❑ Stop, drop, and roll if on fire.
❑ Call the fire department from outside your home.
❑ If you live in an apartment-style building, don't use the elevators and don't go into smoke-filled stairwells or corridors. If you have to stay in your unit, tape around entrance doors to keep out smoke and hang a white sheet out a window or on a balcony rail to attract the attention of firefighters.

Fire Prevention: Electrical

Live within the capacity of your home's electrical system or have it upgraded

❏ Don't make permanent use of extension cords or "octopuses."
❏ Don't use oversized fuses.
❏ If fuses or circuit breakers blow repeatedly, have the circuit checked by an electrician.

Unless your home has just been built, have the wiring checked by an electrician

❏ Determine whether or not you have aluminum wiring.
❏ Find out whether original wiring and any changes made to it are safe.

Have the wiring checked by an electrician if

❏ electrical outlets or switches are unusually warm
❏ you have had trouble with mice or squirrels in your home

Use appliances correctly

❏ Don't run electrical cords under carpeting.
❏ Don't use higher than 60-watt bulb unless the light fixture says so.

Fire Prevention: Heating

Furnaces

❏ Have your furnace professionally inspected and cleaned once a year.
❏ Keep flammable materials away from the furnace.
❏ If you smell gas from your gas furnace, open the windows or leave the house. Call the gas company.

Space Heaters

❏ Space heaters are very dangerous. Treat them as you would a live fire.
❏ Never use a kerosene, propane, or butane heater indoors.

Fireplaces

❏ If you use your fireplace, have it professionally inspected and cleaned once a year.
❏ Use a fireplace screen or glass fireplace door to keep sparks away from carpeting and wood floors.

❏ Don't start a fire with gasoline, lighter fluid, or any other flammable substance.

❏ To prevent build-up of flammable substances in your chimney, burn seasoned hardwood rather than softwood or firelogs.

❏ Never leave a fire unattended.

❏ Don't dispose of ashes until they are cold.

Fire Prevention: Cooking

❏ Keep a class ABC fire extinguisher, or a class B fire extinguisher (designed to put out grease fires) in the kitchen.

❏ Don't leave food, especially grease or fat, cooking unattended.

❏ Keep the entire stove and oven area clean of grease.

❏ If you have a grease fire, do not throw water on it. Use your fire extinguisher, baking soda, or salt; if the fire is small enough, smother it with a pot lid.

❏ If your microwave sparks or the door does not seal tightly, have it professionally checked before using it.

❏ If a fire starts in your oven or your microwave, don't open the door—that will simply give the fire more oxygen.

Fire Prevention: Flammable Materials

❏ Careless smoking is a major cause of home fires. If you must smoke in your home, take these precautions:
  • Don't smoke in bed.
  • Don't smoke anywhere if you are drowsy.
  • Set out and use ashtrays.
  • Empty ashtrays into a toilet or metal container, not into wastepaper baskets.

❏ Keep matches and cigarette lighters out of the reach of children.

❏ Do not use flammable products (container will have flammable sign) near open flames or heat sources such as stoves, furnaces, fireplaces, cigarettes, pilot lights.

❏ Christmas trees are flammable. Don't leave them unattended with the lights on.

Here's more detailed information about the items mentioned in the fire safety checklist.

Smoke Alarms

Every home should have one smoke alarm on each floor. In fact, many municipalities require homeowners to install smoke alarms. Check with your local fire department to find out if you have to install a smoke alarm—and then install one even if you don't have to.

Types of Alarms

There are two types of smoke alarms. An **ionization** alarm can detect fire in its first stage before there is any smoke visible. A **photoelectric** alarm can detect a fire in its second stage, the smouldering stage, when smoke has appeared but there are not yet flames. The third stage of a fire is the flame stage, and the fourth stage of a fire is the heat stage. If you do have a fire, you want to know about it before the third or fourth stages.

Smoke alarms can be powered by battery or by electricity. A battery-powered alarm can be installed fairly easily by the homeowner, but an alarm powered by electricity should be installed by an electrician. If you choose an electricity-powered alarm, make sure it is not wired to a circuit that can be turned on and off by a switch. Also, make sure the alarm has an auxiliary battery in case of a power failure.

Where to Install

Where should you place a smoke alarm? On the ceiling, first of all, because smoke rises. But since they can be triggered accidentally by such things as shower steam or burning toast, alarms should not be too close to either a bathroom or a kitchen. You wouldn't want to frighten your teenage son who is taking his first shower in months, or discourage your spouse who has decided to make you breakfast in bed. An alarm should be placed near the bedrooms or sleeping areas of your home. If your municipality requires you to install smoke alarms, it will probably also tell you where in your home to put them.

Maintenance and Testing

Read the manufacturer's instructions for information about testing and maintenance of your particular alarm. Test your smoke alarm once a month by putting a source of smoke, such as a candle or incense, near the alarm until it sounds. The "Tester Button" usually only tests battery charge. Test your batteries once a month too. Replace batteries when they become low. Use only the exact batteries recommended by the manufacturer. Even if the batteries are not low, replace them once a year. DO NOT use rechargeable batteries in a smoke alarm because they can fail without giving any warning. Vacuum dust from the alarm's smoke chamber and protective cover once a month (more often if someone in your house smokes).

If your alarm isn't working, replace it!

Plan Ahead

Plan an Escape Route

Plan an escape route from every area of your home, and then try it to see if it works. Be sure everyone knows two ways out of their bedroom—a door and a window—if that's possible. You may have to smash windows open, so keep something near each window that can be used to smash it if necessary. "If necessary" is a subtle point you will have to impress upon your children lest they be tempted to test this piece of equipment during one of your fire drills. If you have bars on any windows, they must be easily removable from the inside. If you have a door or window lock that must be opened from the inside with a key, always keep a key hanging near the lock—but not where someone outside can get it by smashing a window.

If your home is in an apartment-style building, locate all the emergency exits and plan an escape route (or two or three) out of the building as well as out of your unit.

Know the Escape Route

Make sure everyone—children, babysitters, and guests included—knows the escape routes and knows that no one is to go back inside for pets, toys, or valuables.

Arrange a Meeting Place

Arrange a place outside your home or building where everyone is to gather in the event of a fire. That way, you will know exactly who is safe and who is missing.

In the Event of Fire

Get Out!

Getting out of a burning building is the first priority. If a fire breaks out, unless it's very small, concentrate on getting everyone out of the home, not on trying to put the fire out, on getting dressed, or on saving your favourite possessions. Don't even stop to call the fire department. Call from a neighbour's home or a cell phone once everyone is out.

Use These Survival Techniques:

CRAWL on your knees to the nearest exit, since the air near the floor is safer to breathe because smoke and dangerous gases rise.

FEEL THE DOOR before entering another room or hallway. Do not open a hot door because there is probably fire on the other side. Close doors behind you as you get out to slow the spread of the fire.

IF YOU HAVE TO ESCAPE THROUGH A WINDOW, SHUT THE DOOR to the room before you open the window, or the air coming through the window may fan the fire.

STOP, DROP AND ROLL. Have everyone in your household learn the "stop, drop, and roll" technique to smother flames if someone's clothes catch on fire. **Stop** instantly—running will fan the flames. **Drop** to the floor and cover your face with your hands. **Roll** on a rug, blanket, or coat to put the fire out. If you are outside, you can use dirt or snow to put the fire out.

IF YOU LIVE IN AN APARTMENT-STYLE BUILDING, take every fire alarm seriously—leave the building if you can when you hear an alarm. Don't just hope that it's a false alarm. Don't try to use the elevators if there's a fire, use the stairs instead. But don't enter a stairwell that's filled with smoke. And if the corridor outside your unit is filled with smoke, you're probably safer to stay in your unit. If you have to stay, tape over cracks between the frame and the entrance door to your unit to keep out smoke (keep a roll of duct tape near the door). Hang a white sheet over your balcony rail or out a window to let firefighters know you're inside.

Contact the Fire Department

Make sure everyone in your family knows how to contact the fire department. In most, but not all, areas of Canada, this is done by dialling 911. Check the number you must use by looking in the front pages of your telephone book under Emergency Numbers.

Fire Prevention: Electrical
Live within Your Electrical Means

Don't exceed the electrical capacity of your home. Do not plug multiple electrical appliances into one outlet, using "octopus" type plugs. Make only temporary use of extension cords: they can cause appliances to overheat.

Do not use oversized fuses in your fuse box. A 15-amp fuse is the one usually required for regular domestic circuits. If your fuses blow repeatedly, have an electrician investigate to find out if you are overloading your system. If you cannot convince the members of your family that they can't watch television, play computer games, listen to the stereo, and dry their hair all at the same time, your system may need upgrading.

Have Your Wiring Checked by a Professional Electrician if:

YOUR HOME IS NOT NEWLY BUILT. The electrician will be able to determine whether you have aluminum wiring (which is found in older homes), and whether the original wiring and any changes made to it by previous owners are safe.

ELECTRICAL OUTLETS OR SWITCHES ARE UNUSUALLY WARM. A hot outlet or switch may be a sign of faulty wiring. Stop using the outlet or switch until it has been inspected.

YOU HAVE ALUMINUM WIRING. Corroded aluminum wiring can get very hot, and aluminum wiring that is under compression can cause sparks.

YOU HAVE HAD TROUBLE WITH MICE OR SQUIRRELS IN YOUR HOME. Visiting rodents may have gnawed off the protective covering on your wires, which could result in a low heat-source fire that your fuse box or breaker may not detect quickly.

Use Appliances Correctly

If you have pot lights in your ceiling, keep insulation, and anything else that may burn, away from them. Do not use a light bulb of higher wattage than recommended in a lamp (you can usually find the recommended wattage on a label on the lamp or shade). If in doubt, do not use a bulb higher than 60 watts.

Do not run electrical cords underneath carpets. If your appliances have frayed or brittle electric cords, replace the cords. If you have an "instant-on" television, unplug it if it's not going to be used for an extended period. Don't unplug any appliance by pulling on the electric cord; always pull out by the plug.

Make sure that all your electrical appliances and electrical cords carry the CSA seal (Canadian Standards Association) or the ULC seal (Underwriters' Laboratories of Canada).

If an appliance sparks, smokes, or has flames coming out of it, turn it off and unplug it, or shut off power to that circuit. Do not put water on electrical equipment that is on fire until it has been unplugged.

Fire Prevention: Heating

Furnaces

Have your furnace professionally inspected once a year by a heating contractor. Between inspections, keep an eye on your furnace yourself. Have it serviced immediately if you notice loose parts, rust, leakage, or any other sign that the furnace is starting to fall apart. Also, change the filters regularly.

Keep the area around your furnace clean and free of dust and lint, which can catch fire if they get close to the furnace. Periodically vacuum out furnace vents and filters on each floor of your home.

If you have an oil furnace and your oil tank is old, have it professionally checked for pinholes that may be about to leak.

If you have a natural gas furnace and you think you smell gas, open the windows immediately, or leave the house. Call the gas company's emergency number or call the fire department. Another thing to remember with a gas furnace is to keep the outdoor natural gas regulator clear of ice and snow—a buildup can cause the fuel flow to become uncontrolled.

Space Heaters

Use only electrical space heaters indoors. Never use kerosene, butane, or propane heaters indoors. You should treat even an electrical space heater as you would a live fire: don't put it near anything that might catch fire, like furniture or draperies. Newer electrical heaters have a switch designed to turn the heater off automatically if it falls over. It is best not to leave an electrical heater unattended, especially if it does not have an automatic shut-off switch. Do not leave children alone with an electrical heater that is turned on.

Fireplaces and Chimneys

INSPECT: Before you use your fireplace for the first time, have the fireplace and chimney cleaned and inspected by a professional chimney sweep. In addition to cleaning the fireplace and chimney flues, the chimney sweep should check that your chimney has a **liner**. If you live in an older house, it may not. Chimney liners reduce the build-up of flammable creosote, which can cause a chimney fire, and they prevent small holes in the chimney mortar from leading to fire in the walls. New homes should have chimney liners because in most areas builders are required by law to install them. Even though owners of older houses may not be required to install a chimney liner, you should have one installed.

The chimney sweep should check that your chimney is tall enough that sparks will not blow onto the roof or back through open windows. You may want to install a **spark screen** or **spark arrester** around the chimney cap. You may also want to install a **rain cap** on your chimney to prevent rain and snow from entering and causing the masonry to crumble.

Have a professional chimney sweep clean and inspect your chimney flues once a year. The spring is a good time, after you've been using the fireplace during the winter. Or have it done in the fall before you start using the fireplace again.

You may think that the lovely smell of wood smoke is the nicest thing about a fire. Unfortunately, wood smoke contains toxic chemicals and allergens and should be going up the chimney, not into the room. If your room smells of wood smoke while you are using your fireplace, have your chimney inspected immediately—don't wait for spring. You should also periodically touch the wall in front of the chimney to check for excessive heat. If it is very hot, have your chimney inspected immediately.

BURN THE RIGHT KIND OF WOOD: Do not burn wood that is green or wet; the wood should have been split and seasoned for six months to a year. It is preferable to burn hardwood logs (such as maple, yellow birch, oak, or elm), not softwood (such as cedar or pine). If you burn green wood, wet wood, or softwoods, you can get a build-up of creosote in the flue that can cause a chimney fire. You should also avoid burning only treated logs in your fireplace. If you use treated logs, do so only occasionally and alternate with natural firewood. If you don't, you can end up with a build-up of paraffin in your chimney, which is also flammable. Also avoid burning painted wood, pressure-treated wood, magazines, cardboard, and coloured paper such as comics. These materials give off toxic fumes.

Do not use lighter fluid or gasoline to get your fire started. Instead use newspaper and small pieces of kindling.

PROTECT AGAINST SPARKS: To protect against sparks and embers setting fire to your rug, floor, or furniture, use a **fireplace screen** or have **glass fireplace doors** installed. You should also have at least eighteen inches of protective tile, brick, or cement between the fireplace itself and wooden floors or carpets. If you don't, use a **hearth rug** made of 100 per cent pure virgin wool, which is naturally fire-resistant up to very high temperatures. Check for the woolmark symbol, as the wool must not be reprocessed. Alternatively, you can treat the carpet you already have with a flame-retardant spray, available at most hardware stores. Keep fireplace implements (tongs, poker, shovel) and heat-proof gloves beside the fireplace and use them to return hot embers that have fallen out to the fireplace. Keep a fire extinguisher handy (an all-purpose class ABC extinguisher or a class A extinguisher designed to put out wood and paper fires)—just in case.

Make sure a responsible person (if you can find one!) is always in the room when a fire is burning. Don't leave your home or go to bed while there are still flames or burning embers. Do not clean out the fireplace until the ashes are cold, and then put the ashes in a metal container outside your home.

Wood-burning Stoves

A wood-burning stove should be properly designed, and should be installed only by a qualified installer.

Have the chimney, flue pipes, and stove inspected regularly for creosote and soot build-up, as well as for ash. Check the colour of the smoke from the chimney; it should be either white or invisible. If it is blue or grey, or any other colour, this is a warning that the stove is improperly vented, or that a fire is smouldering, or that you are burning poor quality wood. (It does not mean that the College of Cardinals has not yet chosen a new Pope.)

As with a fireplace, do not burn softwood or green or wet wood. They may produce creosote that can cause a flash fire in your chimney. Use wood, preferably hardwood, that has been dried and seasoned for six months to a year.

Fire Prevention: Cooking

Fires very often start in the kitchen. You can use this as an excuse not to cook dinner ever again. But if it's cook or starve, take the reasonable precautions that follow.

Fire Extinguishers

Keep a dry chemical fire extinguisher (either an all-purpose class ABC extinguisher, or a class B extinguisher designed to put out grease fires) in the kitchen, in an easily accessible place. Keep it near an exit rather than near the stove. If it's too close to the stove, you may not be able to reach it if there is a stove fire. Make sure it's always in working order. The fire extinguisher should have a ULC seal (Underwriters' Laboratories of Canada). Know how to use the fire extinguisher—remember to **PASS**: **P**ull the pin, **A**im low, **S**queeze the handle, **S**weep from side to side. But don't attempt to fight the fire yourself unless it is very small. If you cannot put the fire out right away or if it is large when you first see it, get everyone out of your home and call the fire department.

You must inspect your fire extinguisher periodically to ensure that the pressure is right, the nozzle is not blocked, and the seal is not broken. The fire extinguisher comes with instructions from the manufacturer saying how often you should inspect. You should also regularly take your fire extinguisher for inspection and maintenance to a servicing agency recommended by the manufacturer. Your instruction manual will tell you how often to do this. If you have used or damaged your fire extinguisher, take it to a servicing agency immediately.

Stove and Oven Fires

Grease is a common cause of kitchen fires. Keep your stove and oven clean of grease, and don't forget to clean grease-traps, vents, and hood filters over the stove too. Any grease in the area will ignite if a fire starts.

STOVES: Do not leave oil or fat, or any food for that matter, on the stove to heat or cook unattended—even for one minute while you answer the phone or investigate why one of your children is strangling the other. Do not even leave a pan of fat or oil on a cold burner. Someone may accidentally turn on the burner. (We bet you're thinking right now who that someone in your household might be!)

If a grease fire breaks out in a pot or pan, you can smother the fire by covering the pan with a large lid. If you see smoke coming out of a covered pot, do not remove the lid because doing so may cause flames to leap out of the pot. Leave the cover on the pot and take the pot off the burner. Do not throw water or flour on a grease fire. The flames will spread rather than die out. Use your fire extinguisher or else throw baking soda or salt on the fire.

OVENS: Do not store anything in your oven. (What are you saving old pizza boxes for, anyway?) Do not use your oven for science experiments or arts and crafts projects, except for products specifically designed for use in a home oven. Do not use your oven as a dryer—especially not for your hair, or for clothing you are wearing at the time.

Do not keep flammable materials near the stove and oven. Find some-place else to keep cleaning supplies, grocery bags, magazines and cookbooks, aprons, potholders and towels, or your collection of wooden spoons. Don't hang curtains on a window near the stove. Instead use venetian blinds or shutters.

If a fire starts in your oven, turn off the oven, but do not open the door—that will only give the fire more oxygen to burn. (Keeping the door closed works on the same principle as the pot lid.) If you leave the door closed, the fire is more likely to die out on its own.

Microwave Oven Fires

Proper installation of your microwave can prevent some microwave fires. Make sure that your microwave is properly grounded by using a three-pronged plug. Do not block the air vents of your microwave; put the oven in a place where it has air space on top and on all sides.

Keep the oven clean of grease (more cleaning!), because you can end up with a grease fire in a microwave oven too. Do not put anything metal in the microwave, including metal bowls, metal-edged or metal-decorated bowls, metal cutlery, aluminum foil, and twist-ties. Metal will cause **sparking** (also known as **arcing**) in the oven. If you have a lot of sparking in your microwave, even though you've remembered not to put any metal in, or if the door does not seal tightly, have the microwave professionally inspected and repaired before using it again.

Don't use your oven as a dryer or to heat anything other than food, unless it's a product specifically designed for use in the microwave.

If a fire does start in your microwave, do not open the door until the flames are gone. As with a conventional oven, opening the door will simply give the fire more oxygen to burn. Instead, keep the door closed and unplug the unit.

Fire Prevention: Flammable Materials

Smoking and Matches

Smoking is not only bad for your health in the long run, it can be an immediate danger to you and those who live with you if you are careless. You should consider banning *all* smoking in your home. This decision is not only good for the health and safety of your household, but it may save you money on your insurance premiums. Ask your insurance agent if there is a reduced premium for non-smoking households. And, as a bonus, a no-smoking rule will cut down on your cleaning—you won't have to vacuum your smoke alarm as frequently!

If you must smoke in your home, never smoke in bed. Do not smoke anywhere if you are drowsy. If you fall asleep with a lighted cigarette, a sofa or chair can catch fire as easily as a bed. Set out lots of deep ashtrays and empty them regularly. Do not empty ashtrays into wastepaper baskets; empty them into a toilet or a metal container.

Do not smoke while you are using, or have just been using, flammable materials. Even such seemingly harmless products as hair spray, nail polish, or nail polish remover can catch fire.

Keep matches and cigarette lighters out of the reach of children. Train your children to hand over to an adult any matches or cigarette lighters that they may find.

If there is a power failure, do not use matches or a lighter to find your way around in the dark. Use a flashlight. Keep a flashlight on each floor of your home in an easy-to-find location (easy to find in the dark, that is), for this purpose. There are rechargeable flashlights on the market that are designed to stay plugged into an outlet. Some of them light up when there is a power failure.

Other Flammables

Most flammable materials are marked by this sign:
Examples of flammable materials are:

- hair spray
- nail polish
- nail polish remover
- cleaning fluid
- aerosol spray cans
- varnish
- paint
- paint stripper
- sealants
- gasoline
- lighter fluid

STORAGE OF FLAMMABLES: Do not store flammable products near any heat source, including the furnace and stove.

There are certain flammable materials that you should not store inside your home at all, such as gasoline, kerosene, or stove oil. The same holds true for rags that you have used to soak up paint, solvents, oil, fuel, glue, or any product that contains linseed oil. They may suddenly burst into flame. (This is known as **spontaneous combustion**.) Store them outside, if you feel you must keep and cherish them, or take them to a hazardous waste recycling depot.

Do not store trash and paper, or other materials that may burn, in your basement or attic or storeroom. While these things are not particularly flammable by themselves, they will act as fuel for any fire that has already started.

WASHERS AND DRYERS: Clean out the lint-collector in your clothes dryer every time you use the dryer, because the heat in the dryer can set it on fire. Also, check every now and then that the dryer exhaust pipe has no lint in it.

Do not dry foam rubber in the dryer. Do not use your washer or dryer to clean rags soaked in flammable liquids. And since we already told you not to store them in your home dirty, why don't you just throw them away?

CHRISTMAS TREES: Christmas trees can be a fire hazard. Set up your Christmas tree well away from any heat source, including heat vents and incandescent light bulbs. Keep your tree well watered so that it doesn't dry out. Not only will your tree look better longer, it will not turn into firewood while still in your home. Do not turn on your Christmas tree lights and then leave the room—either stay to enjoy them, or turn them off.

Precautions with Natural Gas Appliances

If you have natural gas appliances that require lighting with a match, in order to avoid a gas build-up that might explode you should light the match and put it by the gas valve before you turn on the gas. If you have appliances that have a pilot light, you should be aware that the fumes from flammable materials (see the list above) can be ignited by the pilot light. Turn off all pilot lights if you are using these materials, keep the area well ventilated while you use them, and do not re-light the pilot lights after you finish until all fumes are gone. This is especially important in basements.

CARBON MONOXIDE SAFETY

Carbon monoxide has been called the silent killer. Carbon monoxide is a colourless, odourless gas produced by burning when there is not enough oxygen present. It can be produced by cars and by appliances that run on natural gas, oil, or propane, including furnaces. High levels of carbon monoxide will cause convulsions, respiratory failure, coma—and death.

☑ Carbon Monoxide Safety Checklist

Prevention of carbon monoxide build-up

❑ Have your furnace professionally inspected and cleaned once a year.
❑ Don't leaving your car running in the garage.
❑ Don't use outdoor barbecues inside.
❑ Don't use a propane, kerosene, or butane heater inside.
❑ Let some air into your home!
❑ Consider buying a carbon monoxide detector.

If you suspect carbon monoxide poisoning

❑ Get fresh air immediately: open the windows, or better yet, go outside.
❑ Seek medical treatment.

Prevention of Carbon Monoxide Build-up

To prevent a build-up of carbon monoxide in your home:

- Let some air in, especially if your home is tightly sealed to conserve heat in the winter.
- If your garage is attached to your house, open the garage door before starting your car, and don't leave the car running in the garage.
- Never use any outdoor barbecue or grill (charcoal or propane) indoors.
- Never store a propane cylinder indoors, even if you are storing your propane barbecue indoors.
- Never use a propane, butane, or kerosene heater in your home, even for a very short period of time.
- Have your furnace and chimney checked by a heating-system professional once a year.
- Check that your fireplace has its own outside air source
- Have your fireplace chimneys inspected once a year. A blocked chimney can cause a build-up of carbon monoxide.
- Do not smother a fire in a fireplace or wood stove.
- If you have a propane refrigerator, make sure it is vented directly outdoors. If it is not vented outdoors, move it outdoors immediately. Even if it is vented outdoors, have it checked regularly by a certified propane fitter.

Carbon Monoxide Detectors

Carbon monoxide (CO) detectors are available at hardware stores and cost about $50 and up. They do not need to be professionally installed. They either plug in or run on batteries. They are similar to smoke alarms and are supposed to sound when carbon monoxide reaches an unsafe level in your home. Be sure to buy one that carries one of these approval seals: CGA (Canadian Gas Association), UL (Underwriters Laboratories Inc.), or ULC (Underwriters Laboratories of Canada). A CSA (Canadian Standards Association) seal alone is not sufficient because it only indicates that the device has been tested for electrical safety, not for its efficiency in detecting carbon monoxide. Install your carbon monoxide detector near bedrooms or sleeping areas.

Carbon Monoxide Poisoning

As we mentioned above, high levels of carbon monoxide will cause convulsions, respiratory failure, coma, and death. The symptoms of lower-level carbon monoxide poisoning are similar to those of the flu and can include a headache or tightness across the front of the head, weakness, dizziness, nausea, watering eyes, and loss of muscle control.

If you suspect carbon monoxide poisoning, get the victim into fresh air immediately. Open the windows, or better yet, get the victim outside. Then seek medical treatment.

ACCIDENT PREVENTION

Most accidents in the home can be prevented by doing the things your mother always told you to do, like watch where you're going and clean up after yourself. When you prevent accidents, you are not only protecting yourself and your family from injury, you are also protecting yourself from potential legal liability to any other person who might be hurt on your property.

The following checklist sets out the key steps to make your home safer. You will find more information on safety in the home after the checklist. If you do these things, your mother will be proud of you.

☑ Accident Prevention Checklist

❑ Make sure your street number is clearly visible from the street so that emergency vehicles can locate your home.

❑ Have a list of emergency telephone numbers close to your kitchen telephone.

❑ Keep your home well-enough lit, especially stairways, that people can see where they are going.

❑ Don't leave things that people can trip over or slip on, such as toys, electrical cords, loose rugs, bathroom and kitchen spills, or ice. In the winter, sprinkle salt, sand, or ashes at icy entrances.

❑ Provide sturdy support rails on stairways and in bathtubs and showers.

❑ Prevent scalding by setting your water heater at 130 degrees F (55 degrees C) or less.

❑ Install ground fault circuit interrupters in bathrooms and laundry rooms to prevent electrical shock.

❑ If you have a swimming pool or hot tub and young children or pets, consider an extra fence to enclose it separately.

❑ Consider installing specialized safety equipment to protect children.

What follows is a guided tour of your home, and the accidents which might happen unless you take steps to prevent them. Come on in (if you dare).

Entrance

In case you are not successful in preventing all accidents, it's a good idea to make sure your street number is clearly visible from the street at all times so that emergency vehicles will have no trouble locating it. Use dark numbers against a light wall, or light numbers against a dark wall. Illuminate the numbers with a light on a light sensor so that it comes on automatically at dusk. While we're on the subject of emergency telephone calls, keep a list of emergency telephone numbers near the main telephone so that no time is wasted looking these numbers up if there is an accident at your home.

You don't want people to slip or trip at your door. There are a number of things you can do to make your entrances safe. The area around the door should be well-lit so that people can see where they are going. Keep steps and porch in good repair. Sagging or missing boards should be replaced and any serious cracks or unevenness in the concrete repaired quickly. Keep the entrance way clear of snow and ice. (Can you believe this? You even have to clean outside!) It is a good idea to keep a container of sand, ashes or salt near the entrance so that you can sprinkle icy areas before someone slips. Wet leaves can be almost as dangerous as ice, so rake leaves away from your entrance.

Make sure there are protective railings on all steps, porches and decks, and that they are in good repair. Railings are not only a good idea, they may be required by the municipality depending on the number of steps there are.

Living Areas

If people make it safely through your entrance way, try not to put them into danger once they are inside. Highly polished floors of any kind (wood, tile or marble for example) are slippery, especially when they are wet. Consider covering these surfaces with a rug with non-skid backing. But beware! Having protected your family and guests from slipping, you may be setting them up to trip instead.

To prevent people tripping or slipping on scatter mats or area rugs, hold the mats in place with non-skid backings or double-sided carpet tape. Tidy up toys and other articles left lying around on the floor, so people don't trip over them either. Also, run electrical and telephone cords along the wall, not across the room where people might stumble over them.

To keep people from walking into sliding glass doors, which are hard to see if they're clean (finally, a situation where cleaning doesn't pay!), stick decals on them at adult and child eye-level.

Kitchen

Set-up

When you set up your kitchen, think about safety. If you are buying a stove, choose the one that has the safest controls for your family. If the controls are located at the front or side rather than on the back panel, you won't have to reach over the burners to get to them, but they may be within easy reach of young children. If you are buying an electric kettle, toaster or iron, choose one that has an automatic shut-off.

In arranging your cabinets, try not to place things you will need all the time on shelves out of easy reach. (For the 5-foot 2-inch authors of this book, this is anything above the first shelf.) Make sure your kitchen has a stable stool with four legs to allow the height-challenged to reach high shelves. Consider the risks of placing goodies out of the reach of your children. If you know that they will get to the goodies no matter where you put them, don't keep them where your children can injure themselves on the way, over the stove for example.

Maintenance

Once your kitchen is safely set up, make sure that you work safely in it. This involves (you guessed it) more cleaning. If you spill something on the floor, clean it up right away before you or somebody else slips in it. Do not leave cooking food or heating kettles on the stove unattended. Turn the handles of pots and pans in towards the centre of the stove, rather than out, so that you or your children do not accidentally knock them over. When you're cooking, don't wear clothes that hang loosely, especially in the sleeves, because they can get caught on pot handles or even catch on fire. Always make sure all burners and the oven are turned off when you've finished cooking.

Don't let the cord of any electrical appliance, especially a kettle, dangle over the counter so that the appliance can be pulled down. If a plugged-in electrical appliance falls into the water, do not put your hand into the water! Unplug the appliance immediately or cut off power to the circuit.

Stairs and Hallways

Stairs should have a solid hand-rail in good repair and should be well-lit. There should be a light switch at the top and at the bottom of the staircase. Do not use stair coverings that make it difficult to see where each step ends such as flowered or striped carpets or checkerboard tile. Repair or replace stair coverings that are loose or that have holes in them.

Put night lights in the hall and the bathroom, so that no one trips or runs into something when they're prowling around in the dark.

Bathroom

Slipping

Slipping is a common cause of injury in the bathroom. Most bathroom tile is slippery, and the more highly polished it is, the more slippery it is. Put a rubber-backed bath mat next to the bathtub, and clean up spills of water, soap or lotions on the bathroom floor right away. Install horizontal or angled grab bars in the bathtub or shower stall, and put down a rubber mat or rubber safety-strips on the bathtub or shower floor.

Scalding

Scalding is another common bathroom injury. The risk of scalding can be reduced by turning down the thermostat on your water heater to 55 degrees C (130 degrees F), or even less if there are young children or elderly people in the household. You can get a second-degree burn from two seconds of contact with water that is 65 degrees C (150 degrees F). Whatever temperature your thermostat is set at, it is wise to test the temperature of the water with your forearm before getting in or putting in a child.

Electrical Shock

Having safely escaped injury by slipping or scalding, you probably would also like to avoid injury by electrical shock. Don't plug in your hair dryer or electric razor if your hands are wet—and especially don't do this if all of you is wet, for instance if you are still in the bathtub. The shock you get may be your last. If your plugged-in hair dryer or razor or any other electrical appliance falls into the water, do not put your hand into the water. Unplug the appliance immediately.

Have an electrician install a **ground fault circuit interrupter** in bathrooms and your laundry room. This device will not prevent a shock altogether, but it will interrupt the power fast enough to prevent a fatal shock.

Basement

If you have a basement that you use only for storage, it is very easy to take an "out of sight out of mind" attitude towards it. Keep in mind however, that you will have to venture down those stairs some time, and that you should follow the same safety guidelines there as you do in the rest of a house. Your basement stairs should be solid, with a sturdy handrail, and well-lit. Store your possessions so that you don't fall on them and they don't fall on you.

Outdoors

Inspection

Inspect the garden and outside of your home several times a year, and following any major storms, to make sure that there are no objects which are likely to fall, such as bricks, shingles, eavestroughing, shutters, antennas and satellite dishes, wires and tree branches.

Ladders

If you use a ladder during your inspection, be very careful! Lean it against a solid wall or tree (instead of against your next-door neighbour who's giving you a hand), with the feet on solid ground. Place the feet of the ladder a distance of one quarter of the ladder's length away from the wall. Make sure that the ladder is not touching overhead electric wires.

If you have a wooden ladder, check to see that it won't give way as you climb. Before you use the ladder, lay it on the ground and walk along the rungs to test that each rung will support your weight. Don't stand on the top rung of a ladder, and don't lose your balance trying to get at something that's just a bit out of reach.

If you don't have a good head for heights, or you get dizzy sometimes, stay off ladders completely.

Swimming Pools and Hot Tubs

If you're putting in a backyard swimming pool or hot tub, check with your municipality about fencing. You will almost certainly be required to install a locked fence of a minimum height around your entire yard. Consider fencing the pool or hot tub area separately following those municipal standards. If you have young children, this arrangement will provide a separate play space in the yard. In addition, you may not have to meet those municipal standards for the fencing around the rest of your yard. No matter how you fence your pool or hot tub, keep the gates locked at all times.

A pool is a year-round source of danger. Even when the pool is closed for the season, it still contains water. Most winter pool covers will not prevent someone from falling into the water, they will just prevent others from seeing that person. (There are pool covers designed to be walked on safely, but they require special installation and are very expensive.) Keep lifesaving equipment and a telephone close to your pool summer and winter in case of an emergency.

Decks

If you have an outdoor deck, inspect it regularly. Loose or rotting boards should be replaced, as should rickety railings. Don't forget to check the supporting timbers under the deck. Even pressure treated wood or cedar will eventually rot and have to be replaced. The lifespan of the average deck is between ten and twenty years.

Garden Tools

Even outside, it is important to pick up after yourself. There's just no escape from cleaning, is there? Don't leave hoses, rakes, clippers or other gardening tools where they can cause injury.

Special Tips for Parents of Young Children

There is specialized safety equipment designed for the protection of young children. These include:

- window guards to prevent windows from opening far enough for a child to get through and fall
- safety latches for cupboard and other doors
- childproof covers for electrical outlets
- childproof barriers for the top and bottom of staircases

Here are some additional tips—by no means a complete list—for making your home safer for your little ones:

- Make sure that the vertical bannister supports on stairs are not spaced so widely apart that a child's head can get caught between them.
- Keep all medications, household cleaning supplies, and anything else you do not want your child to eat in high or locked cupboards.
- Don't put heavy objects such as plant pots, aquariums, or televisions on stands that are not stable and sturdy.
- To reduce the risk of accidental strangulation, shorten venetian blind and drapery cords so that they cannot be reached by young children.

PREVENTING WATER DAMAGE

Although every spring brings news coverage of rivers flooding residential districts, most water damage to homes is caused by clogging or freezing of pipes.

Freezing

Inside Pipes

If the temperature drops below freezing inside your home for an extended period, your pipes may freeze and burst. If the inside temperature does drop, prevent pipes from freezing by turning on your taps just enough to keep a little water flowing out, because running water is not as likely to freeze. If you own a house and are going to be away in the winter, arrange for someone to come in daily to check that the temperature in your house remains above freezing. If you don't, your homeowner's insurance policy will probably not cover damage due to freezing if you have been away for more than four days.

Outside Taps

If you have outside taps, the water pipes leading from the inside to those taps may freeze unless the tap is shut off and properly drained. Before the arrival of cold weather, turn off the inside tap controlling the flow to each outside tap. Then, because water may still be left in the pipe, open the outside tap and leave it open to allow room for expansion if the water freezes.

Clogging

To prevent your pipes from clogging, don't let food or fat go down your kitchen drain unless the drain is equipped with a garbage disposal system, and don't let hair go down your bathroom drains. If you do have a clog, use a plunger. Use caustic chemical drain cleaners with care because some of them (for example, those containing lye) may eat through your pipes as well as through the clog. Don't try to clear a clog by sticking wire down the drain, because you may make a hole in the pipe. If you can't clear the clog with a plunger or a drain cleaner (use one or the other, not both) it's best to call a plumber.

Know where your home's **main water shut-off valve** is, and mark it clearly so that anyone can turn it off if pipes flood. Keep a pair of pliers nearby in case the valve is stuck. If a toilet is overflowing or a sink faucet gushing, there is also usually a shut-off valve at each sink and toilet.

Shut off the electric power supply before entering a flooded room, or there is a chance you could be electrocuted. If the main circuit controls are located in the room that is flooded, call your local electric company to switch off the power.

"TO DO" LISTS

As you probably noticed, home safety means a lot of work. Many of the home safety steps set out in this chapter need to be taken only once, soon after you've moved into your new home. For the ongoing tasks, get into the habit of following a home safety timetable. Taking safety precautions will seem less overwhelming if you choose a particular day of the month to do routine safety maintenance and if you spread your annual safety checks out over the whole year (instead of over one nightmarish weekend). To help you, the following "To Do" lists organize tasks by how important they are and how often they need to be done.

☑ To Do Immediately

❑ Install smoke alarms.

❑ Plan a fire escape route.

❑ Buy a fire extinguisher (all-purpose class ABC, or class B for grease fires).

❑ Have your electrical wiring inspected if you live in an older home and did not have the wiring looked at when you moved in—or if you have had any problems with electricity in your home.

❑ Look around your home to make sure that no heat source has flammable materials near it.

❑ Put a list of emergency telephone numbers near your main telephone.

❑ Make sure your street number can be seen easily from the street by day or night.

❑ Turn down the thermostat on your water heater to 55 degrees C (130 degrees F).

❑ Install ground fault circuit interrupters in bathrooms and the laundry room.

❑ Keep life-saving equipment and a telephone near your swimming pool all year round.

☑ To Do Monthly

❑ Test smoke alarms and batteries.

❑ Clean smoke alarms.

❑ Inspect your fire extinguishers.

❑ Replace furnace filters during heating season.

❑ Vacuum up the dust around your furnace during heating season.

☑ To Do Once a Year

Fall

- ❏ Turn off inside valves for outside water taps and leave outside taps open.
- ❏ Have your furnace professionally inspected.
- ❏ Have your fireplace and chimney professionally inspected and cleaned.
- ❏ Vacuum furnace vents on each floor of the house.

Winter

- ❏ Prepare containers of sand, salt, or ashes to set out near each entrance to your home.
- ❏ Keep your Christmas tree watered.

Spring

- ❏ Inspect the outside of your home for damage to bricks, roofing, and eavestroughing.
- ❏ Inspect your garden for trees or branches that may fall.

Summer

- ❏ Take a break.

Things Not to Do—Ever!

- Do not throw water on a grease fire.
- Do not throw water on a fire involving a plugged-in electrical appliance.
- Do not use oversized fuses.
- Do not open an oven door if there is a fire in the oven.
- Do not smoke in bed or when you are sleepy.
- Do not use flammable materials around any flame, including cigarettes and pilot lights.
- Do not try to start a fire with gasoline, lighter fluid, or other flammable.
- Do not use an outdoor barbecue indoors.
- Do not use a propane, kerosene, or butane heater indoors.
- Do not leave a car running in the garage.
- Do not use an electrical appliance when you are wet.
- Do not put your hand into water in which a plugged-in electrical appliance has fallen.
- Do not leave water or spills on bathroom, kitchen, or entrance floors.

Well, you made it safely to the end of the chapter! Take a five-minute break until your panic attack passes. Then get started on your home safety improvement plan—and don't forget your cleaning!

EMERGENCY PHONE NUMBERS

If an emergency arises in your household, you don't want to waste time looking up phone numbers. Fill out this list of emergency phone numbers right away. Securely attach one copy next to each telephone in the house. Keep a copy with your cell phone too.

Emergency Phone Numbers List

Fire Department
Police
Ambulance

Poison Control Centre
Natural Gas Company
Family Doctor
Pediatrician
Emergency Veterinary Services

Family Member #1 to Contact
Family Member #2 to Contact
Family Member #3 to Contact

Nearest Neighbour #1
Nearest Neighbour #2
Nearest Neighbour #3

Municipal Water Emergencies
24-hour Plumber
Hydro Company
Taxi
Stress Counsellor/Travel Agent

14 VISITORS WELCOME AND UNWELCOME

Y ou've moved in, unpacked, renovated, made your home safe and secure, and now you are ready to receive guests. Before you mail out your housewarming party invitations, you should know that you have responsibilities to your guests, to the mail carrier who delivers their replies, and to the caterer who will bring in the food. You may also have responsibilities to the guy who crashes your party and the burglar who tries to steal your housewarming gifts.

WHO CAN COME ONTO YOUR PROPERTY?

There are people you want on your property and others you don't. You need to know whom you can keep off your property (and how).

Welcome Guests

If you invite someone to your home, that person has a right to come onto your property and into your home, and then has the right to stay there until you say it's time to leave. Once you've told your guest to leave, he or she must do so as soon as possible and must take the most direct route out. A guest who does not leave when ordered becomes a **trespasser**, and you have the right to remove him or her—by force, if necessary. (Clearly, this is not an etiquette book that you're reading—Emily Post would not approve of taking this approach with your guests.) Don't go overboard in the force department. You can't injure your now-unwanted guest, you can only push or carry your guest off the premises. (If you think you may have to resort to carrying your guests out the door, it would be wise not to serve them a heavy dinner.)

People with a Right to Be There

There are certain people who have a legal right to be on your property (some even have the right to come into your home) even though you do not specifically invite them.

There may be telephone, cable TV, or electrical wires that run across your neighbours' land and yours to provide service to the homes in your area. The utility companies probably have an **easement** over your land (and your neighbours') which allows the companies to have their wires there. Their easement also allows employees of the utility companies to come onto your property to service the wires. These employees don't need your permission each time they come onto your property.

If someone nearby is having a land survey done and the land surveyors have to come onto your property to complete the survey, they can do so without your permission.

In the case of an emergency, police, firefighters, and other emergency workers have the right to come onto your land and even into your home if it's necessary to save lives or property or to pursue an escaping criminal. If it's not an emergency, these people need your permission, a search warrant, or court order to come onto your land or into your home.

People with a Reason to Be There

There are people who arrive at your door unexpectedly but who have perfectly legitimate reasons to be there—people like the Girl Guide selling cookies, the political canvasser, and the door-to-door salesperson. While these people have no right to enter your home without your permission, they do have the right to make their way to your door. If you tell them to leave, they must get off your property as soon as possible and by the most direct route. If they don't, they become trespassers, and you can remove them by force. If you have to use force, use only the minimum amount of force necessary to get them off your property.

People with No Good Reason to Be There

Some people may come onto your property for reasons that have nothing to do with you at all—they're not trying to sell you anything or deliver anything to you. They come onto your property for their own purposes—to take a shortcut, to pick your flowers, or to snowmobile in your field. These people have no legal right to be there. They are trespassers from the moment they set foot on your property, even if they did not use force to enter and are not threatening you in any way. You can remove these people by force, but only after you have told them to leave and they haven't left immediately. Even if you've posted a "No Trespassing" sign to keep such people out, you must tell them to leave before you use force to remove them. Use only the minimum amount of force necessary to get them off your property.

The rules are different if someone uses force to get onto your property or has come there to commit a crime. You don't need to tell a burglar to leave before using force to get rid of him. If the person is only after your property and is not threatening you or any other person, you may only use as much force as necessary to remove the intruder. You may not unnecessarily injure the intruder—your guard dog may bite him, and you may hit him if you have to, but you shouldn't beat him to a pulp or shoot him.

If the intruder is threatening you or any other person, you have the right to use force, not only to get the intruder off your property, but to protect yourself or another. You should not use any more force than is reasonably necessary to defend yourself, but the law allows you to use a greater amount of force to protect lives than to protect property. If you have good reason to think that your life is in danger, you can even kill the intruder.

Even though the law may give you the right to use force to get people off your property, you should only do it as a last resort. Your first choice should always be to call the police.

WHAT CAN YOU DO TO KEEP PEOPLE OUT?

There are limits to what you can do to keep people off your property. You can put up signs that say "No Trespassing" (to keep everyone out) or "No Soliciting" (to keep salespeople out) or "No Canvassing" (to keep political candidates and volunteers for charity out); these signs will discourage some people but not everyone. You can fence your property. You can keep a dog on your property.

You can't deliberately harm people in trying to keep them off. You cannot set a deadly trap, such as a gun that would automatically go off at someone who climbed your fence or broke into your home. And your fence or dog must be designed to keep people out rather than to trap them there once they're inside.

WHAT CAN YOU DO IF SOMEONE GETS IN?

What you do if someone gets onto your property or into your home depends on whether or not the situation is an emergency.

If It's an Emergency

If you have an intruder in your home or on your property, call the police if you feel at all threatened by the person's presence. Some kinds of trespass are criminal offences, for example, trespassing at night, or standing on your property and looking through your windows at any time.

If It's Not an Emergency

You may be able to lay charges against someone who trespasses on your property. It is a provincial offence for someone to trespass at your home in Alberta, British Columbia, Manitoba, Nova Scotia, Ontario, and Prince Edward Island. If someone trespasses on your property repeatedly, or if someone trespasses and damages your property, you might want to lay a charge—if you know who the trespasser is. Contact the police for information about how to lay a charge. (They might do it for you.) If the trespasser is convicted of the offence, he or she may have to pay a fine. In British Columbia, Nova Scotia, Ontario, and Prince Edward Island, a convicted trespasser may also be ordered to compensate you for any damage done to your property.

You have the right to sue someone who trespasses on your property. (As with laying a charge, you have to identify the trespasser first.) If you win the lawsuit, a court may order the trespasser to pay you compensation for any actual damage caused to your property and for interference with your enjoyment of your property. If the trespass has been frequently repeated, the court may give you an **injunction**, an order telling the person to stop trespassing. If you've acquired a frequent trespasser, you should ask your lawyer for advice about what to do. But unless the damage to your property is major or the trespasser is a neighbour who is trying to get a claim of some kind over your property, it's probably not worth the time, money, and aggravation to start a lawsuit.

HOW SHOULD YOU TREAT THE PEOPLE WHO COME IN?

What do you do with the people who do come onto your property, whether you invited them or not? How you treat these people is more than a matter of etiquette and courtesy—it's a matter of law. This area of law is called **occupier's liability**. It is a very complex and confusing area of the law (are there any other kinds?), especially since it's slightly different in every province.

You're more responsible to some kinds of visitors than to others, and we could tell you about the fine distinctions that lawyers and judges love to make between "classes of visitors." But it's best to treat everyone (except maybe an intruder) with the highest level of care that the law requires of you. When someone comes to your door, you can't tell what class of visitor he or she belongs to, and even if you could, you're just going to have one standard of safety in your home anyway. The legal distinctions between visitors only come into play when you're standing in a courtroom defending a lawsuit started by somebody who was injured on your property.

So—What's Your Responsibility?

You have some responsibility for the safety of everyone who comes on your property—even a trespasser. (You have less responsibility to a trespasser—but more about that later.)

As a homeowner, you hope that nobody will be hurt on your property. And if someone is, you hope like hell that you can't be successfully sued. The way to avoid both injury and lawsuit is to treat everyone who comes on your property with the highest level of care that the law requires. This is what the level of care is:

You must take reasonable care to make sure that anyone on your
property will be reasonably safe.

That's not particularly helpful, is it? The law is intentionally vague so that there's room to compensate people who are injured, through no fault of their own, on other people's property. A judge may have to choose between protecting you (who have homeowner's insurance—see Chapter 8) and helping the injured person who has bills to pay. Assuming neither you nor the injured person did anything wrong, what choice would you make if you were the judge?

If you take reasonable steps to make your home and property safe for yourself and your family, you reduce the chance of anyone being injured there. We gave you advice on how to make and keep your home safe in Chapter 13 on home safety. If you make your home safe and someone is hurt anyway, in theory you should be protected from legal responsibility for that person's injuries. Keep in mind, though, that nothing can prevent a person injured on your property from suing you. And if a lawsuit gets as far as a trial, the judge may want to help the injured person by awarding him or her **damages** (money compensation) that you—or your insurance company—will have to pay.

Here are some examples of situations where homeowners have had to pay damages when someone was injured. In each case the homeowner did not take reasonable care to make sure that people were safe on the premises. The homeowners failed to

- remove snow and ice from steps
- repair a stairway railing
- warn that a floor was freshly waxed and slippery

(Because you read and took to heart Chapter 13 on home safety, we know that you would never be this careless.)

You can be ordered to pay damages if someone is injured because you didn't fix dangerous conditions that you knew about (or that you didn't at least warn your visitors about). You could even be ordered to pay damages if you didn't know about the danger but you should have known about the danger. A homeowner is required to inspect his or her premises to find out if something needs fixing—and then to fix it.

What If a Person Is On Your Property Without Your Permission?

Lots of people come onto your property without your specific permission. For most of them—for example, the mail carrier, the Girl Guide selling cookies, and the political candidate who's asking for your vote—you have the same responsibility to keep them reasonably safe that you have towards invited guests.

Your responsibility is different to trespassers. There are special rules that apply to burglars and to people like snowmobilers, dirt-bike riders, and skate-boarders who use your property without your permission. While you don't have to keep them reasonably safe, you can't deliberately harm them more than is necessary to remove them from your property. You also can't create a danger with the intention of harming anyone who might trespass. You can't put up obstacles or traps designed to injure these people if they get onto your property.

What About Children Who Come Onto Your Property Without Permission?

If you have something on your property that you know is likely to attract children yet could be dangerous, such as a swimming pool or playground equipment, you either have to take effective steps to keep children off your property or you must make sure that children will be safe if they get on your property—even if they get onto your property by trespassing.

It is not enough for you to post warning or "No Trespassing" signs. You have to put up a fence capable of keeping the children out. When it comes to swimming pools, most municipalities have by-laws requiring them to be surrounded by locked fences of a minimum height. If you don't have a child-proof fence and you have playground equipment, you have to make sure that your equipment is reasonably designed and maintained to prevent injuries to children.

SOCIAL HOSTS AND DRUNK DRIVERS

What if you have a party and serve your guests alcohol, and one of your guests is in a car accident on the way home? Will you be held legally responsible to the guest or anyone your guest injures?

In some places in the United States, the answer is yes. Homeowners have been ordered to pay damages to people who have been injured in an accident caused by the drunken guest. In Canada, homeowners have been sued but no court has yet held a homeowner responsible. To make sure that you're not the first homeowner held responsible, don't let your guests drive away if you have any doubt at all about their ability to drive. Call them a cab, have a sober guest drive them, or let them sleep at your home.

ANIMAL VISITORS

Some unwanted visitors have more than two legs. What you can do to try to keep them out or to get rid of them depends on whether the animals are domestic or wild. What will work is another matter altogether.

Your Neighbour's Animals

If fate is good to you, you will never have your neighbours' dogs and cats digging up your garden or using your children's sandbox as a toilet. Fate only smiles on some people, and unfortunately, controlling your neighbours' animals is really a matter of controlling your neighbours.

If you find a dog or cat in your yard or on your lawn, it may be that the animal has escaped from its owner and is lost. The owner will probably be delighted if you return the pet. If you don't know who the owner is, you can call the Humane Society or your municipality's animal control department to pick the animal up and take it to the local shelter, or you can take the animal there yourself.

But a neighbour may let his dog or cat wander loose around the neighbourhood even though many municipalities in the country prohibit this. What can you do if your home is on the animal's daily route?

- If you can figure out whose dog or cat it is, you can consider talking to the animal's owner. However polite you try to be, confronting a neighbour with a complaint about her pet is likely to be awkward.

- You can call the municipal animal control department. They may come and pick the animal up, they may speak to the animal's owner, or they may do nothing. Even if you make the call anonymously, your neighbour may suspect that it was you (especially if you previously complained to your neighbour directly).

- You can fence your property. If you weren't planning on having a fence for any other reason, this is a very expensive solution. Fences work better at keeping out dogs than cats.

- There are various chemical sprays on the market that are designed to discourage dogs and cats from coming onto your property without harming the animal. You have to keep reapplying the sprays and they're not very effective. Ask at your hardware store about animal-repellent sprays.

- You can shout at the animal and chase it every time you see it. You can even spray the animal with your garden hose (this works quite well with cats). After the animal encounters your wrath a few times, it may finally get the idea that it should visit elsewhere.

- Try not to attract the animals to your property. Don't leave your garbage outside in garbage bags. Keep it in your garage or in an animal-proof container.

- If the animal is using your property as a toilet, consider collecting the droppings (if you have the stomach for it) and dumping them on the pet owner's lawn, either singly or in a batch. (If you catch a dog in the act and it's accompanied by its owner at the time, try politely offering the owner a plastic bag for clean up purposes.) Many municipalities have "stoop and scoop" by-laws that require dog owners to clean up after their dogs. Contact the by-law department of your municipality to ask them if they have such a by-law and how it's enforced.

- Unless you want regular visits, don't feed neighbourhood animals.

As much as you may want to, you cannot harm or kill the animal. Not only is it illegal but, in trying to kill the animal, you may injure a child or your own pet. And sorry, but you can't harm or kill the animal's owner either.

Wild Animals

You don't have to go to the country to find wild animals in their natural habitat. There are probably more wild animals of certain kinds living in Canadian towns and cities than in the woods and fields. Stop thinking about how to get rid of your animal neighbours permanently, though—the most you can do is to get them out of your home and keep them from getting back in. And if they're just in your garden or the ravine behind your home, all you can do is prevent them from moving inside with you. Other than that, you'll have to learn to live in peace with them.

Keep your distance from wild animals, even when they're sharing an address with you. Any wild animal that is cornered or feels threatened may attack. Furthermore, rabies exists everywhere in Canada (except the Pacific coast of British Columbia) and is always fatal without early treatment. Make sure your pets are vaccinated against rabies. If you are bitten or scratched by a wild animal, speak to your physician.

Don't Let Wild Animals into Your Home in the First Place

It is easier to keep wild animals out of your home than to get rid of them once they've decided to move in. While, for the most part, outdoor animals prefer to live outdoors, there are certain times of the year when your home will seem particularly attractive to them. Field mice like to move inside for the winter, and squirrels and raccoons look for indoor accommodations during the spring nesting season. To keep raccoons, skunks, squirrels and bats or what have you from taking up residence in your attic, crawl space, chimney, or under your deck or porch, you should do the following:

- Cap chimneys.
- Screen open vents and soffit intersections with rust-proof screening.
- Repair holes or cracks in foundations or siding immediately.
- Repair holes in your roof and eaves immediately.
- Enclose the bottom of your porch or deck so that animals can't get underneath.
- Keep your garage and shed closed at all times, and check that there are no holes or weak spots where an animal can get in.
- Keep trees near your house trimmed back, and take down your unused TV tower so that animals who are aerial artists can't jump onto your roof.
- Keep your garbage in animal-proof containers—use metal or heavy plastic containers with a cover that cannot be easily removed (a twist-top cover, or one secured by a bungee cord), and store the containers in a rack, or tied into an upright position so that animals can't tip them over.
- Store your garbage in your garage or in a shed and make sure the doors and windows are closed tight.
- Do not put your garbage out the night before collection since animals often prefer to dine on your garbage at night.

- Ask neighbours to make their garbage animal-proof too.
- Maintain your lawn properly so that it doesn't get grubs (a favourite food of raccoons and skunks).

Evict Them If They Get In

If, in spite of your best efforts, animals do move into your home, get rid of them either yourself (we offer some tips below) or with the help of a wildlife removal service. Once you do get rid of them, unless you want to get rid of them again and again you should identify all potential entrance points and animal-proof them.

If you think that the animal living in your home might be a mother with dependent babies, don't try to evict the family until the babies are old enough to leave on their own (nesting season is late winter to early summer). This is not just soft-heartedness. If the babies are not old enough to leave on their own, they probably won't leave at all. If you evict the mother and the babies starve to death, you will then have to deal with the smell of— well, you get the picture.

If you want to try to evict the animal yourself, locate the entry to the animal's nest. Then, when the animal has left on an errand, do these three things all together:

- Put a transistor radio in the nest or near the entry, tune it to a talk station, and turn the volume up high.
- Put a commercial animal repellent (or you can use cayenne pepper or naphtha flakes) in the nest or entry way.
- Point a bright flood light or spot light at the entry.

Most animals will not want to live under these conditions for long. To find out if your animal has left, roll up some paper into a ball and put it in the entry way (don't plug the entry with the paper, though). Check the entry daily. If the ball has been pushed out, it means that the animal has left but it doesn't necessarily mean the animal has left permanently. Put the ball back into the entry and check it again the next day. Continue checking and putting the ball back until the ball hasn't been moved for two full days. Then, you can be fairly sure that the animal has left the nest.

Once the animal has left, put on a pair of rubber gloves and clean out the nest. (This is another reason to use an animal removal service—they'll do the cleaning for you.) Take away the repellent, the radio, and the bright lights. To make sure the animal does not get back in, seal up the entry to the nest with thick wire mesh that animals can't chew through. To be effective around a foundation or a deck, the wire may need to go down into the ground—as much as three feet for raccoons. If you don't like the look of the mesh, you can cover it with whatever material goes best with the rest of the wall or the porch (brick, wood, etc.). While you're at it, check for other likely entrances and seal them up too.

If you use a wildlife removal service, they will evict your animal and identify and seal up possible entrances. They may not take the animal away, though. In some urban areas, wild animals that have been trapped have to be released in the area. That's because it turns out that trapping and relocating is both cruel and ineffective. A trapped animal will probably injure itself trying to escape from the trap, and will likely die when relocated to a new territory. And sending one animal away doesn't help very much...if your animal were released in Greenland instead of your back yard it would just be replaced by a couple of its cousins who'd been living across the street but were on the lookout for better digs. You can't win this battle.

If your animal was nesting in a chimney, have a chimney sweep inspect and clean out the chimney before you cap it. If it was nesting in your walls or attic (especially if it was a squirrel), have an electrician check your wiring because it may have been nibbled on.

Pests

If the wildlife with which you are sharing your home are of the insect or vermin variety, you have our permission to use deadly force to get rid of them. Depending on the nature of the pest, the seriousness of the infestation, and your own bloodlust, you can call an exterminator or take on the beasts yourself. Your local hardware store will be able to recommend the appropriate pest removal products.

If you have an infestation of carpenter ants, termites, or rats, you should call your municipality, which may help you to get rid of them.

Pests

In this section we'll tell you about various pests and

- why you don't want them around
- where to look for them
- how to avoid them in the first place

ants (the kind that don't chew wood)

- They can carry disease.
- Inspect your kitchen counter; they may be marching into your sugar bowl.

- Clean up food crumbs and spills; keep food (especially sweet food) in sealed containers; close off possible outside entry points, such as cracks and holes around doors and windows.

carpenter ants

- They tunnel in wood and can cause structural damage to your home; they can carry disease; they bite.
- Inspect damp areas of your home for chewed wood that looks like sawdust; look for black ants 6 to 13 mm long.
- Keep your home well ventilated and dry; do not store firewood inside your home; do not leave lumber, logs, or other wood lying around your property; keep food in sealed containers, and clean up crumbs and spills immediately.

carpet beetles

- They eat wool, fur, and animal hair (we're talking fur coats rather than your pooch).
- Inspect clothing and carpets regularly for holes; inspect furs and brushes made of animal hair for uneven surfaces; keep an eye out for oval black beetles 3 to 5 mm long.
- Keep your home clean and free of other pests since beetles also feed on dead insects.

clothes moths

- They eat wool and fur.
- Inspect clothing and carpets regularly for holes; inspect furs for loose and clipped hairs; have a fit if you find a beige or golden moth, or a larvae tube, among your woollen clothes or on your carpet.
- Clean clothing, furs, and carpets regularly; inspect used furniture or clothing before you bring them into your home; if you're away from home, inspect any bureau or closet before you put your clothes into it.

cockroaches

- They spread disease (and your mother-in-law will think less of you).
- Inspect cupboards for dead cockroaches or for black ground-pepper-like droppings; even if you've never seen a cockroach before, you will instinctively recognize it when you see your first. Remember this ancient wisdom: there is no such thing as one cockroach.
- Keeping your kitchen and the rest of your house clean will help to reduce a cockroach infestation if one gets started—but a cockroach can live very happily on a drop of water and the glue in the spine of a book, so try to keep them out by inspecting food, including produce, packages, and boxes that have held food, as you bring it into your home.

fleas

• They transmit disease; their bite can cause an allergic reaction.
• Watch pets for scratching and examine their skin for ground-pepper-like flea droppings (if your pet has a bad case of fleas, you may actually see a flea—but even adult fleas spend some of their time away from their host); watch yourself for itchy red bites; put on a pair of white socks and walk around your carpets (you'll see the fleas jumping if they're in your carpet).
• Keep pets from starting a flea infestation by using flea-collars, flea-pills, or flea shampoos (speak to your veterinarian); do not allow stray or wild animals to sleep in or near your home.

flies

• They carry disease.
• They'll be buzzing around your kitchen.
• Keep doors and windows shut or screened; keep garbage and food debris in closed containers, and empty the containers to your outdoor garbage cans often.

mice

• They spread disease and parasites.
• Inspect for droppings near food and for gnawed holes in food bags and boxes.
• Keep possible food sources (human food, pet food, birdseed, etc.) in sealed jars or tins, and keep garbage in sealed containers; close up or block with steel wool all possible outside mouse entry points, particularly spaces around doors and around outside water taps—a mouse can get through a very small hole or crack.

rats

• They spread disease and can gnaw through electrical wires and wood—and they bite.
• Inspect for droppings, gnaw marks, and greasy marks on walls.
• Keep possible food sources (human food, pet food, birdseed, etc.) in sealed jars or tins, and keep garbage in sealed containers; close up possible outside rat entry points (they need more room to get in than mice do); keep your home free of possible nesting sites, like rubbish in your basement or attic.

spiders

• They're actually beneficial since they eat other insects (the two poisonous North American species, the Black Widow and the Brown Recluse, are rarely seen in Canada), but there are limits to the number and size of spiders most people are willing to put up with.

- If you are afraid of spiders, you don't have to look for them—they'll find you; otherwise look around windows, lighting fixtures, and ceiling corners.
- Vacuum, dust, and "disturb" your house regularly; keep your home free of other insects; clean your basement and crawl spaces; get rid of wood piles and litter, which are attractive nesting sites, and cut high grass around your home.

termites

- They chew wood.
- Inspect for runways or tunnels over the surface of wood; inspect for chewed wood that looks like sawdust; check for infested wood by probing beams with a sharp instrument (the wood will be spongy or almost hollow).
- Keep your home well ventilated and dry; do not store firewood inside your home; do not leave lumber, logs, or other wood lying around your property; remove dead trees and rotting decks and porches.

wasps and hornets

- Wasps and hornets sting (and may cause a fatal allergic reaction in some individuals), and if you disturb their nest they can swarm and sting in great numbers (which can be fatal even if you have no allergies); they also hang around parties and won't leave when asked.
- They can build their nests in the ground or in rock gardens, under or behind steps, under the eaves of a building, in cracks in a house's siding or foundations; they can also build nests in trees (the nest looks like it's made from greyish mummy wrappings).
- If you have fruit trees, clean up fallen fruit immediately; clean up any garbage that would attract wasps or hornets (especially any sweet food or drinks); seal off holes and cracks in the exterior of your home or in your deck or garden where wasps or hornets might want to build a nest.

This is not a complete list of pests. You may be visited by other insects, such as sowbugs, silverfish, and earwigs, none of which will cause you much harm. (Despite their threatening appearance and their unpleasant habit of dropping onto your head when you least expect it, earwigs are not harmful to humans—only to garden plants.) If you have these or any other pests, ask at your hardware store for a product that will rid you of them, or call an exterminator.

Now that you've got rid of your unwanted visitors, it's time to get out of your home—and do battle with your neighbours. In the next chapter, we'll talk about problems you may have with the people who live next door and nearby.

15 NIGHTMARES WITH THE NEIGHBOURS

W hen you were choosing your home, we told you to pay close attention to the neighbourhood and your neighbours. We told you to look for people who are quiet and who take good care of their homes. People like this may or may not turn out to be your best friends, but at least they probably won't annoy you.

If you did not choose your neighbours wisely (or if the lovely people next door move and are replaced by the neighbours from hell), there are more ways than you can imagine for them to make your life miserable—as you will see.

When you have problems with your neighbours, there are different options available for dealing with them, ranging from a friendly chat to a lawsuit to a fistfight. Whatever option you choose, we want to warn you from the outset that it may not be easy. Even when the situation and your rights are clear, and you are being reasonable and civilized, the reaction you get from your neighbour may not be what you hope for. It is only human nature for people to become defensive (and even nasty) when confronted with a complaint about themselves.

Sometimes, no matter what you do, you won't be able to make the problem go away. In fact, trying to solve the problem may create other problems with your neighbour. In any situation, you will have to weigh your options. When we set out options for you to consider, keep in mind the following:

- Whether we mention it or not, doing nothing is always an option.
- If you contact a lawyer, it doesn't necessarily mean starting a lawsuit—a lawyer will first try to solve the problem without litigation.
- If you win a lawsuit and the court orders your neighbour to pay you money, it's up to you to collect the money—officials like the sheriff will help you, but don't think that the judge just hands you a wad of cash at the end of the trial.
- Whatever you decide to do, you're going to have to continue to live with your neighbour—unless one of you moves.

NUISANCES AND ANNOYANCES

How can your neighbours annoy you? Let us count the ways. Your neighbours can

- hold loud parties
- yell at each other on their driveway
- own a dog that barks and howls all day and all night
- keep chickens, plus a rooster that crows (and not only at sunrise)
- have young children who seem to be screaming all the time
- have older children who believe they are disc jockeys broadcasting to the neighbourhood
- run an air-conditioner that clanks, whines, and thumps
- tear up their driveway with a jackhammer

Or your neighbours may be quiet but they

- cook smelly fish every day
- sit on their balcony smoking cigars whose stink wafts over onto your balcony
- have seventy-two cats and never change the cat litter

Then again, your neighbours may be quiet and odour-free but they

- store two or three wrecked cars in their backyard (and one on their front drive)
- let their grass and weeds grow five feet tall
- haven't painted or repaired the outside of their house within living memory

- have painted their house—bright fuchsia with lime-green trim
- have an army of flamingoes and garden gnomes on their front lawn in assorted colours and sizes

We hope that none of this sounds familiar to you. But if it does, what can you do?

Call the Police

If your neighbour's conduct is not only annoying but also dangerous or illegal, call the police. If the police think that the situation is serious, they will act. If they don't think it's serious enough for them to act, ask them what you ought to do. They may have some useful suggestions. The police may also respond to complaints about noise, especially at night, and about domestic arguments.

Get Help for Your Neighbour

Whatever your neighbour is doing that's annoying you may really be a symptom of a larger problem that your neighbour is having. The lady with the seventy-two cats may not be able to take care of herself, much less the seventy-two cats. The neighbour who hasn't painted his house may not have enough money for food, let alone property repairs. The neighbours' children may be screaming or their dog may be howling because they're being beaten.

If you have a neighbour who seems unable to look after herself, you can call the department of social services or the medical officer of health. They'll investigate the situation and may get your neighbour whatever help is needed. If you have a neighbour who is having financial problems, you (or you and a group of neighbours) can offer to do some repairs and maintenance or assist the neighbour in getting money for essential repairs from the government (see Chapter 16). If you suspect that your neighbours are abusing their children, you should contact the local Children's Aid Society. If you suspect animal abuse, call the local Humane Society.

Speak to Your Neighbour

If your neighbour's conduct is annoying but not dangerous or illegal, size up the situation before you act. First of all, consider that the conduct is probably not aimed at you. Your neighbour has his own reasons for doing what he's doing and they probably don't include trying to raise your blood pressure to 250. It may be that your neighbour doesn't even realize that what he's doing is bothering you and would stop if he knew.

If you think that a politely phrased complaint might stop the conduct, you may want to speak to your neighbour. But first take a few deep breaths to calm yourself down. It's not a good idea to confront your neighbour when you're fuming. Your neighbour is more likely to get angry too than to fix the problem. You might also remember that you're probably not a candidate for sainthood yourself—you probably make noise occasionally that disturbs the neighbours. Tell your neighbour what the problem is but act as though he or she has no idea that whatever it is might be bothering anyone. Then suggest how the problem could be solved.

For example, if your neighbour is having a loud outdoor party, do not storm over shouting "Shut up you @#$%&* idiots!" Instead, telephone your neighbour (if you have the phone number) or, if you can't phone, go over and find your neighbour and speak to him privately. He probably already knows that the party is loud so say something like, "This looks like a really good party, and everyone seems to be having fun. I'm sure you don't realize that we can hear you all the way to my place. Could you turn down the music or move the music inside?" With luck, your neighbour will turn down the music—or he may invite you to the party. But he may just tell you to get lost. Unfortunately, no matter how pleasant you are when you make a complaint, you don't know how your neighbour is going to react.

Sometimes it works better if you ask someone else to act as a go-between. It may be easier for both you and your neighbour. For example, a neighbour whom you don't know well may have a dog that is left outside and barks to get in. Instead of speaking to the neighbour yourself, you might ask another neighbour who is friendly with the dog-owner to mention that she knows that the dog's barking is bothering you.

In some situations, you can communicate with your neighbour without using words. If the neighbour's children play noisily in their yard or on the balcony or on the street outside your home, bring out your radio and turn up the volume to drown them out. Your neighbour may get the message. Similarly, loud coughing and choking fits in response to the cigar smoke may help your neighbour realize that the smoke isn't staying on her property.

Make an Official (although maybe anonymous) Complaint

Your neighbour's annoying behaviour may be a breach of a municipal **by-law** or a provincial law. Most municipalities have by-laws prohibiting excessive noise and foul smells and setting property standards. Most provinces have laws (which are usually enforced by the municipality) requiring property owners to control certain weeds. Some provinces also have laws prohibiting property owners from polluting air, water, or soil.

If talking to your neighbour has done no good, or if you have (on reflection) decided to bypass that stage altogether, call the municipal by-law enforcement department. Tell the by-law enforcement officer what your neighbour is doing and ask if there's a by-law against it. If there is a by-law, ask how it is enforced. The municipality may send someone to investigate the matter and to speak to your neighbour, and then may lay a charge under the by-law if the neighbour's conduct continues. However, in some municipalities, it is up to you to lay a charge under the by-law and then to prosecute it. If your neighbour is convicted of a by-law offence, he will have to pay a fine and may be ordered to stop the conduct.

If you live in a condo your neighbour may be breaching a condominium corporation by-law. Speak to the condo manager or security personnel, or bring it to the attention of the condominium's board.

If you're concerned about pollution coming from your neighbour's property (for example, if there are leaking containers of you-have-no-idea-what in their yard), contact your provincial ministry of the environment.

If you think you may have to make a complaint and you want to do it anonymously when the time comes, it's not a good idea to speak to your neighbours first. They'll know it was you who turned them in. Actually, somehow or other, neighbours always seem to know who turned them in.

Start a Lawsuit

If your neighbour's conduct has not only annoyed you but has caused actual harm to you or your property, or has significantly interfered with your use of your property, you may wish to start a lawsuit to get financial compensation for the harm. The court can also grant you an **injunction** ordering your neighbour to stop the annoying conduct. This area of law is called **nuisance**.

Lawsuits are time-consuming and expensive. You should only consider litigation if you can't live in your home because of your neighbour's conduct or if you have lost a great deal of money because of it.

Just Live with It

You may decide that doing anything at all will only make matters worse because your neighbour is a total lunatic. Or you may find that you have no legal right to stop your neighbour's conduct. There are some things that the law won't help you stop. In either case, you have to learn to live with the conduct—or move.

If the annoying conduct is one-time-only, or very occasional, you will probably not find by-law enforcement or a lawsuit effective. If a call to the police or a word with your neighbour won't bring you relief, you probably have to put up with it for the moment.

PROBLEMS WITH YOUR IMMEDIATE NEIGHBOURS

If you live in a house, people can come from all over the neighbourhood to annoy you, but your immediate neighbours have special ways to drive you crazy. Only they share a boundary with you. The **boundary** or **property line** is the invisible dividing line between your land and the land belonging to the people on all sides of you. Unless you and your neighbours have a legal right to be on each other's property, you're supposed to stay off each other's property. You and your immediate neighbours may have disputes about staying off or getting onto each other's land. Common disputes involve

- the location of the property line
- fences on the property line
- trees
- shared driveways
- unauthorized use of another's land

The Location of the Property Line

If there are no boundary fences between you and your neighbours, you can't tell by simply looking at the ground where your property line is located. Even if there are fences, you can't tell just by looking at them whether they're actually located on the property line.

Property line questions can arise between neighbours when, for example:

- You want to put up a boundary fence for the first time or check whether an existing fence is on the boundary.
- You think your neighbour has taken over part of your yard.

If you want to put up a fence between your property and your neighbour's, you must locate the property line on the ground so that you know where to build the fence. If you don't have a survey of your property, you will need to have one made. Tell the surveyor that you intend to put up a fence and ask for survey stakes to be placed in the ground to mark the boundary. Even if you already have a survey, you will need a surveyor to come to your property to mark the boundary with survey stakes. If there is already a fence in place between the properties and you are happy with its location, you can simply build the new fence in the same location as the old one. If you are not certain that the old fence is on the boundary line (and you care enough to go to the expense), you'll have to call in the surveyor.

You may think that your neighbour is acting as though part of your yard belongs to him or her, for example, by planting a rose garden or by putting up a shed that you strongly suspect is located in your backyard. Before you confront your neighbour with your suspicions, make sure you're right by having a surveyor check the property line. If you *are* right, ask the surveyor to mark the boundary by placing survey stakes at the property line. Then have a chat with your neighbour. Your neighbour may have used your yard without realizing it, but even if it was an innocent mistake, the reaction you get may not be an apology.

If your neighbour doesn't retreat behind his or her property line, you have several options:

- You can put up a small or large fence or plant shrubs to mark the boundary, and treat whatever's been planted on your side by your neighbour as your own. You can keep it or tear it out. Grass or flowers or shrubs or trees planted on your land become part of your land, so they belong to you.

- If a structure has been placed partly on your property, you can move it back to your neighbour's property, as long as you can do so without damaging the structure. This would work for swing sets, picnic tables, or a small shed.

- If a more permanent structure like a deck, garage, or fence has been built partly on your property, don't try to tear any of it down before you speak to a lawyer.

Fences on the Property Line

You or your neighbour may want to put up a new fence on your property line or repair or replace one that is already there. You may want a fence to keep your dog in, or your neighbour may have to put up a fence to enclose a swimming pool. The question is: Who should pay? If it's your neighbour's idea, you probably think that he should pay, and if it's your idea, she probably thinks that you should pay. It's not that simple.

Either owner has a right to build a **boundary fence**. More important, in most provinces, no matter who wants the fence and no matter what the reason for wanting it, both property owners have to share the cost of building, replacing, or repairing a fence put up on the boundary between properties.

If you want to put up a fence, speak to your neighbour. Your neighbour may surprise you by being willing to share in the expense, and you can cooperate in choosing the style of fence and the contractor.

If your neighbour is reluctant, do not despair. In almost every province there is a method in place for appointing someone to look into the matter and to decide questions about the type of fence, its location, and how much each of you should contribute. In some places, you and your neighbour will choose the person, and in other places, the municipality will choose the person who will decide these questions.

Before you discuss the fence with your neighbour any further, go away and do some homework. First of all, call your municipality to find out how fence disputes are dealt with in your area. Next, call some contractors to get estimates for different kinds of fences, from the cheapest to the kind you really want. Then, knowing what the law is and what a fence will cost, speak to your neighbour again. Once your neighbour knows his or her legal responsibility, he or she may be willing, although not necessarily eager, to share in the cost of the fence.

If your neighbour still won't agree to contribute, contact your municipality again to ask how to arrange to have your dispute resolved. A person may be appointed to investigate and make a decision in the matter. Once the decision is made, your neighbour will probably go along with it.

If your neighbour still does not cooperate, you will have to build and pay for the fence and then try to collect the amount ordered in the municipality's decision from your neighbour. Contact your lawyer or the municipality for advice.

Trees

How can something as lovely as a tree cause trouble between you and your neighbour? Well . . .

- A tree right on the boundary between neighbours may need to be trimmed or cut down.
- One neighbour's tree branches can hang over into the other neighbour's yard.
- One neighbour's tree roots may spread into the other neighbour's yard.
- You may have a problem with a tree that belongs to the municipality.

Trees planted on the boundary between neighbours belong to both neighbours equally. Both must agree before either one can trim the tree or cut it down. But if the tree is likely to injure you or cause damage to your property (for example, if it is rotting and about to fall down, or its roots are working their way through your foundation), you can act without your neighbour's permission. However, you can only do what is necessary to solve the problem. And what if your neighbour trims or cuts down a boundary tree without your permission (if your permission was required)? Your only remedy is to sue your neighbour for damages to compensate you for losing the tree. In most cases, the damages involved will not justify the expense of a lawsuit.

If a branch from a neighbour's tree hangs over your property and injures you or causes damage to your property, your neighbour is legally responsible for the damage. If you see a tree branch that you're worried may cause you damage, you can ask your neighbour to have it removed. If your neighbour doesn't want to remove the branch, she may change her mind if you point out that she will be responsible for any damage it causes, for example, if it comes crashing through your roof during a storm. If you don't want to talk to your neighbour or if your neighbour refuses to do anything, you have the right to cut the branch off. You can only cut off the part of the branch that is hanging over your property, and you can't go on your neighbour's property to do the cutting.

If roots from a neighbour's tree are invading your property (or your pipes, weeping tile, or basement), you have the right to cut the roots out. You can only cut out the roots that are actually on your property, and you can't cut out the roots in such a way that you kill the tree if there's a way of removing the roots without killing the tree. Your neighbour may be legally responsible for damage caused by the tree roots.

The neighbouring tree whose branches or roots are causing you trouble may belong to the municipality. Call the municipality and ask them to remove the offending branches or roots. You'll probably find that your municipal neighbour is more reasonable than your human neighbours. However, the municipality may not be legally responsible to pay for any damage that the branches or roots have caused to you or your property (check this out with your lawyer).

Trees on your lawn that you think belong to you may in fact belong to the municipality. In many areas, the municipal road allowance comes quite a distance up onto front or side lawns, and a tree on municipal property is the municipality's tree—no matter who planted it. You can't trim or cut down a municipal tree.

In some municipalities, you may not even be able to cut down your own trees because of by-laws that protect mature trees. Check with the municipality before you get out the saw.

Shared Driveways

Sometimes neighbouring houses share a driveway just wide enough for one car, with the property line running right down the middle of the drive. You have an **easement** over your neighbour's half of the driveway, and your neighbour has an easement over your half. The easement gives each of you the right to drive from the street to the garage or parking space on your own property.

Neither neighbour can block the driveway, either permanently or temporarily. This means that you can't build a fence on the property line. You can't park your car in the driveway either, unless you and your neighbour specifically agree to this. If your neighbour blocks the driveway, you can remove the obstacle as long as you act reasonably and do only a minimum amount of damage. If removing the obstacle would cause a lot of damage, don't do it yourself. Speak to a lawyer because you may have to sue to get the obstacle removed.

You cannot force your neighbour to maintain or repair his or her half of the driveway—and your neighbour can't force you to maintain or repair your half either. If the driveway needs maintenance or repair, you have the right to go onto your neighbour's half to do the work (and vice versa). If the driveway needs to be resurfaced or if the snow needs to be shovelled, speak to your neighbour about getting the work done. If the neighbour won't agree and you want it done anyway, you'll just have to do it (and pay for it) yourself.

Unauthorized Use of Your Land

Adverse Possession

We talked about what to do if your neighbour takes over part of your yard. You may want to take steps against your neighbour simply to get the use of your own property back. In some parts of the country, there is another reason to take action—if you let your neighbour continue to use part of your land for a long enough time, you can lose ownership of that part of the land. The right to become the owner of another person's land in this way is called **adverse possession**. For someone to become the owner of your land by adverse possession, that person must be the only person using your land, must use it openly, and must use it without your permission for a continuous period of at least ten to twenty years (the time period varies from province to province).

If, for example, your neighbour puts up a fence that encloses part of your property on his side of the fence, he will become the owner of that part of your property after the end of the time period unless you do something. You can prevent him from becoming the owner of the property by

- removing the part of the fence that's on your property (and putting a new one up on the property line)
- suing your neighbour for **trespass** (see Chapter 14)

Before you do anything, speak to your lawyer.

Whether or not it is possible for someone to become the owner of your land by adverse possession depends on the system under which ownership of your land is registered. There are two systems in Canada: the **registry system** and the **land titles** (or **Torrens**) system, and the right to become an owner by adverse possession exists in the registry system but not in the land titles (Torrens) system. If you live in Alberta, British Columbia, or Saskatchewan, all the land is registered under the land titles (Torrens) system. If you live in Nova Scotia, Newfoundland, Prince Edward Island, or Quebec, all the land is registered under the registry system. In Manitoba, New Brunswick, and Ontario, your land could be registered under either system. When you speak to your lawyer about getting the use of your own property back from your neighbour, ask whether or not you need to be concerned about adverse possession.

Prescriptive Easements

We've told you several times about easements. If your land is registered in the registry system and a person uses your land as if there were an easement over it for a long enough period of time (usually twenty years), that person will eventually get a legal right to that easement by **prescription**. (A prescriptive easement is kind of like adverse possession.) This is more of a concern in rural or cottage areas (where someone crosses over your land on a regular basis to get on and off their land) than it is in urban areas. If someone is crossing over your land on a regular basis, speak to your lawyer. Even if you are not concerned about your neighbour getting a permanent right to cross your land, you may simply want to stop him from crossing it all the time.

THE CONSTRUCTION ZONE

If your neighbour decides to renovate, you can be annoyed by the design of the renovation or by the construction process itself.

Objecting to the Design

As long as the design for your neighbour's renovation complies with municipal zoning and other by-laws, you have no say in what the renovation looks like. If, however, the proposed renovation does not comply, your neighbour will have to apply for an **exemption** from the by-law. Once she makes an application for the exemption, close neighbours will be given notice and an opportunity to oppose the application. If you get notice of an application, look carefully at the details of the proposed renovation. If the renovation will have an unwanted effect on you, you should follow the procedure set out in the notice of application for opposing the renovation by filing a **notice of opposition**. You may also want to speak to your lawyer about opposing the application.

You may want to try to work out your objection privately with your neighbour. Even so, it's important to file your notice of opposition within the required time so that you don't lose your legal right to protest if you and your neighbour can't come to an agreement. When you're discussing your objections with your neighbour, find out what the alternative designs are. It may be that she could legally do something without your permission that you would hate even more—and that that's what she intends to do if your objection succeeds.

If you don't receive any official notice before your neighbour starts construction, it usually means that she didn't need an exemption in order to do the work. But it could also mean that she is building without official permission from the municipality. If you don't see a building permit displayed in an obvious place on your neighbour's property, you might wish to call the municipal building department to find out whether or not a permit has been issued. It's a wise idea to check, because if your neighbour is proceeding without a permit, she may also be proceeding with a design that is contrary to the by-laws.

Objecting to the Construction

Even if your neighbour's building permits and permissions are all in order, you may object to aspects of the construction process, such as:

• construction noise or dirt
• damage caused to your property
• an unsafe construction site

Construction noise and dirt are like any other kind of noise and dirt. You can speak to your neighbour or call the municipal by-law enforcement department. (You may be surprised at how early in the morning construction work is allowed to start.)

If you live in a house, the construction workers may tear up your grass by driving their mini-bulldozer across your lawn, or they may excavate so close to the property line that your driveway collapses. If your property is damaged by the construction, your neighbour is responsible for repairing the damage caused or paying for it to be repaired. Speak to your neighbour. He may be as appalled about his contractor's conduct as you are. If you can't come to an agreement with your neighbour about how the damage will be repaired, you may have to sue him for compensation.

In the course of renovating or re-landscaping, your neighbour may have changed the drainage patterns on his property so that run-off from rain or melting ice floods your property. Your neighbour will be responsible for the damage if you can prove that he changed the drainage patterns and that the change caused the flooding. Contact your municipality because the change may be contrary to a by-law. You may have to hire your own engineer to examine the site and give you an opinion about how the flooding was caused.

IF THE TABLES ARE TURNED

You, of course, are a responsible and thoughtful neighbour and you always take care not to disturb your neighbours by mowing the lawn at 6 a.m. on Sunday morning, having smoky barbecues, and decorating the outside of your home in bad taste. And when you do something that might annoy your neighbours, like hold a noisy party, you let them know about it in advance and thank them afterwards for putting up with it.

However, if a neighbour should happen to come to you with a complaint about your annoying conduct, try to be reasonable about the complaint. Don't take it as a personal attack on you. Listen to what your neighbour is saying and, if there's a valid reason for the complaint, see what you can do to make your neighbour happy without making yourself too unhappy.

16 MONEY TROUBLES

When you run into serious financial trouble, everything is affected—including your home. Even though we hope that you are never in the position of having to use the information in this chapter, it's a good idea to know exactly what effect money troubles can have on you as a homeowner.

In this chapter we discuss such pleasant topics as:

- mortgage foreclosure
- unpaid property taxes
- separation and divorce
- lawsuits
- insolvency and bankruptcy
- expropriation

Yes, this is yet another chapter that will make you want to crawl into bed and hide under the covers.

SOME SOLUTIONS TO MONEY TROUBLES

Before we proceed to the really gloomy stuff, we'd like to suggest a few ways of using your home to make, save or get money. Making, saving or getting money won't help with all the troubles we discuss in this chapter, but could be useful for some of them. In this section we'll talk about:

- setting up a home office
- renting out a room or apartment in your home
- getting a reverse mortgage
- saving money on property taxes
- getting assistance with home repairs and renovations

Setting Up a Home Office

If you have a business of your own, you can set up a home office. A home office saves you money in two ways. First, you don't have to rent or buy office space to carry on your business. Secondly, you get an income tax deduction for part of the cost of running your home. Canada Customs and Revenue Agency (formerly Revenue Canada...but whatever they're calling themselves they're still the federal income tax authorities) allows a home-owner to deduct a percentage of the following expenses for business use of the home:

- mortgage interest
- property taxes
- heat
- electricity
- water
- maintenance and repairs
- home insurance

The catch is that either your home must be your principal place of business *or* you must both use the space in your home only to earn your business income *and* use it on a regular and ongoing basis to meet your clients, customers or patients. The catch is also that you'll have to file a Statement of Business Income or Professional Income with your annual tax return in order to claim the **business-use-of-home deduction**.

When you calculate the percentage of expenses to deduct, use a reasonable basis, such as the area your home office occupies divided by the total area of your home. For example, if your home is 1,500 square feet and your home office is 100 square feet (a 10' x 10' room with your desk, computer, phone, fax, files, etc.), you could deduct 6.6 per cent of expenses. If you get greedy and try to deduct too big a percentage of your expenses, Canada Customs and Revenue Agency may decide to audit you. For more about the home office deduction, get a copy of the Business and Professional Income Guide, available through Canada Customs and Revenue Agency's offices or on Canada Customs and Revenue Agency's website at www.ccra-adrc.gc.ca.

A warning about using your home for business purposes: In many municipalities the by-laws forbid homeowners to carry on business in areas that are zoned residential. If your neighbours complain about you to the municipality (and they will if your business is noisy or your customers take up too much parking space), you could be investigated by municipal inspectors and shut down. If you live in a condominium, the condo by-laws may say you can't carry on any kind of business in your home. Again, the neighbours will be watching.

Renting Out Part of Your Home

You can make some money from your home by renting out a room or a flat. You can also save some money by claiming the same kinds of deductions as you can for a home office (again, you'd have to fill out a Statement of Business Income to claim them against the rental income received).

If you've experienced a sudden thrill and sense of fulfilled destiny at the thought of becoming a landlord in your own home and raking in a few hundred dollars a month, we have to say a few words to restrain you.

For one thing, if you're thinking of renting out more than a room or a basement flat, you should speak to an accountant. If you chop your home into self-contained apartments, or start deducting expenses that increase the value of your entire property (like the cost of a new roof or an addition) you could lose some of your **principal residence exemption** on any gain in the value of your home when you sell. Then you'd end up paying **capital gains tax** on part of any profit from the sale. Normally homeowners don't have to pay any tax when they sell their principal residence. (Your principal residence is the place you ordinarily live.)

For another thing, there are *several* other things to consider—we lay them out for you below.

Is Renting Out the Answer for You?

Renting out part of your home may be against the municipal by-laws, especially if you live in an area that is zoned single-family residential. If you rent out in contravention of the by-law, your neighbours may snitch to the municipality. Your neighbours are less likely to make a complaint if you rent only one room—for example, to a student whom you treat as part of your family or to a quiet person. Avoid taking in a biker who likes to rev her hog in the driveway before tearing off up the street.

The room or flat you want to rent out may not be safe—for example, a basement room with no windows is a firetrap. Anyway, you don't want to endanger someone's life for a few bucks a month. Check with your local fire department to find out if the space you're thinking of renting has enough exits, or high enough ceilings or enough smoke detectors.

Your homeowner's insurance may need to be adjusted if you rent out space. You may need extra insurance coverage if there are going to be additional cooking and heating sources on the premises. Check with your insurance agent. Also ask whether your insurance will pay for repairs to your home if a tenant starts a fire or causes a flood. It could be that you'll want your tenant to take out insurance, so that you can be sure the cost of repairs will be covered.

If You Decide to Go Ahead

Before you let someone share your home, make sure you can live with him or her. Hold an interview, and find out about the person's lifestyle—does she smoke whereas you're a non-smoker? Does he get up at 4 A.M. to go to work...or come home at 4 A.M. from parties? Does he have a girlfriend who's going to end up living in the room or flat too? Does she have a pet that you object to? Ask for references from the person—preferably from a present employer and previous landlords—and then call the references up for a frank chat.

You'll want to set ground rules for living under the same roof, and you'll want a short written contract to set out your rights and your tenant's rights. If you're renting out a room, for example, the ground rules should cover things like use of a shared kitchen or bathroom, use of appliances such as (their) air conditioner or (your) washer, dryer and refrigerator, installation of a phone line for the tenant, keeping the rented room and any shared rooms clean, whether smoking is allowed indoors, when visitors can drop by, acceptable hours for coming in at night (or leaving in the morning). Whether you're renting out a room or a flat, the contract between you and the tenant should set out the amount of the regular rent payment, when it's due, whether the tenant is to make any extra payments (for example, a share of the hydro or telephone bill), and how much notice either of you has to give the other before ending the rental arrangement. Before your tenant moves in, get a payment that includes first month's rent and last month's rent.

If you're a little worried that you might not be able to get rid of a problem tenant because of provincial laws that protect tenants, you'll be encouraged to hear that in most provinces residential tenancy laws do not apply to rooms (as opposed to self-contained apartments) rented out in a home. To make sure that yours is one of those provinces, check with the department of your provincial government that handles landlord and tenant matters.

Getting a Reverse Mortgage

Another way to get some cash out of your home is by getting a **reverse mortgage**. A reverse mortgage is a loan you take out against your home. You have to repay the loan and interest, but you normally don't have to make a single payment until you sell your home—or die. Then the money you owe is paid out of the proceeds of sale of your home or out of your estate. (It's also possible to make arrangements to pay the mortgage off before sale or death occurs.) Reverse mortgages are available only to seniors living in areas where real estate prices aren't likely to fall.

If you qualify for a reverse mortgage, you can borrow up to 40 per cent of the value of your home. How much you'll be able to borrow depends on things like your age (the older you are, the more you can borrow), sex, marital status, type and location of your home, and going interest rates. If you've already got an ordinary mortgage, it has to be paid off out of the funds provided under the reverse mortgage, unless you can get your mortgage lender to agree that its rights against your home will come behind the rights of the reverse mortgage lender.

The average amount of a reverse mortgage is about $50,000. You can choose to take the borrowed money as a guaranteed monthly payment, as a lump sum of cash, or as a combination of the two. Most people take the cash. And you can do whatever you like with the money—fix the roof or hit the casinos at Vegas.

The Cost of a Reverse Mortgage

Income earned on the borrowed money is taxable, but at the same time the interest you owe on the borrowed money is deductible. So there won't be much tax to pay on the income. Speaking of interest, though, the interest that builds up on the borrowed money can be rather intimidating. The accumulated interest after ten years on a $50,000 reverse mortgage with an interest rate of 9.15 per cent will be approximately $70,000. That means you'd have to repay about $120,000 for the $50,000 borrowed. If you have to sell your home before you die (say to finance your care in a nursing home), you might find that the reverse mortgage has eaten up the home's equity and that your home is worth much less than you thought.

For more information, about reverse mortgages pay a visit to the Canadian Home Income Plan website at www.chip.ca.

Saving Money on Property Taxes

Homeowners pay property taxes to the municipality, and it uses the tax to pay for municipal services. So paying property tax is a worthy thing to do—but you may feel *too* worthy. If you think your property taxes are higher than they should be, you may be able to get your tax bill reduced.

Within a municipality, property taxes can vary from home to home. Property taxes are calculated for each property as a percentage of the value of that property. The percentage is the same for every home in the municipality, but the value of each home is different. So the higher the value placed on your home, the higher your taxes will be.

If your tax bill seems out of whack, the first thing to do is check the records for your home at the municipal assessment office. There may be a clerical error in the description of your home or property, or there may be an error in the calculation of your **assessment**. Errors like these should be corrected without your having to make a formal objection.

Objection, Your Worship!

If there's no error, you can formally object to your assessment. You can't dispute the percentage that is applied throughout the municipality, but you can dispute your home's assessment, which is the value your municipality has assigned your home to calculate your taxes. The value that the municipality has given to your home may bear little or no resemblance to its actual market value. In theory, the assessed value is based on your home's market value, but it may be based on the market value ten or twenty years ago, depending on when the municipality last assessed your home.

If you object to your assessment, you have to show that the assessment was not "fair and equitable" because of at least one of the following things:

- Your home is not actually worth as much as the municipality says it is.
- Similar homes in the neighbourhood have been assessed at a lower value because the municipality was using different standards.
- Your home has been reassessed but other nearby similar homes were not reassessed at the same time.

Beware! Once you ask for your property to be reassessed, not only can it be reassessed downward as you hope, it can be reassessed upward. If you want to make an objection to your assessment, contact your municipality to find out what steps you must take.

If You Flat-Out Don't Have Any Money

If you're really in a bad financial situation, in many municipalities you can ask for your property taxes to be reduced or for payment to be put off until you sell your property. You're most likely to get a "yes" answer if besides having a low income you're a senior or you have disabilities, or if your home has been destroyed. Contact your municipality for information.

Getting Help to Pay for Repairs or Renovations

If your income is low and your home needs fixing up so you can go on living in it, there are some programs that can offer you help. You may be able to get a low-interest loan, a forgivable loan or a grant to

- make urgently needed repairs (for example, repairing the heating, plumbing or electrical systems, or the roof)
- if you're a senior, make adaptations so you can go on living there (for example, installing grab bars and handrails)
- if you're disabled, make modifications so you can live there (for example, installing ramps)

These programs may be administered in your area by the federal Canada Mortgage and Housing Corporation (CMHC), or by your province or territory, or by your municipality. For information, contact your CMHC regional office or see CMHC's website at www.chmc.ca, or get in touch with your municipality.

MORTGAGE FORECLOSURE AND SALE

Now we're finished with the cheerful content of this chapter. After this point, the gloom is pretty much unrelieved. So where better to start than with mortgages?

As we told you in Chapter 7, a mortgage is a loan agreement. We also told you that the mortgage agreement gives the mortgagee a claim on your house as security to make sure that you repay the loan. If you don't repay the loan, in most provinces the mortgagee not only has the right to sue you on your promise to repay, it also has the right to take your home.

Now we're going to tell you in more detail what can happen if you don't repay your mortgage loan. Not everything we talk about can or will happen in every province. Ask your mortgagee or your lawyer what is likely to happen to you.

Default

Failure to make your mortgage payments on time is a **default** under your mortgage. It is also a default under your mortgage if you don't pay your property taxes, if you don't have insurance on your home, or if you don't keep your home in good repair. If you demolish all or part of your home it can be a default under your mortgage too—even if it's part of a renovation. The default most mortgagors make is failure to make mortgage payments, and that's the default a mortgagee is most likely to notice right away.

When you default on your mortgage, the full amount of your mortgage becomes payable immediately if the mortgagee wishes. The mortgagee has the right to collect that amount either by suing you on your promise to repay the loan or by taking steps to seize your home.

Legally, the mortgagee has the right to take action against you within a very short time after you miss a mortgage payment. Usually, though, the mortgagee will not actually do anything until you have missed more than one payment, but this is not to suggest that you should feel no concern at all about missing a mortgage payment.

If you default on your mortgage, it's never a good idea simply to wait and see what happens instead of getting in touch with your mortgagee. In fact, if you know that you are going to miss a payment, you should contact your mortgagee before the next payment is due. Maybe your inability to pay is only a short-term problem—you're off work for a while because of illness, or there's been an unexpected major expense. If you know that you will be missing only a payment or two and then everything will be back to normal, your mortgagee may be willing to let you make up the missed payments later. Some mortgages have a special feature that permits you to miss occasional payments without penalty.

Even if your problems are long-term and you have no realistic hope of being able to afford your mortgage payments in the foreseeable future, it still makes sense to speak to your mortgagee. Your mortgagee will not turn a blind eye and allow you to stop paying your mortgage for an indefinite period of time. But your mortgagee may agree not to take action against you for a reasonable time to allow you to sell your home—and in this way to get the money to pay back the mortgage. This might not seem to you like a big favour, but your home will probably sell for more if *you* sell it than if the mortgagee sells it. And the more you get for your home, the more money is available to pay off your mortgage. With luck, there may even be money left over that goes into your pocket.

When you default on your mortgage, the mortgagee has various options and can pursue one or more of them. The options are:

- foreclosure
- judicial sale
- power of sale
- getting possession
- suing on the covenant

They all sound quite nasty, don't they? Details follow.

Foreclosure

When a mortgagee chooses to **foreclose** under your mortgage, it is choosing to take your property in full satisfaction of the mortgage debt. If the mortgagee forecloses and your home is worth more than the amount of the mortgage, the mortgagee doesn't owe you anything. If your home is worth less than the amount of the mortgage, in most provinces the mortgagee can't make you pay the shortfall.

How Does Foreclosure Work?

A mortgagee has to start a court action in order to get foreclosure. You will receive documents telling you that the mortgagee has started a foreclosure action. The documents will set out (although not necessarily in language you can understand) what you can do in response to the action. We tell you something about your possible options below, but to know exactly what to do in your situation, speak to your lawyer.

What Can You Do?

Here are the options.

YOU CAN PAY OFF OR PAY UP YOUR MORTGAGE: You can pay back the full amount of the mortgage. If you pay the mortgage, not only is the foreclosure action stopped, but your mortgage will be **discharged** and you won't owe anything anymore. (Of course, if you couldn't even make your monthly payments, how on earth are you going to pay off the whole mortgage?) In almost every province, you may be able to stop the foreclosure action simply by making the mortgage payments you missed (plus a penalty). In that case, your mortgage is put back in good standing and it continues as before.

YOU CAN ASK TO REDEEM: You have the right to **redeem** the mortgage. (In most provinces you have to ask a court for this right.) If you ask for the right to redeem, you will be given a period of time, from two to six months depending on the province, to come up with the money to pay the full amount of the mortgage (plus interest and your mortgagee's legal costs). You would ask to redeem if you thought you could find someone else to lend you the mortgage money (and you would be able to pay that new mortgage). During the **redemption period**, you can also try to sell your home for at least enough money to cover the amount owed to the mortgagee.

YOU CAN ASK FOR A SALE: You can ask a court for your home to be sold under court supervision. (In some provinces, you don't even have to ask, there will automatically be a sale.) Your home must be offered for sale if you ask, and then the mortgagee must try to sell your home before it can foreclose. If your home is sold, the proceeds from the sale will be used to pay the mortgage, plus interest, and the mortgagee's legal costs. If any money is left, it will be used to pay off any other mortgages against your home; whatever is left after that is yours. If the proceeds are not enough to pay the mortgage, interest, and costs, in most provinces the mortgagee can go after you for the difference.

YOU CAN DEFEND: In rare cases, you may be able to defend the foreclosure action by disputing the mortgagee's legal rights under the mortgage. For example, you may not have signed the mortgage in the first place—your signature was forged. Or you may already have paid the mortgage off.

Judicial Sale

In some provinces, instead of foreclosing the mortgagee may from the outset choose to have your property sold under court supervision.

What is a Judicial Sale?

If your home is sold under **judicial sale**, the proceeds from the sale will be used to pay the mortgage, interest, and the mortgagee's legal costs. Any money left over will be used to pay off other mortgages against your home, and anything left after that goes to you. If the proceeds of sale don't cover what you owe, in most provinces the mortgagee can recover the difference from you.

A mortgagee has to start a court action to get a judicial sale. You will receive court documents setting out what you can do in response to the action. Again, you should speak to your lawyer, but we'll tell you about your options. There aren't many.

What Can You Do?

Well, not a heck of a lot.

YOU CAN PAY OFF OR PAY UP YOUR MORTGAGE: You can pay back the full amount of the mortgage and stop the judicial sale that way. In most provinces, all you have to do is make the mortgage payments you missed (plus a penalty) to stop the sale.

YOU CAN ASK TO REDEEM: In some provinces you can ask a court for the right to redeem the mortgage (see above), and the sale can't take place until the time for redemption has passed.

YOR CAN DEFEND: You can defend a judicial sale action on the same grounds as you can a foreclosure action (see above).

Sale Under Power of Sale

Almost all mortgages contain a provision that gives the mortgagee the power, if you default on your mortgage, to sell your property without having to go to court. As with a judicial sale, the proceeds from the sale will be used to pay the mortgage, plus interest, and the mortgagee's legal costs. If any money is left, it will be used to pay off any other mortgages against your home, and whatever is left after that is yours. If the proceeds of sale are not enough to pay the mortgage, interest, and costs, the mortgagee can look to you to pay the difference.

Before your property can be sold under **power of sale**, your mortgagee must give you written notice of its intention to sell. Once you receive the notice, you have a set period of time (it will be stated in the notice) to pay off the mortgage. In some provinces, you may be able simply to make the missed payments. If you don't pay, the mortgagee can sell your home after a specified period of time.

Sale under power of sale is used often in Manitoba, Newfoundland, Ontario, and Prince Edward Island.

Getting Possession of Your Home

Whether the mortgagee is selling your property or foreclosing, it will want you gone. The mortgagee has the right to ask the court for an order giving it **possession** of your home. You can't stop the mortgagee from getting an order for possession if it gets an order to foreclose or sell. But even after getting an order for possession, most mortgagees won't actually take possession of your home if it looks as though you are going to redeem the property. If the mortgagee does decide to act on the order, force can be used to get you and your belongings out of your home, if you don't go peacefully.

If the mortgagee is suing for foreclosure or judicial sale, the claim for possession will be included in the same lawsuit. If your mortgagee is selling under its power of sale, the mortgagee will have to start a separate lawsuit for possession.

Suing on the Covenant

In most provinces the mortgagee can simply choose to sue you on your **covenant** (promise) to pay the mortgage loan and not try to take or sell your home. A lawsuit on the covenant alone is unlikely, however, because few mortgagees will ignore the other rights they have against your property.

Mortgagees usually combine suing on the covenant with selling the mortgaged property. They do this so they will have a judgment that will let them collect the shortfall from you if the proceeds from the sale of your home are not enough to pay off the mortgage. If the mortgagee is proceeding by way of judicial sale, the claim for payment on the covenant will be included in the same lawsuit. If the mortgagee is proceeding under its power of sale, it has to start a separate lawsuit—usually combined with the lawsuit for possession.

Words of Wisdom

If you cannot make your mortgage payments now, and in your heart of hearts you know you will not be able to make them soon, your future as a homeowner is in the hands of your mortgagee. You may hope that you can negotiate a deal with your mortgagee, but the mortgagee is only going to do something for you if that something will also get the mortgagee what he, she, or it wants. What the mortgagee wants is to get back as much of its money as possible in the fastest, cheapest way.

Allowing the mortgagee to get his or her money in the fastest, cheapest way is usually in your best interest too. That's because the longer and harder you fight, the more interest accumulates on your unpaid debt and the higher the mortgagee's legal fees go. The interest and all of the mortgagee's legal fees get added to your mortgage debt and are ultimately paid by you. If your home is worth more than the mortgage, you want the amount you owe to stay as low as possible so that there will be some money left for you when the home is sold. You also want to sell your home for as much money as possible. You'll probably get more money for your home if you sell it yourself rather than letting the mortgagee sell it. So the best you may be able to do when you run into financial trouble is to persuade the mortgagee to let you sell your home yourself. The mortgagee is more likely to agree to this proposal if you make it early on.

PROPERTY TAXES

If you don't pay your property taxes, the municipality will add interest charges and penalties to your property tax bill. If you *still* don't pay your property taxes, the municipality has the right to sell your home, similar to your mortgagee's right to sell if you don't pay your mortgage. (The municipality doesn't get to keep all the money from the sale, only the amount that you owe in taxes.) Before your home is sold, the municipality will send you a notice in writing and will give you an opportunity to pay up. You may be able to leave your bill unpaid for several years before your municipality actually takes steps to sell your home. Municipalities aren't as quick on the trigger as mortgagees.

FAMILY LAW CONSIDERATIONS

Being married or getting divorced may have an effect on your home.

If You Want to Sell or Mortgage Your Home

If you and your spouse are both **registered owners** of your home (see Chapter 6), you will not be able either to sell or mortgage it unless both spouses agree and sign all the necessary documents.

If only one of you is the registered owner but you are legally married, in most provinces you will almost certainly need the consent of your spouse before you can sell or mortgage your home. If your spouse won't consent to the mortgage or sale, speak to your lawyer. You may be able to get a court to approve the mortgage or sale without your spouse's consent. Of course, starting a lawsuit will not do wonders for your relationship. And the court may well order that your spouse is entitled to receive some of the mortgage money or sale proceeds.

Divorce and Separation

When husbands and wives separate or divorce, they must divide their property between them, including the home in which they live. Depending on the province you live in and your particular circumstances, the following may occur:

- Your home may have to be sold as part of an overall property settlement or order.
- Your spouse may have a right to a share in the home whether or not that spouse is an owner or made any financial contribution to it.
- Your spouse may be able to get an order to stay in the home and to keep you out of it, whether or not that spouse is an owner or made any financial contribution to the home.

Even if you are not legally married and your spouse is not a registered owner of your home, your spouse may still be able to make a claim against it. For example, your spouse could seek a share of the home because he or she made a financial contribution to buying it, or paid household expenses while you paid the mortgage, or did work on the property that increased its value.

If it looks like you and your spouse are going to separate you should speak to a lawyer.

HOW LITIGATION MAY AFFECT YOUR HOME

If you are involved in a lawsuit, it may have some effect on your home whether or not the lawsuit is about your home.

Construction, Builders', or Mechanics' Liens

We told you in Chapter 11 about **construction, builders'**, or **mechanics' liens** and how a lien can be registered against the title to your home. As long as a lien is registered against your home, a prospective purchaser will not want to buy it because your home can be sold to pay off the lien. For the same reason a prospective mortgagee will not want to give you a mortgage.

Notices of Pending Litigation

If you are sued by someone who is claiming an interest in your property, the person who is suing you may be able to register a **notice** on the title to your home that the lawsuit has been started. Such a notice advises any potential purchaser or mortgagee that the ownership of the property is in dispute. Most purchasers and mortgagees will not want anything to do with your property while this kind of lawsuit is outstanding.

Judgments Against You

If you lose a lawsuit and a judgment is made against you ordering you to pay money, the judgment may affect the title to your home. This is so even if the lawsuit had nothing to do with your property, for example, if you were sued for not making your credit card payments or for injuring someone in a car accident. The person who wins the lawsuit and gets the judgment against you has the right to take and sell as much of your property as necessary to pay off the judgment. In most provinces one of the things they can take and sell is your home, even if you own the property with another person. (They'd only get to keep your share of the money from the sale.)

After a judgment has been registered against you, the person who got the judgment keeps the right to sell your home even if you sell it or mortgage it to someone else. Anyone who is buying your home or giving you a mortgage will check to see whether there are any judgments outstanding against you. If they find any, they will insist that the judgment be paid off before or at the time you close the deal.

BANKRUPTCY AND INSOLVENCY

A lot of people are confused about the difference between **bankruptcy** and **insolvency**. If you owe money and the amount you owe is greater than the value of what you own, or if you cannot pay your debts as they come due, you are **insolvent**. You are not **bankrupt** unless a court declares you bankrupt. A court can make a declaration that you are bankrupt at your own request or at the request of one of your creditors. Before a court can declare you bankrupt you must be insolvent, and you must have debts of at least $1,000.

If you are declared bankrupt, a **trustee in bankruptcy** is appointed by the court. The trustee gets almost all your possessions, sells them, and uses the proceeds to pay your creditors. Because you owe more than you own, your creditors will not be fully paid. If this is your first bankruptcy, unless a creditor or the trustee objects you will automatically be **discharged** from bankruptcy after nine months. Once you are discharged, all your debts, with a few exceptions, are wiped out.

What happens to your home if you go bankrupt? If you own a home, in most provinces the trustee will get it. If you own your home together with another person, the trustee can sell it to get your share. If the property is mortgaged, your mortgagee will have the right to sell it or foreclose. If the mortgagee sells your home and there is any money left over, that money will go to the trustee to pay the rest of your creditors. But if your home is sold for less than you owe the mortgagee, the mortgagee will not be able to sue you for the shortfall because you are bankrupt. Actually, not only will you lose your home, you will also lose most of your furniture and belonging. You are allowed to keep only furniture worth $2,000 and **personal effects** (like clothing and jewellery) worth $1,000. You can also keep "tools of your trade" worth $2,000.

If you are insolvent, going bankrupt may be a blessing because it will get you out from under your debts and let you make a fresh start. On the other hand, bankruptcy may be very bad for you, depending on your financial position. If you are insolvent, you should seek the advice of a lawyer who specializes in bankruptcy or of a trustee in bankruptcy. They will be able to tell you whether or not it makes sense for you to choose to go bankrupt. If bankruptcy would be bad for you, they may be able to help you prevent it by assisting you in making a **consumer proposal** to your creditors that will allow you to repay your debts over time and, perhaps, at a reduced rate.

EXPROPRIATION

The government (federal, provincial, or municipal) may up and decide that it needs all or part of your land for some public purpose or project, such as widening the street in front of your home, or building a highway or public building. They can get your property, whether you agree or not, by **expropriating** it. But they do have to pay you for it.

Expropriation is not an area of law for do-it-yourselfers. If you get notice of an intention to expropriate your property, you should speak to a lawyer who specializes in expropriations.

Can You Prevent the Expropriation?

The government has to give you notice of its intention to expropriate your property. Once you get that notice, you have some right to object to the expropriation. It's almost impossible to argue that the public project for the expropriation is not necessary. All you can really argue is that your property is not needed for the project. As you can imagine, this is a hard argument to make if your house is located smack in the middle of the proposed six-lane highway.

Unless you can convince the government to change its mind, the expropriation will go ahead whether you agree to it or not. The government will simply make itself the legal owner of the part of your property that it wants. Then, all you can do is to try to get a fair price for what was taken.

How Much Will You Be Paid?

If your land is expropriated, the government will pay you for it. Generally speaking, you will be paid an amount for your property that is calculated according to the property's market value before the expropriation. In some cases, though, giving you the market value of your property would not be the appropriate compensation. For example:

- There may have been no market for your property before the expropriation, in which case you might be entitled to the cost of buying a replacement property.

- The land may be worth more than market value to you because you are using it for a special purpose, in which case you might be entitled to compensation for that extra value to you.

- You may suffer economic losses because you have to move, in which case you might be entitled to compensation for those losses.

• Only part of your property may be expropriated and the value of the rest of your land may therefore decreased, in which case you might be entitled not only to compensation for the part of your land that is taken but also to compensation for the decrease in value of your remaining land.

In some cases, you may also be paid interest and some of what you spent on legal fees and on fees to determine the value of your property.

When Will You Be Paid?

In almost every province, the government must at least make you an offer of compensation or enter into negotiations with you before it has the right to take possession of your land. In fact, in some provinces if an offer is made you may be able to take the money and still fight for more.

If you don't accept the government's offer, or if you and the government do not agree on the amount you should be paid, you have the right to a hearing before a court or a special board to decide how much you should be paid. In that case, you won't be paid until the hearing is finished.

Don't think that you can delay the government taking possession of your property by prolonging negotiations or by asking for a hearing. It's possible for the government to take possession of your property before the amount of compensation you are entitled to has been settled and paid to you.

All right, it's safe to come out from under the covers now. We have nothing more to say to you about money troubles—in fact, we have nothing more to say about being a homeowner. All that's left to talk about is what's involved when you decide to sell your home.

selling your home

17 GETTING READY TO SELL

People decide to sell a home for many different reasons. Your family may be growing in number and size, and your present place has become too small. You may want to retire to a warmer climate now that your children have moved away. (Do it quickly before they decide to move back!) You may have to move because of a new job. You may have won the lottery and now feel an urge to live in a monster home. Or you may have to sell because of less pleasant reasons, such as financial problems, divorce, or a death in the family.

WHEN IS THE BEST TIME TO SELL?

You've probably heard various kinds of advice about the best time to sell your home. Some people say that you should time your sale based on the state of the economy. Others say you have to choose the right time of year. We talk about some of the more common advice below. If your need to sell is not urgent, you can take some of the advice. But if for some reason you must move right away, the best time for you to sell is now, no matter what the economy or season. Ultimately, your own circumstances determine the best time for you to sell.

Trends in the Real Estate Market

Over the past few decades, real estate prices have gone up and down in cycles, but the general movement has always been upward. Even with the various ups and downs in the market, real estate is worth far more now than it was in the 1950s. However, current wisdom holds that the days of steadily increasing real estate values are over in many parts of the country. In fact, in many parts of the country we may even be facing a long-term decrease in values when there are more ageing baby-boomers selling their homes than there are younger people buying them. But even if long-term trends in real estate don't look great, there may still be short-term changes or local conditions in the real estate market that you can take advantage of, depending on your location and other circumstances.

What we're saying is that real estate is not as attractive an investment as it was when people could make money speculating in houses. So for most people the best reason these days to buy a home is to live in it, not to make a killing on the sale of it. However, since a home does represent such a large investment, it's only reasonable for you to want to get as much home as possible for your money when you buy, and as much money as possible for your home when you sell.

On the national level, housing prices tend to be higher when the economy is strong and also when interest rates go down. On the local level, the popularity of a particular area of the country or within a city may also cause home prices to go up. Or the closing of a major employer in a community will cause prices to drop as people who have lost their jobs try to sell.

Here's something else to keep in mind. It's only natural to think that you should always try to sell your home when prices are high. That's fine if you are getting out of the housing market altogether, or if you're planning to buy a less expensive place. But if you are trading up to a more expensive home, selling when prices are lower may be a better idea. While the home you are selling may not be worth as much as it might be in a better market, neither is the home you are buying. The more expensive home you're thinking about buying will probably go down in price more than the less expensive home you're thinking of selling.

Time of the Year

In Canada, the weather and the time of year have an effect on how many home buyers are out there looking. The more buyers there are, the higher the sale prices will be.

Almost no one wants to think about buying a house during Christmas or summer vacations. On the other hand, people with school-aged children like to move when school is over, and so are more likely to buy in the "spring." The spring real estate market in your area may or may not arrive at the same time as the tulips. In some regions, the spring market is over by the end of February. So, if you're hoping to take advantage of the spring market, ask a real estate agent when that would be.

Buy First or Sell First?

If you are selling your present home in order to buy a new one, you should start looking for your new home as soon as your old one is listed for sale, if not before. That way, you will know how hard or easy it's going to be to find a new home in your price range. Knowing what your new home is likely to cost will help you decide how much you need to get for your current home.

What if you find the new home you want before your old home is sold? If you sign an agreement to buy the new home, you are legally bound to buy it, even if you cannot find a buyer for your old home. You can end up owning and paying for two homes at the same time.

What if you sell your old home before you find a new one to buy? Even if you don't find a new home before the sale of your old home is scheduled to close, you are still legally bound to go through with the sale. You may have to rent until you find a place to buy. That means rental payments and moving twice.

There are ways to avoid these two nightmare scenarios.

Buying First

If you find a home you want to buy before your present property is sold, you can make your offer to purchase conditional on your being able to sell your old home within a fixed period of time. If your offer to buy is accepted and you don't sell your home by the end of the fixed period, you can choose not to go through with the deal.

The vendor may not want to agree to a condition like this. Or the vendor may insist that the fixed period be very short. Even if the vendor does agree, you may only be putting off having to make your decision if you haven't sold by the time the fixed period runs out.

Selling First

If someone offers to buy your home before you have signed an agreement to purchase a new home, you can sign back the offer to make it conditional on your buying a new home within a fixed period of time. If you don't sign an agreement to purchase a new home by then, you can choose not to go ahead with the sale of your old home. A purchaser is more likely than a vendor to agree to make a sale conditional. Even if you haven't found a home by the end of the period, you may choose to go ahead with the sale if you believe that you won't have a problem finding a new home before the sale actually closes.

Think about this too: As a buyer, you will be in a stronger bargaining position if you can put in an unconditional offer to purchase. (In a hot market it may make the difference between getting the home or losing it.)

The ultimate decision whether to buy first or sell first depends on which scenario you find more frightening—owning two homes or owning none.

GOOD NEWS ABOUT TAXES ON THE SALE OF A HOME

When you sell your home, you want to get as much money as possible. So you don't want to give any to the government if you don't have to. Well, you don't have to.

The sale of real estate can trigger **capital gains tax** if the property has gone up in value since the time it was purchased. But homeowners almost never have to pay tax on the sale of their home. As long as your home has been your **principal residence** (very briefly, the housing unit you ordinarily inhabited for the entire time that you owned it) you probably won't have to pay capital gains tax on any profit from the sale. (If instead of triggering a capital gain we've now triggered your paranoia about taxes, contact Canada Customs and Revenue Agency for a more detailed explanation of what a principal residence is and whether your home meets the definition.)

GETTING YOUR ACT TOGETHER

Once you decide that you are ready to sell, there are documents and other material that you should collect. Your real estate agent will need some of them, and your lawyer will need others.

What Your Real Estate Agent Will Need

Gather together documents that affect ownership of your home (title documents, mortgage documents, and claims against the property), any plan of survey, old property tax and utility bills, and anything you have lying around that might help sell your home.

Title Documents

Your real estate agent will want to know the names of all the **registered owners** of your home (see Chapter 6), because all registered owners must consent to the sale. Your agent will also want information about whether the owners are married, because the owners may need their spouses' permission before selling (see Chapter 16). Gather together any of the following documents that you have:

- your **deed** or transfer of title document
- any separation agreement affecting your home
- any court order or judgment affecting your home
- any will or probate documents relating to your home (if an owner has died)

If you live in a condominium, you should also give your real estate agent copies of your condominium documents.

If your home is in a development with commonly-owned land or recreational facilities, give your real estate agent a copy of the homeowner association rules and fee schedules.

Mortgage Documents

If there is a mortgage on your home, your real estate agent will want to look at the documents to find out whether a purchaser could **assume** (take over) the mortgage. A purchaser might look on a mortgage that could be assumed as a plus if the mortgage was for the right amount of money and had a good interest rate. It's also useful for you to know whether the mortgage can be **discharged** (paid off and ended) without a penalty to you if a purchaser insists on the discharge of all mortgages. See Chapter 7.

Claims Against Your Home

If you are aware of any claims or liens (see Chapter 16) against your home, you should tell your real estate agent so that the claims can be dealt with in an agreement of purchase and sale. These claims might include

- construction, builders', or mechanics' liens
- unpaid judgments against you
- unpaid taxes
- unpaid utility bills
- notices of pending litigation

Plan of Survey

If you own a house and have a plan of survey of your property, give it to your real estate agent too. Be sure to tell your agent whether there have been any changes made to your property since the date of the survey. If there haven't been any changes, then you have an **up-to-date survey** and the purchaser won't have to pay to get a survey done. That's nice for a purchaser to hear because it could save him or her up to a thousand dollars.

Property Tax and Utility Bills

Give copies of your tax and utility bills to your real estate agent. A potential purchaser will want to know the cost of taxes and utilities.

Things That Might Help Sell Your Home

You may have information that your real estate agent can use to market your home, such as:

• pictures or videos of the garden or pool at different times of year (especially if you are selling during the winter)

• contracts or receipts that prove recent repairs or renovations

• the home inspection report that you had done when you bought the place

• any plans or drawings for renovations that you were considering

Private Sales

If you have decided to sell your home without using a real estate agent, you will need the same documents that you would give to a real estate agent. In addition, you'll need information to help you decide what price you should ask for your home. Gossip with your neighbours to find out what similar homes have sold for recently in your area. Or, for a fee, you can get an opinion from a real estate agent or real estate appraiser as to the value of your home. It's not enough to know the asking price of homes in your neighbourhood—that information is easily available from ads and vendor's agents—because the selling prices could be higher or lower.

What Your Lawyer Will Need

Your lawyer will want to see everything that you have collected for your real estate agent, other than the things that will help your agent to market your home.

If you are not using the same lawyer who acted for you when you bought your home, your new lawyer will also want to see the **reporting letter** that your former lawyer gave you when you bought the home (see Chapter 6).

GETTING YOUR HOME'S ACT TOGETHER

Real estate agents have always given vendors advice about the little things they can do to make a home attractive to the people who come to view it. Lately, things have gotten rather out of hand. Real estate agents now have pamphlets and videos with detailed instructions that, if followed slavishly, would totally transform your ordinary home into a decorator's dream. You could wake up one morning and wonder where on earth you are! You might even decide that you'd be crazy to sell and let someone else enjoy this palace of delights.

Let's face it. Your home is not perfect. If it were perfect, you wouldn't want to move. There are things that have needed doing for some time which you've kept putting off. In fact, you're probably moving to avoid doing these very things. Well, now you'll have to do some of them. Just don't go overboard.

Look at Videos and Pamphlets

By all means, look at the pamphlets and videos and get some ideas. But don't actually do anything until you talk to your own agent. He or she will probably tell you not to get carried away and will give you advice on what steps it makes sense for you to take. If your real estate agent is a little too enthusiastic for your taste, follow your own instincts and wait for feedback from people who view your property.

Clean and Unclutter

The first things you should do to get your home ready for sale are the ones that cost nothing except time and energy. Start by cleaning and getting rid of unnecessary clutter. If you clean your home thoroughly, it will look better and smell better, and if you get rid of the clutter it will look bigger. Pay special attention to the kitchen and bathrooms. Consider having rugs professionally cleaned. If you're daunted by the cleaning—it's certainly something we keep harping on in this book—you can hire a cleaning company to come in for a few hours. It might cost less than $200 and be well worth the cleaning anguish you save yourself.

When cleaning and uncluttering, keep in mind that, unlike polite house guests, prospective buyers will be looking in the cupboards and closets, under the sink, in the refrigerator, all around the basement—even in the garage. So don't just stuff things away and think they're hidden. Clean and organize these areas too. Get rid of junk you've been saving for reasons long forgotten. (We apologize for giving you all this painful advice.)

Repainting can also make a home look clean and fresh, and you may find that it's more effective to repaint dirty walls than to wash them. It doesn't have to be the world's greatest paint job—*you* won't have to live with it. If your rugs are beyond help from the vacuum or rug-cleaning machine, think about replacing them (with something inexpensive). If tile floors refuse to look anything but old and grimy, cover them with carpeting. If you have bulky furniture in the main rooms, think about re-locating some of it, maybe even to storage facilities.

Neutralize

A potential buyer doesn't want to see your home, she wants to see her own home. So make it easy for a buyer to imagine that this is her place, not yours. Consider putting away things that reflect your family's strong personal tastes a little too much, like posters of favourite horror movies, extensive knick-knack collections, or animal-skin rugs. If some of your rooms are particularly dramatic in colour (a teenager's black bedroom, or a bright orange den with dark brown accents), you might consider repainting them in boring beige. Extremely vibrant wallpaper might need to be replaced with something less lively as well.

Make Necessary Repairs

After your home is clean and clutter-free, have a look around to see if there's anything that would put off a buyer. If you see something, think about what's involved in changing it. If it's a small problem that can be quickly and cheaply fixed, do it. We're thinking of things like dripping faucets, tears in window screens, loose or broken door handles, squeaky hinges.

If fixing the problem would take a lot of work or money, speak to your real estate agent first. (Here we're thinking of things like a roof that needs re-tiling, a malfunctioning furnace, plumbing that leaks, a wet basement.) Ask whether he or she thinks it is worthwhile for you to do the work. Will the problem affect the sale of your home? Will it make it take longer to sell, or even prevent your home from being sold at all? Will it reduce the price a buyer will pay? If your home won't sell until you fix the problem, then clearly you have to fix it. But if the problem will only delay the sale or reduce the price, you'll have to decide whether to make the investment required to fix it.

Don't Try to Hide Serious Problems

Whatever you do, do not try to hide a major problem in your home. Either repair the problem properly or tell your real estate agent about it so that it can be disclosed to prospective buyers. For example, do not simply plaster and paint over a crack that you know is caused by a structural problem. If you have a pipe that leaks whenever you take a shower, don't just stop taking showers and then paint the stained wall.

☑ Prepare Your Home Checklist

You can use this checklist to give you some ideas about what to do to get your home looking its best for prospective buyers. In each category we start with things that are easy and cheap to do and move on to things that are more time-consuming or expensive.

How far should you go in beautifying your home? It's up to you, but we recommend that you stop when you feel yourself being overcome by a Martha Stewartish urge to create a spare bedroom out of a cantaloupe.

On the Outside of a House

Gardens, Drives, and Walkways

- ❑ Depending on the season, mow your lawn, weed your flowerbeds, rake leaves, or shovel snow.
- ❑ Clean up any litter.
- ❑ Clean up after pets.
- ❑ Clean and arrange lawn furniture.
- ❑ Remove garden gnomes and pink flamingoes.
- ❑ Repair fences and gates.
- ❑ Repair or resurface driveways and walkways.

The House Itself

- ❑ Clean windows, window ledges, and doors.
- ❑ Clean eavestroughs.
- ❑ Clean siding.
- ❑ Plant flowers in the garden or put out flower pots or window boxes.
- ❑ Landscape with some shrubs.
- ❑ Put down a new doormat.

❑ Paint trim, shutters and garage door (you can go artistic here, with contrasting or coordinating colours).
❑ Add lights around house or in garden
❑ Repair broken windows or doors.
❑ Repair leaking roof.
❑ Repair crumbling chimney.

On the Inside of any Home

Walls, Ceilings, Windows, Doors, and Floors

❑ Remove ceiling cobwebs.
❑ Make sure all light fixtures are clean and change burnt-out light bulbs
❑ Clean windows, frames, sills, and blinds.
❑ Leave drapes and blinds open (or, if it's evening, turn on lights) during showings to make the home look bright.
❑ Make sure windows open and close properly; repair as necessary.
❑ Clean or replace window coverings.

❑ Wash walls.
❑ Touch up chipped paint.
❑ Plaster over minor cracks and holes and repaint.
❑ Repaint one or more rooms in neutral colours.
❑ Paint over any water damage (after you fix the leak).

❑ Clean doors and frames and polish doorknobs.
❑ Make sure that doors open and close properly and quietly; repair as necessary.
❑ Replace door hardware and knobs.

❑ Clean and polish floors.
❑ Vacuum carpets and steam clean, if necessary.
❑ Put down runners on worn carpets in high traffic areas.
❑ Replace flooring or carpets.

Closets and Storage Areas (including Basement)

❑ Remove clutter.
❑ Throw out or recycle junk.

❏ Organize clothes, shoes, and other items neatly.
❏ Clean and deodorize pet areas.

Living Areas and Bedrooms

❏ Remove clutter, and possessions that shout "I'm me!"
❏ Dust and vacuum everything.
❏ If you have a fireplace, clean it and stack logs neatly.
❏ Set out flowers and plants.
❏ Rearrange furniture to make rooms appear larger.
❏ Store large items of furniture elsewhere.
❏ Purchase more attractive curtains and bedspreads.

Kitchens and Bathrooms

❏ Clean to a sparkling shine.
❏ Clear off counter tops.
❏ Make sure everything smells good—remove garbage and don't cook smelly food just before a showing (bake cookies instead!).
❏ Remove embarrassing personal items from the bathroom before a showing.
❏ Replace mildewed shower curtain.
❏ Set out flowers, potpourri, or scented soap.
❏ Buy matching shower curtain and towels.
❏ Replace cracked toilet seat covers.
❏ Repair leaky faucets and toilets.

18

PUTTING
YOUR HOME
UP FOR SALE

You can sell your home with or without a real estate agent. In this chapter, we tell you about the sale process with an agent and without one. Since most people do use a real estate agent, the chapter focuses on selling your home with an agent.

THE SALE PROCESS WHEN
YOU USE A REAL ESTATE AGENT

There is no legal requirement to use a real estate agent to sell your home, but the process is generally easier and faster if you do have one. A real estate agent will

- help you set a realistic asking price
- find the greatest number of potential buyers
- market your home
- arrange showings to potential buyers
- help negotiate the terms of sale

Setting a Realistic Asking Price

When you put your home on the market, it is up to you to set an **asking price**. The asking price is an indication of what you would like to get for your home, if possible. An interested buyer doesn't have to offer the asking price.

The first step in setting your price is finding out what your home is worth. To find that out, you need information about recent sales of similar homes in your neighbourhood. (You especially need to know what actual sale prices have been, and it's very useful to know the average time between homes being listed for sale and being sold.) A real estate agent has access to this information that you do not. A real estate agent also has the knowledge and objectivity to tell you how your home is different from those similar homes that have sold—whether it's worth more or less. However, knowing what your home is worth does not automatically tell you what price to ask. Real estate agents can give you advice about how much higher or lower than your home's market value to set the asking price.

Real estate agents say that a home that is properly priced sells more quickly than one that is improperly priced. If you price your home too high, it will take longer to sell. If your home stays on the market for too long, potential buyers may think that there are problems with it. They'll either not come to look at it at all, or they'll offer you far less money than they would have otherwise. Even if you reduce your asking price after a while, you may end up with less money than you would have received if you'd priced your home properly in the first place.

Real estate agents (and therefore their house-hunting clients) are most interested in a home when it first comes onto the market. They want to see what's new, not what's been hanging around for weeks or months. If your home doesn't sell within a couple of weeks (in a hot market) or a month (in a cool market), your agent may recommend reducing the price to try to re-spark interest in your property.

If You're Selling in a Seller's Market

A **seller's market** is a hot market. Your chances of selling right away for a decent price are pretty good already. If you want to heat the market up even further—to get competing offers that will jack up the sale price—your real estate agent may recommend that you set your asking price in the middle of the range of recent sale prices for similar homes. That's right, you don't start by asking for the maximum you hope to get. Overpricing will put potential buyers off rather than reel them in. Buyers will be attracted to your well-priced property because the price looks like a bit of a deal, comparatively speaking. And if there are several people interested, they won't mind bidding higher because they know the property could be worth more than the asking price. Another strategy your agent might recommend is to tell potential buyers that you won't accept any offers until your home has been on the market a certain length of time—say three, four or five days. Potential buyers will feel like they're at an auction and will bid against the competition.

If You're Selling in a Buyer's Market

A **buyer's market** is a cool market. If there are a lot of homes similar to yours on the market and they're not getting snapped up, your agent might recommend that you ask a slightly lower price than other vendors in the neighbourhood are asking. Just a slightly lower price, not a steeply lower price or buyers will think there's something wrong with your home. Potential buyers will take notice of your nicely underpriced property because it looks like a bargain.

Finding Potential Buyers

When you put your home on the market with a real estate agent, you have the option of using the **Multiple Listing Service** (MLS) in your area. Only homes listed with real estate agents can appear on the MLS database. Details about your home will be made available to all real estate agents in the area, so every agent with a client looking for a home like yours can easily find out about it. Your home will almost certainly be sold to someone whose real estate agent found out about it through the MLS.

Access to the MLS is the major advantage in using a real estate agent to sell your home. Without access to MLS, you are limited to a "For Sale" sign on your lawn and ads in the newspaper or on the Internet. Clearly, you cannot reach the same number of prospective buyers all by yourself as you can through the MLS.

Marketing Your Home

Although a real estate agent's major marketing tool is the MLS, there are other things that your agent can do to help market your home.

Making Your Home Attractive

The first thing your agent will do is advise you on how to make your home as attractive as possible to buyers. In Chapter 17 we talked about some of the things that people do to spruce up their homes at sale time. Your agent should help you work out a plan for your home.

The Feature Sheet

Most agents prepare a **feature sheet** that describes the home for sale. A feature sheet is handed out to people who have viewed your home to help them remember it. It usually provides information about the size of the lot and the number and size of the rooms, and it highlights any especially attractive features, like a newly renovated kitchen or bathroom. The feature sheet may also provide information about realty taxes, utility costs, and any mortgages. Some feature sheets are works of art, with colour photographs of your home and sparkling prose.

Open Houses

If your home is listed on the MLS, your agent will probably suggest an **open house** for real estate agents only. Experienced real estate agents constantly review the MLS for information about new listings that might appeal to any of their clients. When an agent finds an interesting listing, he or she will make a point of going to the open house to check the property out. Since your home is most likely to be bought by a client of another real estate agent, it is important to give other agents this opportunity to see it. If your home is attractive and well priced, many of the agents at the open house will make arrangements to bring their clients over immediately.

In addition to open houses for other real estate agents, your agent may suggest that you have one or more open houses for the general public. Don't feel you have to agree. Just as you suspected, this kind of open house mostly attracts browsers and nosy neighbours. Agents like this kind of open house because it gives them a chance to find more clients. But you are not likely to find a buyer for your home through this kind of open house.

If you do have an open house, it's best for you not to be there. Your agent will ask for the name, address, and telephone number of everyone who drops by and will try to walk through the home with each visitor. Even though your agent will be keeping an eye on things, you would be wise to put away valuable or fragile items.

Advertising Your Home

If you're selling a house, your agent will suggest that you place a "For Sale" sign on your lawn. Even though your home is most likely to be bought by a person who found out about it from a real estate agent, many buyers do drive around neighbourhoods looking for "For Sale" signs. Don't worry too much that dozens of people will knock on your door because they have seen the sign. Your agent's name and telephone number will be on the sign, and most prospective buyers will either call your agent or their own agent. If someone does come to your door asking to look around, politely tell them to call your real estate agent.

Many vendors are very anxious to have their home advertised for sale in the newspaper or on cable TV or a website. In fact, some real estate agents market themselves by promising to place lots of ads. However, experienced real estate agents will tell you that advertising does not usually sell your home. It's more a way for the agents to market themselves. The thing that is going to sell your home is not ads but a listing on the MLS.

Showing Your Home

Unless you are really fortunate, your home won't be sold until after a lot of people have looked at it. You can go through a period of weeks of people traipsing through your home on very little notice. You will be under constant pressure to keep everything looking its best. You'll have to keep the cat and the dog off the living-room sofa and pick up the socks and underwear that usually decorate the bedroom floors. You won't be able to cook fish *a la garlic* in case you get a call that someone wants to view your home after dinner. After the initial thrill of living in neat, clean, sweet-smelling premises wears off, having your home up for sale can seriously get on your nerves!

If someone wants to view your home, your real estate agent will call you first to make an appointment. All appointments are made through your agent's office, even though most of the people who come to see your home will not be clients of your agent. With luck you will be given enough warning to tidy up, and put away any valuables. If the prospective buyer is asking to come at a very inconvenient time, you can say no, but you shouldn't make it too difficult for people to view your home.

At the time of the appointment, the prospective buyer will arrive with his or her own agent. Your agent will not be there. If your agent has prepared a feature sheet for your home, give it to the visiting agent. Then get out of the way—if the agent and the buyer have questions, they'll come and find you or will contact your agent. Avoid any temptation to follow them around as they tour—it will make them uncomfortable. The agent will stay with the buyer, and this offers you some protection against theft or damage.

The prospective buyer's agent will give you a business card. Keep the cards of all the agents who come to your home so that your agent can collect them to make follow-up calls. Your agent should give you feedback from the other agents, so you'll know what people who visited your home did or didn't like about it. The feedback may encourage you to make additional repairs or slap on a coat of paint—or to consider lowering your asking price.

If you are away a lot of the time, you may want to give your agent permission to let other agents take buyers through when you're not there. In this case, give your agent a key and make sure your home is always neat.

Negotiating the Terms of Sale

If someone wants to make an offer to buy your home, his or her real estate agent will contact your agent to make an appointment with you to review the offer. At that time, your agent and the buyer's agent will meet with you, usually at your home, to show you the offer and go over its terms with you.

If you want to discuss the offer privately with your own agent, you can ask the other agent to leave the room. You can ask your own agent to leave too, if you want to have a private discussion with family or friends.

You can accept the offer, reject the offer, or sign back a **counter-offer**—in which you make changes to the offer (for example by changing the total price or the amount of the deposit or the closing date). Your agent will help you evaluate an offer, or draft a counter-offer.

We tell you more about reviewing an offer and negotiating a sale in Chapter 19.

HOW TO FIND A REAL ESTATE AGENT

Your real estate agent's job will be to get you and your home set up for sale, but it's most likely going to be another agent who actually finds a buyer for your home. So you don't need an agent who has extra-special talents at selling. You want someone whose judgment you trust about pricing your home, making it attractive to buyers, and accepting or rejecting an offer. You also want an agent who is pleasant to work with. If you are buying and selling at the same time, you may use the real estate agent you are house-hunting with to help you sell your present home. (In Chapter 3 we talked about what to look for in an agent to help you house-hunt.) If you don't have an agent or you need a different agent to sell your home (for example, if you're buying and selling in different areas), ask relatives, friends and neighbours for recommendations. Or you can collect names of agents from "For Sale" signs in your area or from advertisements. When you have a few names, interview at least three agents at your home. Ask each agent

- What experience he or she has in the real estate market in your local area. Within a city, there can be different markets with different conditions— the agent you choose should be familiar with your neighbourhood and able to choose the selling strategy that will work best there.

- What his or her view is of the local real estate market. Is it a buyer's or seller's or balanced market right now? What's it likely to be in the near future? Is this a good time to sell?

- What asking price he or she would suggest for your home. If you interview several agents, one of them may tell you that your home is worth a lot more than the others indicated. Don't choose an agent just because he or she suggests a high asking price. The agent may only be doing this to get your listing, and very soon after signing a contract with you may recommend that you lower the price.

- What he or she would suggest you do to make your home attractive to buyers (you may get fairly general answers since at this point you're asking for free advice).

- What his or her usual rate of commission is. Commission rates are negotiable. If you talk to a few agents before you sign an agreement with one, you may find one who is willing to offer a lower commission rate in order to get your listing. If you are buying and selling a home at the same time, you may get a better commission rate if you use the same agent for both. (That's because the agent stands to get part of the commission on the home you buy as well as on the home you sell.)

- What his or her marketing plan usually involves MLS, open houses for agents, open houses for the public, a spot on cable television, information about your home on a website, a feature sheet for prospective buyers, newspaper advertisements.

- How often he or she will be in touch with you to provide feedback from house-hunters and agents who have viewed your home.

- For references, if you didn't find the agent through the recommendation of someone you trust.

THE LEGAL RELATIONSHIP BETWEEN YOU AND YOUR REAL ESTATE AGENT

When you list your home for sale with a real estate agent, you and the agent enter into a legal relationship via the listing agreement that you both sign.

The Listing Agreement

The **listing agreement** is the written contract that sets out the relationship between a vendor and a real estate agent. It contains a number of important things.

Agent's Duty to You

A listing agreement creates in law an **agency relationship** between you and your real estate agent. Your legal agent has certain duties to you, first and foremost to look after your best interest. Some listing agreement forms set out the duties in detail and others don't. The duties exist whether they're mentioned in the form or not.

Agent's Authority to Offer

The listing agreement gives your agent **authority to offer** your home for sale for a fixed period of time. If it is sold during that period, no matter who actually finds the buyer (you, or your agent, or another agent), you agree to pay a commission to your agent. If the property is sold within a certain time after that period ends, you still agree to pay a commission to your agent if the buyer is someone who first saw your home through your agent or another real estate agent who found out about your home on the MLS.

Agent's Commission

The agreement also sets out what the agent's **rate of commission** will be. Real estate commissions are calculated as a percentage of the sale price of your home. Agents may ask for a commission as high as 6 per cent or even more. If you sell your home for $100,000 with a commission of 6 per cent, the commission is $6,000. This is a lot of money, especially if your home sells quickly, and you may feel that your agent is being very well paid for not doing very much.

If it makes you feel any better, your agent doesn't get to keep all that money. First of all, if your home is sold on the MLS, the commission is split between your agent and the agent working with the buyer. Then, those agents only get to keep some of the money. A good chunk of it goes to the real estate agency that each works for. On a $6,000 commission, your agent might end up getting as little as $1,500. Actually, now that you know where the commission is going, you probably feel even crankier than before.

To add to your crankiness, let us mention that real estate agents are required to charge GST (HST where applicable) on the commission received. Some agents absorb the GST and pay it out of the commission; others don't. Be sure to find out what your agent is planning to do.

Multiple Listing Service Listing or Exclusive Listing

When you enter into a listing agreement, there are two kinds of listings to choose between, a **Multiple Listing Service listing** and an **exclusive listing**. A Multiple Listing Service listing puts your property on the Multiple Listing

Service (MLS) database. Your agent gets paid a commission no matter who finds a buyer for your property. An exclusive listing gives your agent the exclusive right to find a buyer for your home. Again, your agent gets paid a commission no matter who finds the buyer. However, your home won't be listed on the MLS.

For most people, an MLS listing is the sensible way to go. The MLS database can lead a lot more potential buyers to your property than a single agent, however hard-working that agent is, because the MLS automatically gives every agent in the area information about your property. If you choose an exclusive listing, other real estate agents who know your home is for sale may be reluctant to bring their clients to view it. That's because those agents can't be sure of getting a share of the commission payable when your home is sold. Under an exclusive listing, the whole commission goes to your agent, unless your agent and the agent who brings in a buyer can reach an agreement to share it.

An exclusive listing is not out of the question, though. It's slightly cheaper than an MLS listing, so it can save a vendor money in commission and it can be just as useful as an MLS listing in some situations. A homeowner might choose an exclusive listing if she wasn't really sure she wanted to sell, or wasn't in a big hurry to sell. A homeowner might also go for an exclusive listing if he didn't have his home up for sale but was approached by an agent who had a buyer ready. And in a hot real estate market, a home in a desirable neighbourhood can be sold just by a sign on the lawn—so there's no great need for an MLS listing.

If you start with an exclusive listing, you can enter into a new agreement with the same agent for an MLS listing (usually with a higher rate of commission) at any time. But you can't enter into an MLS listing agreement with any other agent until your exclusive listing agreement ends. So it's probably best to limit an exclusive listing to a short time.

By the way, you may also hear of something called an **open listing**. It's really hardly a listing at all. An open listing agreement gives an agent the right to find a buyer for your home and to earn a commission for doing so, but it also gives you the right to list with other agents or to find a buyer yourself (and pay no commission to your agent if you do). You're not too likely to find an agent who's interested in such a free-and-easy relationship.

Information About Your Property

The listing agreement is used not just to set out your relationship with your agent but also to get information about your home for prospective buyers. The agent will ask you for and write down in the listing agreement information such as

- the legal description of the property
- the price you are asking
- the size of the lot (if you're selling a house)
- the size, construction, and age of the home
- the size and number of rooms
- any fixtures excluded from the sale and any chattels included in the sale (for more about fixtures and chattels see Chapter 19)
- details of your mortgage
- the zoning that applies to your property

It's very important that the information you put in the listing agreement be absolutely correct because prospective buyers will rely on it.

Disclosure Statement

Some real estate agents in some provinces will ask you to complete a **disclosure statement** or **property information statement** which sets out information about the condition of your home—in particular, about any problems you're aware of. This information will be made available to prospective buyers. If the disclosure statement contains any false information, you can be sued by the person who buys your home.

Your real estate agent wants this form as legal protection in case he or she unknowingly passes on false information from you to the buyer. The form makes it clear that you, and not the real estate agent, were the source of the information.

THE SALE PROCESS WHEN YOU SELL PRIVATELY

The reason for selling privately—that is, without a real estate agent—is to avoid paying a commission to an agent. When you sell on your own, you will have to do for yourself all the things that an agent would have helped you with or done for you. You will have to

- set a realistic asking price
- make your home attractive
- find prospective buyers
- show your home to prospective buyers
- negotiate the terms of sale

If the real estate market in your area is hot, you may not have any trouble selling your home privately. But if it's cool, you may find yourself looking for a real estate agent to help you sell, after you've gone two or three months without a decent offer.

Setting a Realistic Asking Price

If you set your asking price too high, you will scare away potential buyers. No matter what you think your home is worth, you would be wise to get a professional to tell you what its fair market value is. You can pay to get an opinion from a real estate agent or a real estate appraiser. You can also ask the professional to help you set your asking price.

Making Your Home Attractive

In Chapter 17, we made suggestions about how to make your home attractive to potential buyers. You can follow any of those suggestions that catch your fancy. You just won't have a real estate agent to give you additional advice.

Finding Buyers

You should know that some buyers will be frightened off by a private sale. They're afraid that private sellers will be unreasonable about the price or that they will be generally difficult to deal with. On the other hand, there are buyers who will be attracted by a private sale. They will think that you may be willing to sell for a lower price because you don't have to pay a real estate commission. It's up to you to decide whether to pass on any part of what you save.

Place a "For Sale By Owner" or "Private Sale" sign on your lawn. You can buy or rent professional-looking signs. The sign should have your phone number on it.

Advertise in the local newspapers. Consider putting your address in the ad so that prospective buyers can drive by for a look. You may want to include a picture of your home, although that will increase the cost of the ad. Don't forget to put your phone number in.

You may also be able to find an Internet site that lets private sellers list their property for a fee—then you'll be able to catch the attention of Internet house-hunters.

Showing Your Home

Prepare a feature sheet and have copies available to give to people who come to view your home. You can collect some model feature sheets by going to open houses.

Show your home by appointment only. For protection against break-ins, don't tell callers when you will be out. If real estate agents phone, tell them it's fine for them to bring a client if they agree that any commission will be paid by the buyer and not by you.

Before the appointment, tidy up. Put away any valuables or breakable items.

When someone is viewing your home, stay with that person at all times. You may also want to have someone else with you for your own safety and to guard against theft and damage.

If you're asked a question, answer it honestly. Don't make any false statements about the property. If someone makes a rude remark about the condition of your home, try not to act offended. (It may be a tactic to get your to lower your price.)

If a potential buyer tries to negotiate the price with you during the showing, say that you will only consider written offers.

Negotiating

Speak to a lawyer before you put up your "For Sale" sign. Ask the lawyer to prepare an offer to purchase which contains blanks for things like the price and the closing date, but which contains all necessary clauses that an agreement to sell your particular home should have in it. These clauses might relate to things like a mortgage you can't discharge or a mutual driveway that gives your neighbour a legal right to drive over part of your property.

If, against our best advice, you don't want to talk to a lawyer, you can get blank "Offer to Purchase" forms from a store that sells office supplies and legal forms.

If someone wants to make an offer, give him or her your offer to purchase form. The prospective buyer can either fill the offer in alone or with the help of a lawyer. To help the buyer draft the offer, provide a copy of your feature sheet. Also provide a legal description of the property, a copy of a survey if you're selling a house and if you have a survey, and details of your mortgage if the buyer asks about assuming it (taking it over from you).

Don't accept any offer, or sign back a counter-offer, without legal advice. Once an offer is presented to you, show it to your lawyer.

19 FROM OFFER TO CLOSING

Someone has actually put in an offer to buy your home! You are (choose one): (a) amazed; (b) relieved; (c) horrified at the thought of moving; (d) all of the above. You can stop worrying about moving—because you've got lots of other things to think about and do first. In this chapter, we will tell you what you need to do from the time you receive an offer to purchase your home to the time that the deal closes. And then you can go back to worrying about moving.

REVIEWING AN OFFER TO PURCHASE

If someone wants to make an offer to buy your home, the offer will be presented to you by your real estate agent and the buyer's agent. The agents will go through the offer with you to make sure that you understand it and that every detail in the offer is accurate.

Your agent may be quite enthusiastic about any offer you get. He or she may prefer not to reject several potential buyers just so you can get a bigger deposit or two or three thousand dollars more for the purchase price. So you need to know what's important to *you* in terms of price, to avoid being swayed by your agent's opinion. After all, your agent will get only a small share of the increase in price.

BIDDING WARS

In certain areas of the country, and at certain times, you may find your home the object of a kind of feeding frenzy among buyers. If your neighbourhood is really hot, you could get several offers at once or in quick succession from people who want to buy your home. You want to deal with the offers in a way that will make the most of the competition among the buyers so that you get the best price and other terms you can. There are several approaches you can take in dealing with **multiple offers**. You can hold onto the best offer and tell the other buyers who've put in offers that they have one more chance to make a competitive offer. Then look at the original best offer together with the resubmitted offers and choose the one you like best. Or you can deal right away with the buyer who put in the best offer but tell the others who put in offers that you'll let them know within a short time whether you've decided to enter into an agreement of purchase and sale or whether the negotiations fell through and you're accepting new offers. Ask your real estate agent for any approach he or she recommends (and why), and then decide how you would like to proceed.

THE ANATOMY OF AN OFFER

Even though the real estate agents will explain any offer to you, we want to stress the importance of having your lawyer review an offer before you accept it or sign back a counter-offer. You're entering into a very important and valuable contract. You want to be sure it's a good contract for you. Once you accept an offer or the purchaser accepts your counter-offer, there's usually no going back.

Every offer contains an **irrevocable date**. You have until that date to decide whether you want to accept the offer, reject the offer, or sign back a counter-offer (see Chapter 18). If you do nothing, the offer will simply end on that date.

The following information will help you understand the key terms of the offer and will help you to decide whether to accept the offer, reject it, or make a counter-offer.

The Names of the Purchaser and the Vendor

All registered owners of the property should be named as vendors. The owners' names are the only names that are important to you when you're selling. It's up to the purchasers to figure out what their own names are.

Description of the Property

If you're selling a house, it's important that the size of your property be accurately set out. The agreement must not set out a lot size that is bigger than the actual property. You also want to make sure that any **easements** over your property are mentioned. An easement is a right that someone else has to use or cross over a portion of another person's property. If, for example, you share a mutual driveway with your next-door neighbour, your neighbour has an easement over your part of the driveway, and you have an easement over your neighbour's part of the driveway.

If the description of the property is not correct or does not mention an existing easement, the purchasers may be able to use that mistake later to get out of the deal or ask for a reduction in the purchase price.

The Purchase Price

The purchase price is probably the part of the agreement that you will look at first. It will probably be lower than your asking price. Just about every purchaser expects you to sign back a counter-offer asking for a higher price. If the offered price is reasonably close to what you want to get, it makes sense to sign back a counter-offer for the higher price, but if the offered price is much too low, it may make more sense to reject the offer.

How Much of That Price is Yours?

Before you accept or reject an offered price—especially if it's much lower than your asking price—it's a good idea to sit down and figure out roughly how much of that money you will actually walk away with. Here's how you do it.

Start your calculation with the purchase price. At the time of closing you will probably have prepaid certain expenses that the purchaser will get some of the benefit of after closing, such as property taxes or fuel oil or condominium maintenance fees. The purchaser will have to pay you back fo her share of these prepaid expenses, so you can add that share to the purchase price.

After that you start subtracting. Out of the purchase price, you'll have to pay the real estate agent and your lawyer, you'll have to pay off your mortgage unless the purchaser is assuming it (taking it over), you'll have to pay off any claims registered against your home, and you'll have to pay any taxes and utilities bills that are **in arrears** (past due for payment). It may turn out that you underpaid rather than overpaid your property taxes, and you'll have to make an adjustment in the purchaser's favour for that and subtract the outstanding amount from the purchase price. Even if the purchaser is assuming your mortgage, the amount of the outstanding balance of the mortgage has to be deducted from the purchase price.

The following table will help you do the calculation.

TABLE 1: ESTIMATING WHAT YOU'LL MAKE FROM THE SALE

MONEY TO BE RECEIVED

Offered price $ _____
Plus adjustments for prepaid expenses
    realty taxes   _____
    fuel oil   _____
    unmetered utilities   _____
    condominium maintenance fees   _____

Total money you will receive   _____ (A)

MONEY TO BE SUBTRACTED

Real estate commission   _____
Legal fees   _____
Money required to discharge mortgages
    principal and interest   _____
    prepayment penalty   _____
    discharge fees   _____
Money required to discharge any claims
    against your property   _____
Money required to pay utilities arrears   _____
Money credited to the purchaser for
    assuming existing mortgages   _____
Adjustment for underpaid realty taxes   _____

Total money to be subtracted   _____ (B)

WHAT YOU'LL GET FROM THE SALE (A − B) $ _____

The Deposit

It's usual for the purchaser to pay a **deposit** if the vendor accepts the offer (it's the purchaser's way of showing he or she is serious about the deal). You want a substantial deposit. Handing over a large deposit makes a purchaser think twice before backing out of the deal without a good reason, because if the purchaser does, you as vendor may be able to keep the deposit. (Don't worry—most purchasers don't want to back out.)

You don't get to cash the deposit cheque. The deposit is held by your real estate agent until the deal is closed. Then it will be used (in whole or in part, depending on how much it is) to pay the commission you owe your agent.

Assumed Mortgages and Vendor Take-Back Mortgages

The offer may state that the purchaser will **assume** your existing mortgage. That means the purchaser wants to pay you less cash but take over your mortgage payments (then you won't have to pay off your mortgage when the deal closes). Or the offer may provide for a **vendor take-back mortgage**. That means the purchaser is asking you to lend some of the purchase price and take back a mortgage (often a second mortgage, with the purchaser's first mortgage given to an institutional lender).

Assumed Mortgages

If the offer states that the purchaser will assume your existing mortgage, make sure that the terms of your mortgage are accurately set out. If you accept an offer promising terms that don't match what your mortgage documents say, the purchaser may later be able to force you to reduce the purchase price, or may even be able to get out of the deal.

The offer should accurately set out the following information about your existing mortgage:

- outstanding principal
- interest rate
- monthly payments
- mortgage due date
- any prepayment privileges
- any limitations on a purchaser's right to assume the mortgage

OUTSTANDING PRINCIPAL: This is the amount of money that is still owing on your mortgage. The amount still owing will be less than the principal amount you originally borrowed (although maybe not very much less!) because you will have paid some of the principal back since you got the mortgage loan. The purchaser is relying on having the outstanding principal available to help finance the purchase. If the actual outstanding principal turns out to be less than stated in the offer, the purchaser will have to find money from other sources.

To find out how much is outstanding on your mortgage, ask your mortgagee. Make sure it's the same amount set out in the offer.

INTEREST RATE AND MONTHLY PAYMENTS: Make sure that the interest rate and monthly payments set out in the offer are the same as stated in your mortgage documents.

MATURITY DATE AND PREPAYMENT PRIVILEGES: The full remaining amount of the mortgage must be paid on the maturity date. At that time, the mortgage will have to be refinanced. It's important to the purchaser to know how long it is until he or she has to refinance the mortgage, so make sure that the date in the offer matches the one in your mortgage documents. The purchaser will also be relying on the prepayment privileges (the right to pay down the principal more quickly) stated in the offer, so make sure that the description of these privileges is exactly the same as in the mortgage documents.

LIMITATIONS ON THE PURCHASER'S RIGHT TO ASSUME THE MORTGAGE: Not all mortgages can be assumed by a purchaser. Some mortgages automatically become payable on the sale of the mortgaged home. If the mortgage on your home cannot be assumed, you should not accept an offer that promises the purchaser the right to assume it. Other mortgages can be assumed by a purchaser only if the mortgagee approves (the mortgagee wants someone who is a good credit risk). If your mortgage gives your mortgagee the right to approve the purchaser, make sure the offer states that. (Then the purchaser usually makes his or her offer conditional on approval by the mortgagee.) If the offer is conditional on the purchaser getting the mortgagee's approval, make sure that the offer states that the purchaser will take all reasonable steps necessary to get that approval (the purchaser usually has to give the mortgagee financial information).

WARNING: You should know that in many provinces you as original mortgagor remain liable on an assumed mortgage. If the purchaser does not make the mortgage payments and the home cannot be sold for enough money to cover the amount of the mortgage, you can be sued by the mortgagee for the shortfall. In fact, the mortgagee does not have to wait for a shortfall to start a lawsuit against you. Unless you get the mortgagee to agree otherwise, in most provinces there's nothing you can do to protect yourself against being sued by the mortgagee if you let the purchaser assume your mortgage. But as long as the home is worth significantly more than the outstanding balance on the mortgage, there won't be a shortfall, and you won't have to pay the mortgagee anything.

Vendor Take-Back Mortgages

If the buyer wants the vendor to lend some of the purchase money and to take back a mortgage, the offer sets out the principal amount of the mortgage the buyer wants, the interest rate, the monthly payments, the due date, and any pre-payment privileges that the buyer wants the mortgage to contain.

You may like the idea of holding a mortgage as an investment. If you are thinking of taking back a mortgage, make sure it's a good investment. Calculate the value of your home. Its value should be high enough for the sale proceeds to cover any first mortgage, your mortgage, and the costs of selling the home, if the purchaser doesn't make mortgage payments and the home has to be sold. You should also ask your real estate agent to help you do a credit check on the purchaser.

If you don't want to hold the mortgage as an investment, you can still agree to take a mortgage back, and then find someone who is willing to buy the mortgage from you. If you sell the mortgage, you will have to do so at a **discount**—the person who buys it will pay you less than the face amount of the mortgage because that person has to wait to be repaid by the purchaser. Your real estate agent or lawyer can probably find someone to buy the mortgage. Before you accept the purchaser's offer, make sure that you have a commitment from someone to buy the mortgage from you.

If you don't want to take back a mortgage, just delete the provision from the offer before you sign it back. (If you make this change to the purchaser's offer, you may lose the deal.)

Chattels and Fixtures

The purchaser may have put into the offer a list of certain **chattels** to be included in the purchase price, such as appliances or window coverings. Check this list carefully and decide whether or not you want to sell these things with the house.

If you want to take with you any items that are attached to the home (like ceiling lights and fans, built-in bookcases or shutters or heavy mirrors that are bolted to the wall), the offer must specifically mention those items. These are **fixtures** and are considered to be part of the home. If the offer does not state that you have a right to keep them, they are sold with the home.

For a longer discussion about chattels and fixtures, see Chapter 5.

If any equipment in the home is rented, for example, a water heater, the offer should say so. Otherwise, it's possible for the purchaser to claim he thought the equipment was being sold with the home and to ask for a reduction in the purchase price equal to the value of the equipment.

The Closing Date

The offer sets out a **closing date** of the purchaser's choice. This is the day you hand over ownership of the home and the remaining amount of the purchase price. It's also moving day. Check the date to see that it satisfies your needs. You may want a longer time before you have to pack up and move, or you may want the sale to close as quickly as possible. If you are not happy with the closing date, change it before you agree to the offer.

Use of the Property

The offer may contain a statement that the **current use** of the property can be "lawfully continued" and may have a space to fill in what the current use is. The purchaser will probably fill in the blank with a description of how you're presently using your property—for example as a single-family residence, or a residence with a professional office, or a residence with a separate apartment. You want to make sure that what the purchaser fills in is an accurate description of how you're using your property. But keep in mind that when you sign the offer and it turns into an agreement of purchase and sale, you're not only stating what the current use is, you're stating that the purchaser can legally continue to use the property that way in the future. In other words, you're promising that your current use of the property is allowed by municipal zoning by-laws (and condominium by-laws if you live in a condo).

The purchaser's lawyer will check the by-laws to make sure the current use is allowed. If it's not allowed, the purchaser may be able to get out of the deal or demand a reduced price. So before you accept the purchaser's statement about the use of the property, be sure that what you're doing with your home is legal. If you have any doubt, check with your municipal zoning department (and look at your condo by-laws).

Conditions

The purchaser may have made the offer **conditional** on certain things, such as:

- being able to sell his or her own house
- being able to obtain financing
- being approved by your mortgagee
- getting a satisfactory professional home inspection report

If the condition is not met, the deal can fall through.

It is very common for a purchaser to make the offer conditional on getting financing and getting mortgage approval within a certain time. Check with your real estate agent that the length of time asked for is reasonable.

More and more purchasers are also making their offers conditional on a satisfactory inspection report. The purchaser can legally back out of the deal only if the report shows significant problems with the home. (Dust bunnies under the beds are not a significant problem, although cracks in the foundations might be.) If you don't agree to an inspection, the purchaser will probably think that you have something to hide—something worse than dust bunnies, that is. Make sure that the offer requires the purchaser to have the inspection done within a few days.

The purchaser may have a home to sell too, and may make the offer conditional on selling it. Whether or not you agree to such a condition will depend on the length of time the purchaser wants to sell, and whether or not other people seem to be interested in your home. If there is a lot of interest in your home, it's silly to agree to this condition for any period of time. Even if the condition gives you the right to continue to list your home for sale and to consider other offers, many prospective purchasers will not even look at, let alone make an offer on, your home if it has been conditionally sold. On the other hand, if this is the only offer you've had in some time, and you have no reason to expect another offer any time soon, what do you have to lose?

Inspection Clauses

The offer may contain clauses giving the purchaser the right to visit the home before the deal closes to take measurements, to get estimates from contractors, or to inspect the condition of the property immediately before the closing. As long as the clauses don't allow the purchaser to come too often and as long as you will be given enough notice of a visit beforehand, there is no reason not to agree to these clauses.

Other Special Clauses

The purchaser may (but realistically, probably won't) put in any number of clauses that could require you to provide things that you don't have, or to make changes to the property that you can't easily make. For example, if you're selling a house the offer might say that you will give the purchaser an up-to-date survey. That's fine if you have one, but if you don't, a clause like this would require you to have one done—at the cost of up to a thousand dollars! Or if the purchaser wants to use the property for a purpose not presently allowed by the municipal zoning by-law, the offer may say that you will have the zoning changed. Agreeing to a zoning change could cost you a lot of time and money, and you still might not be able to get the change.

Be very careful of any special clauses. Don't promise to do things that you can't do easily—and especially don't promise to do things you can't do at all!

THE VENDOR'S LAWYER

We told you before that you should get your lawyer involved as soon as you receive an offer to purchase your home. Whether or not you did so, you will need a lawyer once there is an accepted offer. Your lawyer will prepare all the necessary documents and answer any questions raised by the purchaser's lawyer.

Choosing a Lawyer

If you were happy with the lawyer you used when you bought your home, it is simplest to use that lawyer again for the sale. That lawyer will already have most of the information and documents necessary for the sale. Besides that, this is the lawyer who certified that you had a **good and marketable title** to your home (see Chapter 6). If the purchaser's lawyer finds any title problems, it's your lawyer who handled the purchase who is responsible for correcting those problems.

If for any reason you decide to use a different lawyer, go back to Chapter 6 for information about how to choose a lawyer.

Once you have a lawyer, you should immediately give him or her a signed copy of your agreement of purchase and sale. A new lawyer will also want to see the reporting letter, your deed, and any other documents that you received from the lawyer who helped you buy the home. Your lawyer, new or old, may also need the following documents when he or she starts to work on your sale:

- any mortgage documents
- your most recent plan of survey of the property, if you're selling a house
- your most recent property tax and utility bills
- any separation agreement affecting your home
- any court order or judgment affecting your home
- any will or probate documents affecting your home (if an owner has died)

What Your Lawyer Will Do

Legal fees for selling homes are lower than legal fees for buying homes. They're still at least several hundred dollars, so you should know what you are paying for. Your lawyer will

- review the agreement of purchase and sale
- answer any questions the purchaser's lawyer has about your title to (ownership of) the property

- calculate exactly how much money you should receive from the purchaser
- prepare the documents needed to transfer title to the purchaser and arrange for you to sign them
- close the transaction with the purchaser's lawyer
- review and register any vendor take-back mortgage
- pay off any claims against your home or any mortgages that are not being assumed by the purchaser
- pay the real estate commission
- pay you the balance of the purchase money
- provide you with a reporting letter

Reviewing the Agreement of Purchase and Sale

Your lawyer will be looking mainly at the kind of **title** you promised in the agreement to transfer to the purchaser on closing. Your lawyer needs to know what the purchaser is entitled to ask for so he or she can deal with the purchaser's lawyer on title questions.

Answering Questions about Title

The purchaser's lawyer will search the title to your home. If the purchaser's lawyer discovers any problem with the title, he or she will ask your lawyer to correct it by the closing date. It's up to your lawyer to determine whether or not the problem is one that you as the vendor are responsible for fixing. If so, your lawyer must try to fix the problem. Occasionally there are problems that cannot be fixed easily. If there is a serious problem that you cannot or will not fix, it is up to the purchaser whether or not to complete the deal. Your lawyer will tell you whether a problem is serious enough to give the purchaser a legally valid reason not to complete the deal.

Calculating the Money to be Paid by the Purchaser

Your lawyer will calculate exactly how much money the purchaser must pay to you when the deal closes, and will prepare a document that sets out **adjustments** to the purchase price and give it to the purchaser's lawyer.

The purchaser agreed to pay the purchase price but will be credited with certain amounts against the price. First of all, there is a credit for the deposit. In addition, the purchaser will receive a credit for the amount of any mortgage he or she is assuming. There are other items that must be taken into account which may increase or decrease the amount the purchaser pays, such as property taxes and utility charges. Whether these last items increase or decrease the amount the purchaser pays on closing depends on whether you have overpaid or underpaid tax or utilities bills.

Preparing Documents

In order to transfer ownership of your home to the purchaser, you will have to sign a **deed.** Your lawyer will prepare the deed and will prepare and explain to you any other documents necessary for the sale. Because you will have to sign documents, it's important for you not to disappear—let your lawyer know where you can be reached up to and including the day of closing.

Closing the Transaction

On the day of closing, your lawyer will arrange with the purchaser's lawyer to hand over the deed and the keys to your home. In most provinces, your lawyer will receive the final purchase money then (in some provinces you and your lawyer may have to wait).

Dealing with a Vendor Take-Back Mortgage

If you agreed to take back a mortgage from the purchaser, the mortgage itself is usually prepared by the purchaser's lawyer. Your lawyer will review the mortgage to make sure that it matches the terms you were promised in the agreement of purchase and sale. At the closing of the transaction, your lawyer will register the mortgage on the home's title in the provincial registry office.

Paying off Mortgages and Other Claims

If you have a mortgage that is to be paid off when your home is sold, your lawyer will contact the mortgagee to find out exactly how much money must be paid. (Usually, your lawyer will be able to arrange to pay off the mortgage after you have received the purchase money.) Your lawyer will tell the purchaser's lawyer to make part of the purchase money payable directly to the mortgagee. Your lawyer will then arrange to deliver the money to the mortgagee and get and register a **discharge** of the mortgage.

Occasionally, the purchaser will insist that the mortgage be paid off and discharged before the deal closes. In that case, you may have to borrow money to pay off the mortgage and repay that loan when the deal closes. Whether a purchaser may take this position depends on the wording of the agreement of purchase and sale. Your lawyer will tell you early on in the transaction if the purchaser is taking this position.

If there are any other outstanding claims against the property (such as a judgment against you, a construction or mechanics' lien, back property taxes, or unpaid utility accounts), your lawyer will arrange for these claims to be paid out of the purchase money.

Paying the Real Estate Commission

The purchaser pays a deposit at the time the agreement of purchase and sale is signed, and that deposit is normally held in trust by your real estate agent. When the deal is completed, the real estate commission is paid out of that deposit. If any deposit money is left, it will be sent to you. If the deposit is not enough to cover the commission, your lawyer will pay your real estate agent the balance of the commission out of the purchase money received on closing.

Paying You the Balance of the Purchase Money

After paying off any mortgages and claims, after paying the real estate commission, and after scooping something from what's left to cover legal fees, your lawyer will pay you the balance of the purchase money.

If you are buying another home, the money will be used for that purchase. If you aren't buying another home, think about what you want to do with the money. Make arrangements with your lawyer to deposit it directly into your bank account or into an investment certificate. You want to start earning interest on your sale proceeds as soon as possible.

Providing You with a Reporting Letter

When the sale of your home has been completed, your lawyer will send you a reporting letter. This letter will show how the amount paid by the purchaser was calculated by explaining the adjustments that were made to the purchase price. The letter will also set out in detail what money was received by your lawyer and what money was paid out and to whom it was paid.

YOUR RESPONSIBILITIES UNTIL CLOSING

Signing an agreement of purchase and sale means that on the closing date you not only have to transfer title to the property but also have to hand over possession of your home. The closing date can be weeks or months away, and you remain responsible for the home even though you are not going to own or live in it for very much longer.

You Can't Take It with You
(Unless You Must Take It with You)

You've signed an agreement to sell your home (and perhaps some of the contents too). When you move out, you can't take any of the contents you agreed to sell. You also can't take any fixtures, other than those you specifically mentioned in the agreement of purchase and sale.

When you hand over possession to the purchaser, you have to hand over **vacant possession**. That means you can't leave behind any family members (no matter how much you would like to), and you also can't leave behind any possessions the purchaser did not agree to buy. Resist the temptation to leave your broken-down freezer in the basement or your National Geographic magazine collection (started in 1953) that has been residing in your attic. The purchaser doesn't want to find these things in the home for the same reason you did not want to take them with you—it costs money to get rid of them.

If you remove things that you should have left behind, you may be sued for the value of the items you took. If you leave things behind that you should have taken, you can be sued for the cost of having them removed. As a practical matter, though, it's rarely worth the cost for the purchaser to sue for these items alone. But if the purchaser finds enough problems with the home, a lawsuit against you becomes more worthwhile and therefore more likely.

In the Event of Damage or Destruction

You're not just required to hand things over to the purchaser—you must hand them over to the purchaser at closing in the same condition they were in when the agreement of purchase and sale was signed, except for normal wear and tear. This rule applies not only to the chattels and fixtures in the home but to the home itself.

If something in the home breaks or is damaged, you must fix it. If your roof develops a leak, you must repair it, although you don't have to replace the roof if it is possible to simply patch the leak. You are not required to repair damage the way you might do it if you were going to keep the home. If you have agreed to sell your fifteen-year-old refrigerator and it stops working before closing, you must either repair the refrigerator or replace it. But, you don't have to get a new refrigerator—just a fifteen-year-old refrigerator that works.

If the home is destroyed or suffers major damage before closing, you must tell the purchaser. The purchaser has the right to walk away from the deal and get his deposit back. Or instead, the purchaser can choose to complete the deal and receive any insurance proceeds paid to you as a result of the damage or destruction. You should not make any repairs until you find out what the purchaser wants to do.

As you can see, it's in your interest to keep your home and contents properly insured right up until closing.

THE RESPONSIBILITY TO CLOSE

It takes two to tango, and it also takes two to close a real estate deal. What if either the vendor or the purchaser just isn't in the mood?

If the Vendor Refuses to Close

On the day of closing, you have a legal obligation to transfer your home to the purchaser and hand over possession. If you've changed your mind about selling since you signed the agreement of purchase and sale—maybe because home prices have risen since then and you think you might get more from a new purchaser—you may not be able to get out of the deal.

If you refuse to close, the purchaser can sue you for **specific performance** and if successful will get a court order forcing you to hand over the home and title on exactly the terms set out in the agreement. The purchaser may also be able to get money from you by way of court-ordered **damages**, to compensate for the trouble you've caused. And on top of that, you'll have to pay not only your own legal fees but a good part of the purchaser's too.

While a court action is going on, the purchaser will probably be able to prevent you from selling your home to anyone else by registering notice of the lawsuit against the title to the home.

If the Purchaser Refuses to Close

On the day of closing, the purchaser has a legal obligation also—to pay you for the home. If the purchaser refuses to close the deal without a valid reason, you can claim the purchaser's deposit. You may have to sue to get it. And you still have to find someone to buy your home.

Instead of claiming the deposit, in most provinces you can sue for damages. If you are successful, the money you get in damages will amount to the difference between what the purchaser was supposed to pay and what you actually receive when you sell your home to someone else. You'll also get some of your legal fees paid back by the purchaser.

But if it turns out that you sell the home for the same amount the purchaser was to pay, or for more, you don't have any damages and a court won't order the purchaser to pay you anything. It could turn out that you would get more money by going after the deposit than you would by suing for damages.

Don't Panic

Most deals close without a hitch. Even if a problem does arise, it can usually be solved.

20 GOODBYE AND GOOD LUCK

Well, much to your relief and ours, we don't have a lot left to say. In fact, we really don't have anything left to say. We just thought that the book should have twenty chapters rather than nineteen chapters.

But since we're here, we'd like to give you a bit of a send-off. We hope that our book has given you enough information to let you go into home ownership with your eyes open. And we hope that we have not opened your eyes so wide that you don't go at all.

APPENDIX

SAMPLE INVENTORY LISTS

	Description	Quantity	Original Cost	Date of Purchase
Living room:				
sofas				
chairs				
tables				
desks				
lamps				
musical instruments				
mirrors, paintings, and wall decorations				
ornaments and clocks				
plants				
books				
stereo equipment				
CDs, tapes, and records				
television and VCR				
videotapes				
computer equipment				
draperies				
carpets				
fan				
air-conditioner				
other				

	Description	Quantity	Original Cost	Date of Purchase
Family room:				
sofas				
chairs				
tables				
desks				
lamps				
musical instruments				
mirrors, paintings, and wall decorations				
ornaments and clocks				
plants				
books				
stereo equipment				
CDs, tapes, and records				
television and VCR				
videotapes				
computer equipment				
sewing machine				
draperies				
carpets				
fan				
air-conditioner				
other				
Dining room:				
table				
chairs				
buffet, server, or sideboard				
cabinet				
sidetables				
lamps and chandeliers				
china				
silverware—flatware				
silverware—dishes				

	Description	Quantity	Original Cost	Date of Purchase
glass and crystal				
mirrors, paintings, and wall decorations				
ornaments				
plants				
draperies				
carpets				
wallpaper				
Bedrooms:				
bed, including mattress				
dresser				
chairs				
tables				
lamps				
computer equipment				
stereo equipment				
television and VCR				
radio				
alarm clock				
books				
bed linens				
draperies				
carpet				
mirrors, paintings, and wall decorations				
ornaments				
plants				
wallpaper				
fan				
air-conditioner				
humidifier				
other				
Kitchen:				
table				
chairs				

	Description	Quantity	Original Cost	Date of Purchase
cabinets and countertops				
sideboard or server				
dishes				
glassware				
cutlery				
pots and pans				
utensils				
clock				
radio				
television				
mirrors, paintings, and wall decorations				
wallpaper				
linens				
draperies				
flooring and carpet				
plants				
food				
appliances:				
stove and oven				
microwave oven				
refrigerator				
freezer				
electric kettle				
electric coffee pot				
electric coffee grinder				
toaster				
food processor or blender				
electric juice maker				
electric can opener				
electric knife				
deep fryer				
washing machine				

	Description	Quantity	Original Cost	Date of Purchase
dryer				
vacuum cleaner				
iron				
sewing machine				
other				
Bathroom:				
towels				
mirrors, paint-ings, and wall decorations				
lamps				
table				
chair				
scale				
ornaments				
curtains and shower cur-tains				
plants				
cosmetics				
appliances:				
electric razors				
hairdryer				
electric tooth-brush				
curling iron				
Women's clothing and jewellery:				
dresses				
suits				
skirts				
pants				
shorts				
blouses and shirts				
sweaters				
shoes				
belts				
scarves				
gloves				

	Description	Quantity	Original Cost	Date of Purchase
coats				
hats				
boots				
purses				
undergarments				
stockings				
night clothes				
swimsuits				
other				
jewellery:				
rings				
earrings				
necklaces				
brooches				
bracelets				
watches				
glasses and sun-glasses				
other				
suitcases				
Men's clothing and jewellery:				
suits				
pants				
shorts				
jackets				
shirts				
sweaters				
belts				
ties				
handkerchiefs				
shoes				
gloves				
underwear				
night clothes				
coats				
hats				
boots				
other				

	Description	Quantity	Original Cost	Date of Purchase
jewellery:				
rings				
watches				
cufflinks				
tie pins				
glasses and sun-glasses				
other				
suitcases				
Children's clothing, equipment, and toys:				
pants				
tops				
sweaters				
dresses				
skirts				
shoes				
coats and snowsuits				
hats				
gloves				
boots				
underwear				
night clothes				
swimsuits				
glasses				
toys and games				
equipment:				
carriage				
stroller				
car seat				
playpen				
crib				
swing				
other				

	Description	Quantity	Original Cost	Date of Purchase
Sports equipment:				
bicycles				
camping equipment				
fishing equipment				
golf clubs and bags				
hunting equipment				
outboard motor				
shoes (running, aerobics etc.)				
skis, boots, and poles; ski clothes				
tennis and squash racquets				
other				
Basement:				
pool or ping-pong table				
exercise equipment				
bar and liquor				
furniture				
carpets				
tools				
stored valuables				
appliances:				
furnace				
air-conditioning system				
dehumidifier				
Garage and outbuildings:				
lawnmower				
snowblower				
garden tools				
other				

INDEX

Also by Margaret Kerr and JoAnn Kurtz

Facing A Death in the Family: Caring for Someone Through Illness and Dying, Arranging the Funeral, Dealing with the Will and Estate

Make It Legal: What Every Canadian Entrepreneur Needs to Know About the Law

CONTACT US

If you have comments or suggestions, or are interested in having us give a presentation to your group or association, please contact us through one of the methods below:

Through our publisher

John Wiley & Sons Canada, Ltd.
22 Worcester Road
Etobicoke, Ontario
M9W 1L1

Or by e-mail

joann.kurtz@senecac.on.ca

Or visit our website at

www.kerr-and-kurtz.com

ORDERING

To order any of these titles through the publisher call:

John Wiley & Sons Canada, Ltd
Phone Toll-free: 1-800-567-4797
Fax Toll-free: 1-800-565-6802
Phone in Toronto: 416-236-4433
Fax in Toronto: 416-236-8743

They are also available at your local bookstore or online bookstore.